AN INTRODUCTION TO ECCLESIASTICAL LATIN

Sola Scripturarum ars est, quam sibi passim vindicant:

Scribimus indocti doctique poemata passim.

Hanc garrula anus, hanc delirus senex, hanc sophista verbosus, hanc universi praesumunt, lacerant, docent, antequam discant. Alii, adducto supercilio, grandia verba trutinantes, inter mulierculas de sacris literis philosophantur.... Taceo de mei similibus, qui, si forte ad Scripturas sanctas post saeculares literas venerint, et sermone composito aurem populi mulserint, quidquid dixerint hoc legem Dei putant, nec scire dignantur quid prophetae, quid apostoli senserint: sed ad sensum suum incongrua aptant testimonia.... Puerilia sunt haec et circulatorum ludo similia, docere quod ignores, imo, ut cum stomacho loquar, ne hoc quidem scire quod nescias.

Noli offendaris in Scripturis sanctis simplicitate et quasi vilitate verborum, quae vel vitio interpretum, vel de industria sic prolata sunt, ut rusticam concionem facilius instruerent, et in una eademque sententia aliter doctus, aliter audiret indoctus.

Jerome, Ep. 53.

* * * * *

Saepe et verba non latina dico ut intelligatis.

Augustine in Ps. 123.

* * * * *

Melius est reprehendant nos grammatici, quam non intelligant populi.

Augustine in Ps. 138.

AN INTRODUCTION
TO
ECCLESIASTICAL LATIN

BY

REV. H. P. V. NUNN, M.A.

ST JOHN'S COLLEGE, CAMBRIDGE

OXFORD
BASIL BLACKWELL
1963

First Edition 1922
Second Edition 1927
Third Edition 1951
(with an Appendix of Latin Hymns)
Reprinted 1952
Reprinted 1958
Reprinted 1963

Printed in Great Britain for Basil Blackwell & Mott, Ltd.
by A. R. Mowbray & Co. Limited in the City of Oxford
and bound at the Kemp Hall Bindery

MEMORIAE
MATRIS DILECTISSIMAE
IN CHRISTO DORMIENTIS
DEDICATUM

BY THE SAME AUTHOR

The Elements of New Testament Greek.
Fourth Edition *Crown 8vo.*

A Short Syntax of New Testament Greek.
Third Edition *Crown 8vo.*

A Short Syntax of Attic Greek.

The Authorship of the Fourth Gospel
Crown 8vo.

Christian Inscriptions.
Crown 8vo.

CONTENTS

PREFACE

THIS book is written to meet the needs of a special class of students, namely of those that desire to study Ecclesiastical Latin.

Ecclesiastical Latin may be defined as the form which the Latin language assumed in the hands of the Fathers of the Western Church and of their successors up to the time of the revival of learning.

The book is divided into two parts: first, a summary of such syntactical rules as are necessary for the understanding of the works of these writers, with an explanation of the points in which Ecclesiastical Latin differs from Classical Latin: secondly, a selection of passages taken from the works of some of the principal authors of the period with notes drawing the attention of the student to the appropriate sections of the syntax.

The syntax has been treated on broad lines, and no attempt has been made to trace all the peculiarities of the countless writers of Ecclesiastical Latin who represent so many different countries and degrees of culture.

The examples are taken as far as possible from the Vulgate New Testament, because this is the most readily accessible book belonging to the period.

It must not be assumed from the fact that the examples are taken from this source that the Vulgate is to be regarded as typical of Ecclesiastical Latin.

It is a translation, and often a very literal translation, of a Hebrew or Greek original. The Vulgate is not a Latin Classic in the sense that the Authorised Version of the Bible is an English Classic.

It will however be found that most of the constructions that commonly occur in Ecclesiastical Latin are to be found in the Vulgate, and, generally speaking, examples have been given of these constructions only. A very slight attempt has been made to deal with the great variety of curious distortions of Latin which the translators made use of in the attempt to represent literally obscure passages in the Hebrew.

Those who intend to use this book should possess at the least a knowledge of the conjugations of Latin verbs and the declensions of Latin nouns such as may be got from any primer[1].

They should begin with the Vulgate New Testament which can be procured in the revised text of Wordsworth and White from the Bible Society. A brief dictionary of the Vulgate New Testament by Dr Harden has recently been published by the S.P.C.K.

From this they may pass on to the study of the easier Fathers, such as Cyprian, or to the Latin Hymns.

Unfortunately there are not many editions of the Latin Fathers readily accessible to English readers. The only collection of cheap texts is found in the series "Opuscula SS. Patrum," edited by H. Hurter at Innsbruck. The S.P.C.K. "Texts for Students" series contains some Latin texts.

At present the only texts of Latin Hymns readily available are the *Hymni Latini*, published by Clowes: *The Hundred best Latin Hymns*, published by Gowans and Gray; the *Cathemerinon* of Prudentius in the "Temple Classics" (Dent) and, for more advanced students, *Early Latin Hymns* by Walpole, Cambridge Press.

It is hoped that the book may be of use to ordination candidates; but there is also another class of student that the author had in mind when writing it, namely those who either begin the study of Latin after they leave school, or who wish to continue their study for the purpose of improving their education.

It is to be feared that not many persons carry away enough Latin with them from school to enable them to read the Classical authors with any readiness; to such persons who wish to improve their knowledge of the language by private study the author offers the following suggestions.

John Locke stated that in his opinion the best way for an adult to learn Latin was by reading the Latin Bible, and so great a linguistic genius as Lord Macaulay did not disdain to learn German from a German Bible. The author feels confident from experience that those who begin with the Latin Bible and the easier Ecclesiastical authors will be able to go on to the study of the Classics, if they desire to do so, with far more intelligence and profit than if they had tried to approach them without some previous preparation. He believes that, in the general absence of any opportunity of hearing spoken Latin and speaking the language oneself,

[1] For beginners the author recommends *Latin for Beginners*, by Benjamin L. Dooge. Ginn and Co. *Gradatim*, by Heatley and Kingdon, is also useful.

the next best course is to read as much as possible of such authors as are most easily understood[1].

The Gospels in the Vulgate are very simple and easy to understand, and the same simplicity of style is also found in some of the early Ecclesiastical writers and in many mediaeval writers, especially in the Hymns and Liturgies.

Speaking generally there is a directness and absence of artificiality about the Ecclesiastical writers which makes their works more easily intelligible than most of those of the Classical writers, except Caesar, and they have the advantage over his works in that they contain no long passages in "Oratio Obliqua."

Much of Classical Latin is highly artificial, not to say unnatural, in its modes of expression. The authors whose works are most generally read wrote for a fastidious and highly cultivated society of *littérateurs* who, in most cases, thought far more of style than of matter. Their subject-matter was often borrowed from the Greek; they wrote rather to please than to instruct; and, especially under the early Empire, they wrote with a view to reading their works to admiring circles of friends, whose applause they hoped to arouse by some novel or far-fetched turn of expression. All Classical Latin literature, except the very best, is vitiated by rhetoric, and by the desire to say old things in a new way.

The Christian authors, on the other hand, although most of them had been trained in the rhetorical schools, and although their writings show many traces of their training, were at least men in

[1] The author is pleased to find that his opinion in this matter is confirmed by the high authority of the late Dr J. H. Moulton in the parallel case of an adult who wishes to learn Greek.

Dr Moulton considers that this study may be most easily approached by the way of N.T. and Hellenistic Greek, which, in Latin, is paralleled by the Vulgate and the Ecclesiastical writers.

Dr Moulton's words are as follows:

"Men who have had no educational advantages, called to the work (of the ministry) after many years away from school—how shall we best train them for service in which experience shows they may be surpassingly useful?...Perhaps the writer may contribute his experience of some years. Hellenistic Greek proves a far shorter road than the Classical grammar which the writer used in his schoolmaster days. A short and simple grammar and reader in New Testament Greek, written for the purpose, supplies the forms and syntax needed for intelligent reading of the sacred text; and with this basis it is found that students with an aptitude for languages can go on to Classical Greek when they have become proficient in the far easier Hellenistic." J. H. Moulton in *Camb. Biblical Essays.*

deadly earnest. They did not write to amuse the leisure of their friends: those of the first three centuries wrote with the fear of death always hanging over them to men who needed help and guidance in the face of the same terror: those belonging to the age after the triumph of the Church wrote of things which they held to be of eternal and sovereign importance both to themselves and to those who should read their books. This, generally speaking, gives their writings a simplicity and directness which greatly facilitates the progress of the learner.

Even the Latin of the middle ages, although it is certainly not Ciceronian, and would not have passed current even with Jerome, yet is a wonderfully forcible and pregnant form of speech at its best.

It is foolish to condemn and neglect a whole period of literature, because the style in which it is written does not come up to a purely artificial and arbitrary literary standard.

It is not necessary to deny the great excellence of the Latin of the Augustan age, and of Cicero in particular, in order to see merits in the Latin of other periods. We may heartily agree that the Latin of the Golden Age is supreme and unapproachable. We may all wish to write like Cicero and do our best to imitate him; but this is no reason why we should refuse to see any merit in writers who, carried on by the natural development of the language, and by the strange and novel ideas which they were constrained to express, wrote in a different style, and with a different vocabulary.

There is no more reason for setting up the writers of the Augustan age as models of style, and labelling all that does not conform to their standard as decadent or barbarous, than there would be for setting up Dryden, Pope and Johnson as the only correct writers of English. No language in which it is still possible for an author to express his thoughts with precision and clearness can justly be called decadent or barbarous, even though it does not conform to a given standard; and it is by this test, rather than by approximation to any "Classical" style, that the later authors should be judged.

Although, as has been said, much of the work of the earlier Ecclesiastical authors is vitiated by the rhetorical devices common to the period in which they lived, and although many of the later authors are barbarous enough; yet, with few exceptions, all the best known writings of Ecclesiastical authors of the first rank are worth studying in the original.

There are very few books accessible on this subject. The following have been consulted:

GOELZER. La Latinité de St Jérôme (deals with Jerome's writings other than the Vg.).

REGNIER. La Latinité des sermons de St Augustin.

KAULEN. Sprachliches Handbuch zur Biblischen Vulgata. (New edition, Freiburg im Breisgau 1904.)

ROENSCH. Itala und Vulgata.

DALPANE. Nuovo Lessico della Bibbia Volgata (Firenze 1911).

PEULTIER, ETIENNE, GANTOIS. Concordantiarum universae Scripturae Sanctae Thesaurus. Paris.

None of these books except the first and the last are very helpful.

The author wishes to thank Dr H. J. White, Dean of Christ Church, for kind advice and encouragement.

H. P. V. N.

17 DAVENPORT PARK ROAD,
STOCKPORT

November 1921

PREFACE TO SECOND EDITION

IN several of the reviews of the first edition of this book it was assumed that the author believed that "Ecclesiastical Latin" was a special dialect written by Church writers. It was pointed out by the reviewers (quite unnecessarily) that the opinion that "New Testament Greek" was a special dialect had long been given up and that it was now universally held that the New Testament was written in the colloquial Greek of the time, influenced to some extent by the Semitic nationality of the writers. The reviewers then went on to assume that the author was as much in error about the nature of "Ecclesiastical Latin" as earlier writers had been as to the nature of "New Testament Greek." It was also assumed that he wished to bring all Christian writers of Latin, however much they might differ in date, culture and nationality, under one classification.

It is unfortunate that the necessity of choosing a brief title for the work should have made this supposition possible to those who did not take the trouble to read what the author actually did say on this topic in the body of the book.

If the term "Ecclesiastical Latin" is employed for want of a better one, this must not be taken to imply that anything else is meant than that it is Latin written by men who were for the most part Christians, who studied the Latin Bible rather than Vergil and Cicero and who made use of the spoken rather than the literary idiom of their time when writing for the people.

They of course differed widely from one another in culture, but they had this in common that they all read the Latin Bible with at least as much devotion as the Classical authors read Classical Greek and they (generally speaking) avoided extravagant rhetoric.

The author fully agrees that the basis of the Latin which they used was the spoken Latin of their time, but he believes that their style was as much influenced by that of the Latin Bible as that of the average English writer on religious subjects is by the Authorised Version.

If he has taken his examples almost exclusively from the Vulgate New Testament, this is for two reasons:

(1) The Vulgate New Testament is the most easily procurable and the most familiar of all Christian Latin books.

(2) It is a fact (explain it how you will) that examples of the constructions most common in Christian Latin authors who rise above the level of absolute barbarism can always be found in the Vulgate.

It should be remembered that this book does not claim to be exhaustive in any way. It is only an "Introduction," written for beginners, to the Latin written by Christian authors from the appearance of the first Latin version of the Bible until the revival of learning.

Since it was published, *A Grammar of the Vulgate* has been published by Mr Plater and Dr White at the Oxford Press.

The author has had the advantage of consulting this book and has taken the liberty of inserting a few of the examples there given.

He also desires to thank certain kind correspondents who have pointed out many errors which were left in the first edition owing to circumstances over which he had no control at the time of its publication.

Students of this book will find *Excerpta Biblica* by Messrs Willis and Stephen, published by Dent, very useful. This book consists of extracts from the Latin Bible with the usages which offend most against Classical Syntax removed. *A Primer of Mediaeval Latin*, by C. H. Beeson, published in Chicago, contains some interesting extracts from mediaeval writers. There is also a Latin version of *Robinson Crusoe*, published by Sands and Co., which is likely to be very useful to those for whom this book has been written.

THE ORIGIN AND CHARACTER OF ECCLESIASTICAL LATIN

THE basis, and much of the content, of Ecclesiastical Latin is to be found in the vernacular speech of the Roman people of which but little survives in literature.

The form of Latin which is most commonly studied is that which is to be found in the writings of the great authors who lived in the century before the commencement of the Christian era. To this form of the language the name 'Classical' has been given, and it is often referred to as the Latin of the Golden Age.

All the books of this period that have come down to us were the work of highly trained literary men who were thoroughly acquainted with Greek literature and who imitated of set purpose not only its form, but also its content.

> Vos exemplaria Graeca
> Nocturna versate manu, versate diurna,

was the maxim which all of them followed.

The consequence of this is that 'Classical Latin' is, speaking generally, a very artificial form of language. It may be said of it, as has been said of Attic Greek (as portrayed in the literature of Athens), that it is an artistic language which nobody ever spoke, but which everybody understood.

This form of the language, however, was regarded in ancient, no less than in modern times, as an example to be followed, as far as possible. The writings of Cicero, Vergil, Horace and Ovid were studied in the schools of the Roman Empire in Africa, Gaul and Spain, no less than in Italy, as models of style and vocabulary, and left an ineffaceable mark on the language. They continued to be studied, though with less zeal and intelligence, throughout many periods in the middle ages and at the Renaissance they came in for more than their own.

To write like Cicero or Vergil became the passionate desire of all scholars and the chief end of education: the direction then given to literary study has influenced the course of teaching almost to the present day.

In spite of the protests of Erasmus, style was set up as the end after which the scholar must strive, and that a style not his own, but a style imitated from great writers who lived nearly two thousand years ago under quite a different civilization, and in another sphere of thought. The skill most commended was that which caught some trick of phrase and adapted it to the translation of contemporary forms of expression. It was this 'Ciceronianism,' as it has been called, that did so much to kill Latin as a living language, because it checked all spontaneity and preferred to galvanize a corpse rather than to encourage the growth of a living organism.

During the time when the Classical literature was growing into perfection and passing into the stage of imitation and decay the Vernacular Latin also continued to grow and, like all growing organisms, to absorb many elements from its surroundings.

Those who spoke it were not deterred by any fear of the schoolmaster or the audiences in the recitation rooms from adding new words when they were required to express new ideas.

The genius of the old Latin language, like that of the old Roman people, expressed itself in action and was rich only in verbs and in concrete terms. Abstract ideas were quite foreign to native Latin thought, and, when the introduction of Greek philosophy rendered it necessary to express such ideas in speech, recourse was had either to a periphrasis or to new-coined or adopted words.

Substantives ending in *io*, *ia* and *tas* began to increase in number and also adjectives in *is*; but the Classical writers avoided these new methods of expression as far as possible, or introduced them with an apology. It was not until the old Latin families had been killed off in the civil wars, until Greek became the language of all educated men in Rome and the most celebrated Latin authors began to arise, not in Italy, but in Spain and Africa, that the boundaries of the old Latin speech were gradually broken down, and a flood of new words and constructions, mostly borrowed from Greek, or suggested by it, mingled with the stately current of the ancient diction. Such words as *essentia*, *substantia*, *personalis*, *possibilis* then came into use, all, be it noted, words that have passed into English. The Latin language ceased to be the language of a nation and became the language of an empire.

The language in which the Christian writers first wrote was, of course, Greek. Greek, thanks to the conquests of Alexander, was the *lingua franca* of the East where Christianity took its origin.

When St Paul wished to write to the Church in Rome, he wrote in Greek. When St Clement (a Roman Bishop) wrote to Corinth he also wrote in Greek. Many of the earliest inscriptions in the Catacombs are in Greek. Latin does not seem to have been commonly used in the Roman Church until the end of the second century[1].

It was not for Rome that a Latin translation of the Bible was needed, but for Africa, Gaul and Spain, and perhaps for the country congregations of Italy.

The first Christian writing in Latin of which we have any knowledge is this Latin version of the Bible. It is commonly known as the *Old Latin* version and will be referred to here by the abbreviation O.L. It is not known with any certainty by whom or when this translation was made. It seems to have been a composite work made by several hands, perhaps at different periods. It had one marked peculiarity: it was an extremely literal translation.

"We have already said," writes Gaston Boissier, "that the first persons who translated the Holy Scriptures into Latin were not professional authors, but only scrupulous Christians who desired no other merit except that of being faithful interpreters. Preoccupied before all things with the object of basing their version on the text, they created new words, invented strange expressions, and tortured the ancient language without pity, to make it fit the genius of a foreign idiom. Can anyone imagine what an admirer of Vergil or a pupil of Cicero must have had to suffer when thrown into the middle of this barbarism[2]?"

At the beginning of the third century we find that a generally received translation of the Bible was coming into use at Carthage, and by the middle of the century it was quite established.

This translation underwent many revisions. A rather smoother version circulated in Italy and Gaul: another, still more refined, was used by St Augustine in the fourth and fifth century, and this is sometimes called the *Itala*.

The first of these versions is found in the writings of Cyprian and in the Codex Bobbiensis. The second is found in the Codex

[1] See Sanday and Headlam, *Romans*, p. lii.

[2] *La Fin du Paganisme*, vol. 1, p. 351.

Veronensis. The third is found in the writings of Augustine and in the Codex Brixianus.

In these versions the translation of the O.T. was made from the Greek version known as the Septuagint (commonly called the LXX) which was accepted by the early Church as quite as authoritative as the Hebrew original which few Christians could read. This LXX version was also a very literal translation of the Hebrew, literal to the verge of unintelligibility in many places, especially in the poetical and prophetic books.

Thus the O.L. version of the O.T. was the literal translation of a literal Greek translation of a Hebrew original, and it is not wonderful if not only the beauty, but also the sense, of the original often disappeared under such handling.

The O.L. version of the N.T. was made from the Greek original. Anyone who wishes to see how literal it is may compare the Latin version of the Epistle to the Ephesians with the Greek original and then with Beza's version.

The most potent influences in the formation of early Ecclesiastical Latin were (1) the Vernacular Latin of the period, by which the Fathers allowed themselves to be influenced in order that they might be understood by half-educated people, (2) the O.L. version of the Bible with its many Graecisms and Hebraisms, (3) the Classical Latin as taught in the schools, of which all the Fathers were pupils, or even teachers.

We might perhaps add a fourth source of influence to the above, namely the writings of Tertullian, who was an author of a very original and independent type of genius and who had great influence on all his Christian successors, especially on Cyprian.

The O.L. version of the Bible did not however influence later Ecclesiastical Latin directly.

The text got into such a bad condition at the end of the fourth century that Pope Damasus commissioned the most famous scholar of the day to re-edit it.

This man Eusebius Hieronymus, or Jerome, as he is commonly called, had studied Latin in Rome under Donatus, was well acquainted with Greek and had some knowledge of Hebrew. When he set to work on the task imposed on him by Pope Damasus he found that the translation of the O.T. was so incorrect and corrupt that nothing but a complete retranslation of the whole from the Hebrew could produce a satisfactory result. He therefore set himself to improve his knowledge of Hebrew and, in the face of great opposition and much prejudice, he retranslated the whole of the O.T. from the Hebrew original. But in so doing he seems to have kept as near as he could to the version which he was trying to supersede, and not to have made any attempt to translate it into such Latin as he wrote himself in his letters and commentaries. Perhaps he found it was impossible to bring about any nearer approximation of the languages, or perhaps he feared the storm of obloquy that any such attempt would have aroused; in any case his version is a revision of the O.L. with the help of direct reference to the Hebrew, and not a new translation, such as might have been expected from a man of Jerome's literary powers. It is not in any sense a Latin Classic as the English Bible is an English Classic, and Cardinal Bembo was not altogether without excuse when he warned a brother Cardinal not to read the Vulgate—as Jerome's Latin version is called—lest he should spoil his Latin style.

The popular prejudice against Jerome's version was such that it was found impossible ever to induce the people to accept his version of the Psalms—the part of the O.T. most familiar to them from its use in public worship. To this day in the official edition of the Vulgate the version of the Psalms is not the one that Jerome made from the Hebrew, but a revision of the *Old Latin* version that he made in the early part of his life with the help of the Greek of the LXX only.

Those who wish to get some idea of what the O.L. version of the O.T. must have been will get a good idea by reading the Psalter in the Vulgate.

Jerome did not think it necessary to make a new translation of the New Testament. He revised the Gospels carefully and the rest of the N.T. in a cursory manner.

He did not set much store by the books of the Apocrypha and therefore only retranslated Tobit and Judith, and did not even revise the others. The result of his labours is thus a composite work which after a time won universal acceptance and was declared by the Council of Trent to be 'authentic.' This version, as has been said, is called the *Vulgate*, or commonly received version. An authoritative text was edited by order of Popes Sixtus V and Clement VIII and can be procured in many editions[1]. Of late years

[1] An edition in good type and convenient form is that of Hetzenauer, published by Pustet.

a new edition of the N.T. has been undertaken by the late Dr Wordsworth, Bishop of Salisbury, and Dr H. J. White, now Dean of Christ Church, Oxford.

This is being published in its full form by the Oxford Press, and a small edition is published by the Oxford Press and by the Bible Society.

It was this Vulgate version that had supreme influence in the middle ages when Greek and Hebrew were unknown to all but a very few scholars. The revival of Greek and Hebrew studies at the Renaissance was looked upon with grave suspicion by the scholars of the old learning as leading to heresy.

The old version had such a hold that even Erasmus, when he published a new Latin version in parallel columns with his edition of the Greek text, contented himself with copying the Vulgate version with the correction of a few of the most glaring solecisms. Beza put out a new version in Latin in the seventeenth century which is still published by the Bible Society. It is interesting to an advanced student to compare this version with the Vulgate[1].

The points in which Ecc. L. differs from Cl. L. are principally the following:

The use of a great number of abstract and compound nouns and of nouns denoting an agent and ending in *or*.

The use of diminutives. The use of words transliterated from Greek.

The extended use of prepositions where in Cl. L. a simple case of the noun would have sufficed.

The disappearance of long and elaborate sentences with many dependent clauses. Clauses are often connected simply by *et*, or no conjunction is used at all.

The disappearance to a great extent of the Oratio Obliqua and the Accusative with Infinitive construction.

The substitution therefor of a new construction imitated from the Greek and introduced by *quod*, *quia*, or *quoniam*.

The gradual extension of this construction even in clauses where *ut* would be used in Cl. L. especially in noun clauses.

[1] For further information see articles on Latin Versions and Vulgate in Hastings' *Dictionary of the Bible* and Sir Frederick Kenyon's *Our Bible and the Ancient Manuscripts*.

The Infinitive used to express purpose or result, as in Greek, and also to express dependent commands.

The Subjunctive is used where it would not be used in Cl. L. and vice versa.

The use of periphrastic forms of verbs, especially forms made up with *esse* or *habere*.

In a word we see the process at work which turned the Latin of the Empire into the modern Romance languages.

SYNTAX

SENTENCES.

1. Syntax deals with the methods by which words are combined to form sentences.

A sentence is a group of words expressing a statement, a question, or a desire. (Under the term *desire* commands, entreaties and wishes are to be included.)

2. Every sentence must consist of at least two parts, either expressed or understood:

(1) **The Subject**—the word or group of words denoting the person or thing of which the predicate is said.

(2) **The Predicate**—the word or group of words denoting all that is said about the subject; or the word or group of words which expresses the assertion that is made, the question that is asked, or the desire that is expressed about the subject. The predicate is not necessarily identical with the verb. It includes the complements and extensions of the verb and also the object.

If a verb is transitive it must have an object.

The Object is the word or group of words denoting the person or thing towards which the action of the verb is directed.

The verb agrees with its subject in number and person.

3. Verbs which require a complement to complete their meaning are called **Copulative verbs**. The most important copulative verb is the verb *to be*.

Verbs which signify *to become*, *to appear*, *to be chosen*, *to be named*, and the like are also copulative.

If the complement of a copulative verb is a noun, it agrees with the subject of the verb in number and case; if it is an adjective, it agrees with the subject of the verb in number, gender and case.

This rule is sometimes put in the following form:

The verb 'to be' takes the same case after it as before it.

Examples:

Caesar imperator est. *Caesar is general.*

Metelli facti sunt consules. *The Metelli have been made consuls.*

Rex magnus est. *The king is great.*

Regina magna est. *The queen is great.*
Reges magni sunt. *The kings are great.*
Regnum magnum fit. *The kingdom becomes great.*
Felices appellamur. *We are called happy.*

4. A Simple sentence is a sentence which contains a single subject and a single predicate.

Multiple and Complex sentences are sentences which contain more than one subject and predicate.

In dealing with sentences it will be found convenient to keep carefully to the following terminology:

The name *sentence* should be applied only to a complete statement, command, or question occurring between two full stops.

Groups of words forming part of a multiple or complex sentence, and having a subject and predicate of their own should be called *clauses*.

Groups of words forming an equivalent to some part of speech, and not having a subject and predicate of their own, should be called *phrases*.

5. A Multiple sentence is a sentence which consists of two or more clauses none of which depends on any of the others, but which all make equally important and independent statements. These clauses are said to be combined by co-ordination.

In the Heb. language such co-ordinated clauses are very common, and this peculiarity is faithfully reflected in the Vg. O.T., and, to a certain extent, in the N.T. In Latin, uninfluenced by Heb., clauses are more generally combined into complex sentences.

Example:

Et egressus est rursus ad mare: omnisque turba veniebat ad eum, et docebat eos. *And he went out again to the sea, and all the crowd came to him, and he taught them.* Mk. ii, 13.

6. A Complex sentence is a sentence which consists of a principal or main clause and one or more subordinate clauses depending on it, or on one another as noun, adjective, or adverb equivalents. These clauses are said to be combined by subordination.

Example:

Si quis voluerit voluntatem ejus facere, cognoscet de doctrina, utrum ex Deo sit, an ego a meipso loquar. *If any man willeth to do his will, he shall know of the teaching, whether it is of God, or whether I speak of myself.* Jn. vii, 17.

7. Subordinate clauses are divided into three classes:

(1) **Noun or Substantival clauses** that take the place of a noun.

(2) **Adjectival clauses** that take the place of an adjective.

(3) **Adverbial clauses** that take the place of an adverb.

NOUNS.

8. Cases and their meanings. Inflection is a change made in the form of a word to denote a modification of its meaning, or to show the relationship of the word to some other word in the sentence.

Examples: *bird* becomes *birds* in the Pl. and *man* becomes *men*. The pronoun *he* is used when it is the subject of a sentence; but it is changed into *him* when it is the object. There are however few inflections left in English.

Latin nouns, pronouns and adjectives have inflections to show number and case; adjectives and some pronouns have inflections to show gender as well.

To give a list of these inflections is called *giving a declension*, or *declining a word*, because the cases other than the Nominative were considered by the old grammarians to fall away (*declinare*) from the form of the Nominative. For the same reason cases other than the Nominative are sometimes called Oblique cases.

Hence also the origin of the name *Case* from the Latin *casus* = falling.

The cases actually in use are seven in number.

(1) The Nominative, used to express the subject of a finite verb.

(2) The Vocative, used in addressing a person or thing.

(3) The Accusative, used to denote motion towards and to express the object of a transitive verb.

(4) The Genitive, used to limit the meaning of another noun like an adjective and to denote various relations most of which are expressed in Eng. by the use of the preposition *of* or by the possessive case.

(5) The Dative, used to express that to or for which anything is done. This includes the dative of the indirect object after transitive verbs.

(6) The Ablative, used to express separation or motion from and in many other senses.

(7) The Locative, which is not given in the tables of declensions in grammars, used to denote the place at which anything happens in certain expressions.

9. The Nominative Case is the case of **the Subject** of a sentence or clause in all sentences or clauses in which the verb is not in the Infinitive mood.

Tunc discipuli ejus, relinquentes eum, omnes fugerunt. *Then all his disciples forsook him and fled.* Mk. xiv, 50.

10. The Vocative Case is used in **addressing** a person or a personified thing.

Bone Pastor, Panis vere, *Good Shepherd, true Bread,*
Jesu, nostri miserere. *Jesus, have mercy on us.*

11. The Accusative Case denotes **motion towards** or **extension.**

It is therefore the case of the **Direct Object,** because the object is the name of that towards which the action of the verb goes forth.

So the Acc. is used with or without a preposition to denote **motion towards.**

The Acc. denotes the **time during which** anything happens and also **extent of space.**

12. The Acc. is used to express the direct object of a transitive verb.

Qui videt me, videt eum qui misit me. *He that seeth me, seeth him that sent me.* Jn. xii, 45.

Many verbs which are transitive in English are represented by intransitive verbs in Latin:—Mihi nocet. *He harms me.* Mei obliviscitur. *He forgets me.* Pane vescitur. *He eats bread.*

13. Motion towards is generally expressed by a preposition such as *ad* or *in* followed by a noun in the Acc. case.

The preposition is omitted in Cl. L. before the names of towns and small islands and before certain words such as *domum, rus, foras.*

In the Vg. a preposition is generally used before *domum,* and it is also found before the names of towns.

Non relinquam vos orphanos: veniam ad vos. *I will not leave you orphans: I will come to you.* Jn. xiv, 18.

Sed cum Romam venisset, sollicite me quaesivit. *But when he came to Rome, he sought me out diligently.* II Tim. i, 17.

Venit ergo iterum in Cana Galilaeae.... *He came therefore again to Cana of Galilee....* Jn. iv, 46.

14. The Acc. may denote **extent of time or space,** but in Ecc. L. the Abl. is often used for extent of time. See section 55.

Et mansit ibi duos dies. *And he remained there two days.* Jn. iv, 40.

15. Cognate Accusative. Any verb whose meaning permits it may take after it an Acc. of cognate or kindred meaning.

Bonum certamen certavi. *I have fought a good fight.* II Tim. iv, 7.

Nolite judicare secundum faciem, sed justum judicium judicate. *Do not judge after the appearance, but judge a righteous judgment.* Jn. vii, 24.

See also Lk. ii, 8; I Tim. vi, 12; I Pet. iii, 14.

16. Certain verbs meaning to teach, to ask, to conceal are followed by **two Accusatives,** one of the person and another of the thing.

If a verb of this kind is used in the Passive voice the object noun denoting the thing is retained in the Acc. case.

Ille vos docebit omnia. *He shall teach you all things.* Jn. xiv, 26.

Aut quis est ex vobis homo, quem si petierit filius suus panem, numquid lapidem porriget ei? *Or what man is there of you whom, if his son ask him for a loaf, will he give him a stone?* Mt. vii, 9.

Hic erat edoctus viam Domini. *He was instructed in the way of the Lord.* Acts xviii, 25.

17. Two Object Accusatives are rarely used, in imitation of Gk., after verbs meaning *to put on.*

This is not Cl. The Cl. construction is to use the Acc. of the person and the Abl. of the thing put on.

Calcia te caligas tuas. *Put on thy sandals.* Acts xii, 8.

Induite vos armaturam Dei. *Put on yourselves the armour of God.* Eph. vi, 11.

Induti loricam fidei. *Clad with the breastplate of faith.* I Thess. v, 8.

So in one instance with a verb meaning *to put off*:

Expoliantes vos veterem hominem. *Putting off from yourselves the old man.* Col. iii, 9.

18. The Acc. is sometimes used after **Passive** verbs to denote an action done to oneself. This seems to be an imitation of the Greek Middle voice. This construction is rare in prose, but common in Latin poetry, where it is used with great freedom.

State ergo succincti lumbos vestros in veritate: et induti loricam justitiae, et calciati pedes in praeparatione evangelii pacis. *Stand therefore with your loins girt about with truth, and having put on the breastplate of righteousness, and with your feet shod with the preparation of the gospel of peace.* Eph. vi, 14.

Abluti corpus aqua munda. *With our body washed with pure water.* Heb. x, 22.

19. The Genitive Case is an **adjectival** or **descriptive** case. A noun in the Gen. case is generally connected with another noun which it qualifies very much in the same way as an adjective.

The Gen. case can generally be translated into Eng. by the use of the preposition *of* or by the Possessive case.

The name *Genitive case* means the case of kind or origin; but the case is most frequently used to denote possession.

20. Possessive Genitive denoting possession.

Justorum autem animae in manu Dei sunt. *But the souls of the righteous are in the hand of God.* Wisdom iii, 1.

21. The Gen. may express **authorship, source,** or **material,** or almost any relationship that can exist between two persons or things.

Inter natos mulierum. *Among those born of women.* Mt. xi, 11.

Periculis fluminum, periculis latronum. *In perils of rivers, in perils of robbers...* (i.e. *arising from rivers or robbers*). II Cor. xi, 26.

Ergo evacuatum est scandalum crucis. *Therefore the reproach of the cross has ceased.* Gal. v, 11.

Prae gaudio illius. *For joy thereof.* Mt. xiii, 44.

So the Gen. is used to denote **personal relationship** such as that of son and father, mother and son, or even husband and wife

Dicebat autem Judam Simonis Iscariotem. *But he spake of Judas Iscariot, the son of Simon.* Jn. vi, 71.

Stabant autem juxta crucem Jesu...Maria Cleophae et Maria Magdalene. *But Mary the wife of Cleophas and Mary Magdalene were standing by the cross of Jesus.* Jn. xix, 25.

22. The Partitive Genitive expresses the whole after words denoting a part.

Magister bone, quid boni faciam, ut habeam vitam aeternam? *Good Master, what good thing shall I do that I may have eternal life?* Mt. xix, 16.

See also Mt. xxv, 19; Acts v, 15; Rom. xv, 26; Acts xxiv, 21.

23. The Subjective Genitive. The Gen. is said to be used subjectively when the noun which is in the Gen. case is the name of the doer of the action denoted by the noun with which it is connected.

Quis nos separabit a caritate Christi? *Who shall separate us from the love of Christ?* (i.e. *from the love that Christ feels for us*). Rom. viii, 35.

Propter quod tradidit illos Deus in desideria cordis eorum. *Wherefore God gave them up to the desires of their own heart.* Rom. i, 24.

See also II Cor. v, 14; I Tim. iv, 1.

The Subjective Gen. is also found in the Vg. after adjectives and participles in imitation of the Gk.

Et erunt omnes docibiles Dei. *And they shall all be taught of God.* Jn. vi, 45.

Quae et loquimur non in doctis humanae sapientiae verbis.... *Which also we speak, not in words taught by human wisdom....* I Cor. ii, 13.

24. The Objective Genitive. The Gen. is said to be used objectively when the noun which is in the Gen. case is the name of the object of the action denoted by the noun with which it is connected.

The objective Gen. is used much more freely in the Vg. than in Cl. L., in imitation of the Gk. It is often used with nouns which express the action of an intransitive verb.

Dedit illis potestatem spirituum immundorum. *He gave them power* (*to cast out*) *unclean spirits.* Mt. x, 1.

Sicut dedisti ei potestatem omnis carnis. *As thou hast given him power over all flesh.* Jn. xvii, 2.

Et erat pernoctans in oratione Dei. *And he was spending all the night in prayer to God.* Lk. vi, 12.

Si nos hodie judicamur in benefacto hominis infirmi.... *If we are judged to-day for a good deed done to an impotent man....* Acts iv, 9.

Quidam autem conscientia usque nunc idoli, quasi idolothytum manducant.... *For some men with the consciousness even now of the idol eat it as a thing offered to an idol....* I Cor. viii, 7.

Spiritus autem blasphemia non remittetur. *But blasphemy against the Spirit shall not be forgiven.* Mt. xii, 31.

See also Mk. xi, 22; Jn. ii, 17; Rom. x, 2, xv, 8; II Cor. x, 5; Col. ii, 12; I Tim. iii, 5.

25. The Possessive Pronoun may be used in the sense of an objective Gen.

Hoc facite in meam commemorationem. *Do this in remembrance of me.* Lk. xxii, 19.

Quaecumque enim scripta sunt, ad nostram doctrinam scripta sunt. *For whatsoever things were written were written for our learning*—(i.e. *to teach us*). Rom. xv, 4.

Neque veni Hierosolymam ad antecessores meos apostolos. *Nor did I go to Jerusalem to the apostles who were before me.* Gal. i, 17.

Ita et isti non crediderunt in vestram misericordiam. *So they also did not believe that mercy might be shown to you.* Rom. xi, 31.

Quotidie morior per vestram gloriam, fratres, quam habeo in Christo Jesu Domino nostro. *I die daily, brethren, I protest by the glorying in you which I have in Christ Jesus our Lord.* I Cor. xv, 31.

The question whether a Gen. is subjective or objective can only be decided by the context. Sometimes the decision is not easy.

26. The Descriptive Genitive is used to give a description or explanation of the noun with which it is connected.

In Cl. L. a descriptive Gen. is always qualified by an adjective; but this is not always the case in Ecc. L.

In the Vg. the use of this Gen. is widely extended in imitation of the Construct state in Heb. There are few adjectives in Heb., and a noun in the Construct state is connected with another noun where an adjective would be used in Latin or Gk.

Et facti estis judices cogitationum iniquarum. *And ye become judges with evil thoughts* (i.e. *unfair judges*). Jas. ii, 4.

Quia propter te mortificamur: tota die aestimati sumus ut

oves occisionis. *Because we are put to death for thy sake: all the day we are counted as sheep for the slaughter.*

Rom. viii, 36, quoted from Ps. xliii, 22.

In odorem suavitatis. *For a sweet smelling savour.*

Eph. v, 2.

Annorum enim erat amplius quadraginta homo, in quo factum erat signum istud sanitatis. *For the man was more than forty years old on whom this sign of healing was done.*

Acts iv, 22.

See also Mt. viii, 26; Mk. i, 4; Lk. ii, 14; Jn. v, 29, vii, 35; Rom. xv, 5; Phil. iii, 21.

27. The descriptive Gen. may also be used **predicatively.**

Nescitis cujus spiritus estis. *Ye know not of what spirit ye are.* Lk. ix, 55.

Nam ut impudentis est clamoribus strepere, ita congruit verecundo modestis precibus orare. *For as it is the mark of a shameless person to make a disturbance with his cries, so it befits a modest person to pray with restraint.*

Cyprian, *De Oratione Dominica.*

28. **The Genitive of price or value.** The Gen. of some neuter adjectives such as *magni, parvi, tanti, quanti,* is used to denote the price at which a thing is valued, bought or sold.

Dixit autem ei Petrus: Dic mihi, mulier, si tanti agrum vendidistis? *But Peter said to her: "Tell me, woman, if you sold the field for so much?"* Acts v, 8; Lk. xii, 24.

29. The Gen. is used **after certain verbs** which are not transitive in Latin as they are in Eng.

Most verbs meaning to pity, to remember, to forget, are followed by a Gen. case in Cl. L.

In the Vg. the usage varies. A Dat. is found after *misereor* and sometimes *super* with an Acc.

Ps. cii, 13; Prov. xxi, 10; Mt. ix, 36; Mk. viii, 2.

Recordor is very rarely followed by an Acc.

Hos. vii, 2; Ez. xxiii, 19.

Memini is also rarely followed by an Acc.

Is. xlvi, 8; I Macc. vii, 38.

Obliviscor is followed by an Acc.

Ps. ix. 18, xlix, 22; Heb. xiii, 2.

The following are examples of the normal use.

Misertus autem dominus servi illius, dimisit eum. *But the lord taking pity on that slave, forgave him.* Mt. xviii, 27.

Omnia ostendi vobis, quoniam sic laborantes oportet suscipere infirmos, ac meminisse verbi Domini Jesu, quoniam ipse dixit: Beatius est magis dare quam accipere. *I have shown you all things, that so labouring ye ought to support the weak, and to remember the word of the Lord Jesus, how he said: "It is more blessed to give than to receive."* Acts xx, 35.

Non enim injustus Deus, ut obliviscatur operis vestri.... *For God is not unjust that he should forget your work....* Heb. vi, 10.

30. The following uses of the Gen. which are not found in Cl. L., but which are found in the Vg., in imitation of Gk., should be noted.

Verbs meaning to rule are followed by a Gen.

Reges gentium dominantur eorum. *The kings of the nations rule over them.* Lk. xxii, 25.

See also Acts xix, 16; Rom. xiv, 9.

31. The Gen. of a word may follow another case of the same word to heighten its meaning.

Ecce sum vivens in saecula saeculorum. *Behold I am alive for ever more.* Rev. i, 18.

32. **The Genitive Absolute** is found.

Qui ostendunt opus legis scriptum in cordibus suis, testimonium reddente illis conscientia ipsorum, et inter se invicem cogitationum accusantium, aut etiam defendentium. *Who show the work of the law written in their hearts, their own conscience bearing testimony to them, and their thoughts accusing them, or even defending them to themselves.* Rom. ii, 15.

This is the reading of Wordsworth and White. The SC text reads *cogitationibus accusantibus*, etc.

See also Acts i, 8; II Cor. x, 15.

At first sight it might seem that these passages might be explained differently, more in accordance with Latin usage; but the original Gk. shows that the construction is meant for the Gen. Absolute.

33. The Gen. is used after the comparative of an adjective.

Qui credit in me, opera quae ego facio et ipse faciet: et majora horum faciet.... *He that believes in me, the works that I do he shall do also: and greater than these shall he do....* Jn. xiv, 12.

See also Mk. xii, 31; Acts xvii, 11; Heb. iii, 3, vi, 16; III Jn. 4.

34. The Gen. may be used to express space within which.

Et videtis, et auditis, quia non solum Ephesi, sed paene totius Asiae, Paulus hic suadens avertit multam turbam.... *And ye see and hear that not only at Ephesus, but throughout almost all Asia, this Paul persuades and turns away much people.* Acts xix, 26.

35. The Dative Case denotes that to or for which anything is done. It is generally translated into Eng. by the use of the prepositions *to* or *for*.

N.B. The Dat. does not denote motion to.

36. The Dat. of the **Indirect Object** is used after many verbs which are also followed by a direct object in the Acc. case.

> Pecuniam copiosam dederunt militibus.... *They gave large money to the soldiers....* Mt. xxviii, 12.

37. When verbs which are followed by an indirect object in the Dat. as well as by a direct object in the Acc. are used in the Passive voice, the direct object becomes the subject of the sentence and the Dat. remains.

> Auferetur a vobis regnum Dei, et dabitur genti facienti fructus ejus. *The kingdom of God shall be taken from you and given to a nation bringing forth the fruits thereof.* Mt. xxi, 43.

38. The Dat. is used after many verbs which are not transitive in Latin as they are in Eng.

The most important of these verbs are:

imperare, *to command.*	suadere, *to persuade.*
ignoscere, *to pardon.*	servire, *to serve.*
remittere, *to pardon.*	placere, *to please.*
parcere, *to spare.*	displicere, *to displease.*
credere, *to believe.*	nocere, *to injure.*
obedire, *to obey.*	resistere, *to resist.*

Many verbs compounded with a preposition are followed by a Dat., especially compounds of *esse*.

> Etenim Christus non sibi placuit. *For even Christ pleased not himself.* Rom. xv, 3.
>
> Hujuscemodi enim Christo Domino nostro non serviunt, sed suo ventri. *For men of this kind do not serve Christ our Lord, but their own belly.* Rom. xvi, 18.
>
> Et obtulerunt ei omnes male habentes. *And they brought to him all that were sick.* Mt. iv, 24.
>
> Quid mihi prodest, si mortui non resurgunt? *What doth it profit me if the dead rise not?* I Cor. xv, 32.

Some verbs that are followed by a Dat. in Cl. L. are followed by an Acc. in Ecc. L.

Credere is often followed by *in* with the Acc., *benedicere* and *maledicere* are followed either by the Dat. or the Acc.

39. If a verb which is followed by the Dat. as its sole object is used in the Passive voice, it is normally used impersonally.

Si enim aliquis diceret aliquid de aliqua terra remota, et ipse non fuisset ibi, non crederetur ei sicut si ibi fuisset. *For if anyone should say anything about some distant land, and he himself had not been there, he would not be believed, as he would be, if he had been there.* Thomas Aquinas.

40. The Dat. may denote the person in whose interest, or against whose interest anything takes place.

Et ecce aperti sunt ei caeli.... *And behold the heavens were opened for him....* Mt. iii, 16.

Quomodo aperti sunt tibi oculi? *How were thine eyes opened for thee?* Jn. ix, 10.

Tibi soli peccavi, et malum coram te feci. *Against thee only have I sinned, and done evil in thy sight.* Ps. li, 4.

See also Mt. xxi, 2, 5, xxvii, 21.

41. The Dat is used with *esse* to denote possession.

Quod tibi nomen est? *What is thy name?* Lk. viii, 30.

Argentum et aurum non est mihi. *Silver and gold have I none.* Acts iii, 6.

42. The Dat. of certain nouns (in Ecc. L. these are generally nouns denoting emotions) is used, especially with *esse*, to denote result or purpose. This Dat. is generally accompanied by another noun or pronoun in the Dat. denoting the person interested.

Et eritis odio omnibus gentibus propter nomen meum. *And ye shall be hated of all nations for my name's sake.* Mt. xxiv, 9.

Et nihil eorum Gallioni curae erat. *And Gallio cared for none of these things.* Acts xviii, 17.

See also Col. iv, 11; I Thess. ii, 7.

43. The Dat. is regularly used to express the Agent after a gerundive participle and rarely after a perfect participle.

Audistis quia dictum est antiquis.... *Ye have heard that it was said by them of old time....* Mt. v, 21.

Novissime autem omnium tanquam abortivo, visus est et

mihi. *And last of all he was seen by me also, as by one born out of due time.* I Cor. xv, 8.

Et ecce nihil dignum morte actum est ei. *And behold nothing worthy of death has been done by him.* Lk. xxiii, 15.

44. The Ablative Case may be described as an **adverbial** case, because a noun in the Abl. case generally qualifies a verb, adjective or adverb in the same way as an adverb.

The name *Ablative case* means the *taking away case.* It is a very unsuitable name, as it covers only a small number of the uses of the case.

The meanings of the Abl. case, as we find it in Latin, are derived from the meanings of three different cases which existed in the primitive form of the language:

1. A true **Ablative** case, denoting separation, or the place from which anything is taken.

2. An **Instrumental,** or **Sociative** case, denoting the instrument by means of which anything is done, or the accompanying circumstances of the action.

3. A **Locative** case, denoting the place where, or the time when anything happens.

The particular kind of meaning denoted by a noun standing in the Abl. case depends partly on the **meaning of the noun itself** and partly on the **meaning of the word with which it is connected.**

Thus in the sentence *Roma abiit,* He went from Rome, *Roma* is obviously used in the proper Abl. signification of separation from.

In the sentence *Baculo puerum percussit,* He struck the boy with a stick, *Baculo* is Instrumental.

In the sentence *Proximo anno rediit,* He returned next year, *anno* is Locative.

The student must always consider the **context** in which a word in the Abl. case is found before attempting to translate it.

The meanings of the case are so various, that it is not well to attach too definite a meaning to it in the mind.

In many instances, especially in late Latin, a preposition is placed before a noun in the Abl. case to make its meaning more precise.

45. The Ablative of Separation, generally translated '*from.*' In Cl. L. the Abl. is used without a preposition to denote motion from a place when the place spoken of is a town or small island.

The Abl. of certain words such as *domo* is used in the same way.

In Ecc. L. a preposition may be used with nouns of this kind; with all other nouns a preposition is used to denote motion from.

Et alia die cum exirent a Bethania, esuriit. *And on another day when they came out from Bethany he was hungry.* Mk. xi, 12.

See also Acts xviii, 1, xxv, 1.

46. The Abl. is used with verbs and adjectives denoting separation, deprivation, release or want and also with words denoting descent or origin.

In Ecc. L. a preposition is often used after such words.

Qui veritate privati sunt. *Who are deprived of truth.* I Tim. vi, 5.

47. The Instrumental Ablative and the Ablative of Attendant Circumstances, generally translated '*with.*'

The Ablative of the Instrument. The word that denotes the means by which anything is done is put in the Abl. without a preposition.

Occidit autem Jacobum fratrem Johannis gladio. *But he killed James the brother of John with a sword.* Acts xii, 2.

In the Vg. the prepositions *a* or *in* are sometimes found before a word denoting the Instrument in imitation of Heb., or of Gk. influenced by Heb.

Et commota sunt superliminaria cardinum a voce clamantis. *And the posts of the door were moved by the voice of him that cried.* Isa. vi, 4.

Ego baptizo in aqua.... *I baptize with water....* Jn. i, 26.

Domine, si percutimus in gladio? *Lord, are we to strike with the sword?* Lk. xxii, 50.

See also James iii, 4.

48. The Ablative of Manner. The word which denotes the manner in which anything takes place is put in the Abl., without a preposition if it is qualified by an adjective: if it is not qualified by an adjective, the preposition *cum* is used before it.

At illi instabant vocibus magnis postulantes ut crucifigeretur. *But they were urgent with loud voices demanding that he should be crucified.* Lk. xxiii, 23.

Qui autem supra petrosa seminatus est, hic est qui verbum audit, et continuo cum gaudio accipit illud. *But he that was sown on the stony places, this is he who hears the word, and immediately with joy receives it.* Mt. xiii, 20.

The preposition is used in Ecc. L. even when the noun denoting manner is qualified by an adjective.

Qui susceperunt verbum cum omni aviditate.... *For they received the word with all eagerness....* Acts xvii, 11.

49. Verbs and adjectives denoting filling or equipping may be followed by a word in the Abl. denoting that with which the filling or equipping is done.

Such verbs and adjectives may also be followed by a word in the Genitive.

O plene omni dolo, et omni fallacia.... *O full of all guile and all deceit....* Acts xiii, 10.

Et impletae sunt nuptiae discumbentium. *And the wedding was furnished with guests.* Mt. xxii, 10.

Plenum gratiae et veritatis. *Full of grace and truth.* Jn. i, 14.

50. The Ablative of Price. The word which denotes the price at which anything is bought, sold or hired, is put in the Abl. case.

Quare hoc unguentum non veniit trecentis denariis? *Why was not this unguent sold for three hundred pence?* Jn. xii, 5.

See also Mk. vi, 37; Acts xxii, 28.

51. The Ablative Absolute. A noun or pronoun in the Abl. case with a predicative participle, or adjective, or even another noun agreeing with it, is used to denote an incident that accompanies or explains the action of the verb on which it depends like an adverbial clause. This construction is very common in Latin, and is called the Ablative Absolute, because it is independent of, or loosed from (*absolutus*), the main structure of the sentence.

The Abl. in this construction is an Abl. of accompanying circumstances. A phrase of this kind is generally best translated into Eng. by an Adverbial clause. The kind of Adverbial clause most suitable for the translation of any particular instance of this construction is determined by the context; generally speaking it will be either a clause of Time, a clause of Cause, or a clause of Concession. See sections 153, 156, 166.

The noun in the Ablative Absolute construction should not denote the same person or thing as the subject or object of the clause on which it depends.

This rule is however frequently violated in Ecc. L.

In Eng. there is a similar construction which is called the Nominative Absolute.

It is seen in the following sentence:

This done, he went home.

In Latin this sentence would be:

Hoc facto domum abiit.

A closer parallel is seen in the colloquial use of a phrase beginning with *with*:

"With things being so dear I shall never be able to manage it."

Examples of the Ablative Absolute:

1. Equivalent to a clause of Time.

Et ejecto daemone, locutus est mutus. *And when the devil was driven out, the dumb man spake.* Mt. ix, 33.

Et cum haec dixisset, videntibus illis, elevatus est. *And when he had said this, as they were looking on, he was taken up.* Acts i, 9.

2. Equivalent to a clause of Cause.

In quo admirantur non concurrentibus vobis in eandem luxuriae confusionem. *In which they wonder, because you do not run with them into the same slough of debauchery.* I Pet. iv, 4. See also Acts xxvii, 7.

The following are examples of the ungrammatical use of the Abl. Absolute, where the noun in the Abl. refers to the same person as the object of the clause with which the Abl. Absolute is connected.

Et ascendente eo in naviculum, secuti sunt eum discipuli ejus. *And when he went up into a ship, his disciples followed him.* Mt. viii, 23.

Paulo autem volente intrare in populum, non permiserunt discipuli. *But when Paul wished to go in to the people, the disciples suffered him not.* Acts xix, 30.

See also Mt. viii, 34, ix, 27; Acts vii, 21, x, 19, xx, 1.

Rarely a participle stands in the Abl. by itself in this sense:

Videntes autem Petri constantiam et Johannis, comperto quod homines essent sine litteris et idiotae.... *But seeing the boldness of Peter and John, and finding out that they were unlettered and ordinary men....* Acts iv, 13.

See also Acts xvi, 38.

51 *a*. Ablative of Comparison. A noun in the Ablative case may be used after an adjective in the comparative degree to denote that with which the comparison is made.

Multis passeribus meliores estis.
Ye are of more value than many sparrows. Mt. x, 31.

52. Locative Ablative, or Ablative of Place or Time, generally translated '*in*' or '*at*.'

Ablative of Place. The Abl. case is used to denote the place in which, or the time at which anything happens.

In Ecc. L. it is often preceded by a preposition where one would not be used in Cl. L.

The way in which the place at which anything happens is expressed in Cl. L. is somewhat peculiar.

Generally speaking the preposition *in* is used followed by a noun in the Abl. case; but if the place spoken of is a town or small island the name of the town or small island is put in the so-called Locative case. This ends in *ae* in singular nouns of the 1st declension and in *i* in singular nouns of the 2nd declension. In the plural of these declensions, and in the 3rd declension, the ending of the Loc. case is the same as the ending of the Abl.

Examples:

Romae, *At Rome*. Corinthi, *At Corinth*. Athenis, *At Athens*.

The Loc. case is also found in the words *domi* at home: *ruri* in the country: *foris* out of doors.

In Ecc. L. the Loc. is sometimes found in the names of towns: sometimes *in* with the Abl. is used.

Erat autem quidam discipulus Damasci.... *But there was a certain disciple at Damascus....* Acts ix, 10.

Paulus autem, cum Athenis eos expectaret.... *But Paul, when he was waiting for them at Athens....* Acts xvii, 16.

Et erat vir in Lystris infirmus pedibus.... *And there was a man in Lystra lame in his feet....* Acts xiv, 7.

53. A kind of Loc. Abl. is used to express **the thing in respect of which** a statement is made, especially in words denoting a part of the body or mind. This is sometimes called the Abl. of Respect.

Vir infirmus pedibus.... *A man lame in his feet....* Acts xiv, 7.

Beati pauperes spiritu. *Blessed are the poor in spirit.* Mt. v, 3.

Fratres, nolite pueri effici sensibus: sed malitia parvuli estote. *Brethren, do not become children in sense: but in malice be ye babes.* I Cor. xiv, 20.

Sed ad sua desideria coacervabunt sibi magistros, prurientes auribus. *But at their desire they will heap up to themselves teachers: itching in the ears.* II Tim. iv, 3.

Mattheum nomine. *Matthew by name.* Mt. ix, 9.

See also Acts vii, 51.

54. **Ablative of Time**. The time at which anything happens is denoted by the Abl. when the noun denotes a period of time.

In Ecc. L. a preposition may be used.

Quinta autem vigilia noctis venit ad eos, ambulans supra mare. *But in the fifth watch of the night he came to them, walking on the sea.* Mt. xiv, 25.

In diebus autem illis venit Johannes Baptista, praedicans in deserto Judaeae. *But in those days John the Baptist came preaching in the desert of Judea.* Mt. iii, 1.

55. The Abl. of nouns denoting a period of time may be used to denote the **time within which** anything happens.

This use is widely extended in the Vg. to denote the time during which anything takes place, which is denoted in Cl. L. by the Acc. case.

Quadraginta et sex annis aedificatum est templum hoc, et tu tribus diebus excitabis illud? *Forty and six years was this temple in building, and wilt thou raise it up in three days?* Jn. ii, 20.

Tanto tempore vobiscum sum? *Have I been so long with you?* Jn. xiv, 9.

Quid hic statis tota die otiosi? *Why stand ye here all the day idle?* Mt. xx, 6.

The use of the Abl. to denote duration of time is found in the inscriptions in the Catacombs and is therefore probably a popular usage.

56. The Adjectival Ablative or **Ablative of Description** describes a person or thing. The noun in the Abl. generally denotes a feature of the body or mind and is always qualified by an adjective.

Patres, nolite ad indignationem provocare filios vestros, ut non pusillo animo fiant. *Fathers, do not provoke your children to wrath, that they may not become of feeble mind.* Col. iii, 21.

Beati mundo corde. *Blessed are the pure in heart.* Mt. v, 8.

57. Ablatives used with verbs. The Abl. is used after certain verbs which are not transitive in Latin as they are in Eng.

The commonest of these verbs are:

utor, *I use.*	potior, *I get possession of.*
fruor, *I enjoy.*	careo, *I am without.*
fungor, *I perform.*	egeo, indigeo, *I need.*

Ego autem nullo horum usus sum. *But I have used none of these things.* I Cor. ix, 15.

Pro Christo ergo legatione fungimur. *We therefore perform the office of ambassador on behalf of Christ.* II Cor. v, 20.

Et civitas non eget sole neque luna, ut luceant in ea. *And the city needs not the sun or moon to shine in it.* Rev. xxi, 23.

Egeo is used with a Gen. in imitation of Gk. in Rev. iii, 17.

58. The adjectives *dignus* and *indignus* are generally followed by a noun in the Abl.

In the Vg. they are sometimes followed by a noun in the Gen. in imitation of Gk.

Dignus est operarius cibo suo. *The workman is worthy of his food.* Mt. x, 10.

Amplioris enim gloriae iste prae Mose dignus habitus est. *For he was thought worthy of more glory than Moses.* Heb. iii, 3.

PRONOUNS.

59. A **Pronoun** is a word used instead of a noun to point out or enumerate persons or things without naming them.

Many words classed as pronouns can be used as adjectives to define or point out nouns.

Personal and Reflexive pronouns can only be used in place of nouns. Possessive, Demonstrative, Relative, Interrogative and Indefinite pronouns can be used either in place of nouns or adjectivally.

When a pronoun can be used adjectivally it should be called an Adjectival Pronoun.

As a rule pronouns agree in gender and number with the noun in place of which they are used, but sometimes they agree only in sense with the noun and not with its grammatical number and gender.

Thus a plural pronoun may be used with reference to a collective noun, a neuter plural pronoun may be used with reference to two feminine nouns denoting things without life, a plural pronoun may be used with reference to a country because the thought is directed rather towards its inhabitants.

Euntes ergo docete omnes gentes, baptizantes eos.... *Go therefore and teach all nations, baptizing them....* Mt. xxviii, 19.

Possessiones et substantias vendebant, et dividebant illa omnibus.... *They sold their possessions and divided them to all....* Acts ii, 45.

Et circumibat Jesus totam Galilaeam, docens in synagogis eorum. *Jesus went about all Galilee, teaching in their synagogues.* Mt. iv, 23.

Sed habes pauca nomina in Sardis, qui non inquinaverunt vestimenta sua. *But thou hast a few names in Sardis, who have not defiled their garments.* Rev. iii, 4.

See also Rom. ix, 24.

60. Personal Pronouns. As the ending of a Latin verb shows what person and number its subject is, the Nominative of personal pronouns is seldom used, except when special emphasis is desired.

Nos audivimus ex lege quia Christus manet in aeternum; et quomodo tu dicis: Oportet exaltari filium hominis? *We have heard out of the law that Christ abideth for ever; and how sayest thou: "The Son of man must be lifted up"?* Jn. xii, 34.

Ille erat lucerna ardens et lucens. Vos autem voluistis ad horam exultare in luce ejus. *He was a burning and a shining light. But you were willing for a season to rejoice in his light.* Jn. v, 35.

There are no personal pronouns of the third person in Latin except the Reflexive *se*. Demonstrative and Relative pronouns are used to take the place of the missing personal pronoun.

For examples of the use of the demonstrative pronouns as personal pronouns of the third person, see Jn. ix, 8, 12, 18, 21, 36; Lk. ix, 9; Acts xi, 15, 16.

61. Reflexive Pronouns may be treated as a branch of personal pronouns. They are used when the subject of the verb is described as acting on himself, or in his own interest, or as saying or thinking something about himself.

In the first and second persons, reflexive pronouns are identical in form with the oblique cases of the personal pronouns and are often made more emphatic by the addition of the proper case of *ipse*: in the third person, both singular and plural, the forms *se, sui, sibi, se* are used.

> Nihil feceris tibi mali. *Do thyself no harm.* Acts xvi, 28.
>
> Tu de te ipso testimonium perhibes. *Thou bearest witness about thyself.* Jn. viii, 13.
>
> Et abiens laqueo se suspendit. *And going away he hanged himself.* Mt. xxvii, 5.

When reflexive pronouns are used in a subordinate clause they sometimes refer to the person denoted by the subject of the main clause. This is seldom the case where any ambiguity is likely to be caused, but in Ecc. L. such pronouns are used rather loosely.

> Et cadens in terram audivit vocem dicentem sibi.... *And falling to the earth he heard a voice saying to him....* Acts ix, 4.
>
> See also Acts xxviii, 16; Mt. vii, 11.

Rarely a demonstrative pronoun is used in the Vg. where a reflexive pronoun would have been more correct.

> Exinde coepit Jesus ostendere discipulis suis, quia oporteret eum ire Hierosolymam.... *From that time Jesus began to show to his disciples that he must go to Jerusalem....* Mt. xvi, 21
>
> See also Mk. x, 32; Rom. iii, 26.

62. Possessive Pronouns are used adjectivally and are equivalent to the Gen. case of the personal or reflexive pronoun.

In the first and second persons the Gen. of the personal pronoun is rarely found in the sense of a possessive pronoun. Phil. ii, 12.

In the third person *suus* is used reflexively, that is, when the person or thing to which it refers is the subject of the sentence or clause in which it stands.

Propterea ergo magis quaerebant eum Judaei interficere: quia non solum solvebat Sabbatum, sed et Patrem suum dicebat Deum. *On this account therefore the Jews sought the more to kill him, because he was not only breaking the Sabbath, but also because he said that God was his Father....* Jn. v, 18.

When the person or thing referred to by the pronoun is not the subject of the sentence or clause in which it stands, the Gen. of a demonstrative pronoun (generally *ejus* or *eorum*, etc.) is used as the possessive pronoun of the third person.

Princeps autem sacerdotum Ananias praecepit adstantibus sibi percutere os ejus. *But the chief of the priests Ananias commanded those that stood by him to smite his mouth* (i.e. Paul's mouth). Acts xxiii, 2.

N.B. In Latin, as in French, the gender of a possessive pronoun does not depend on the gender of the word denoting the possessor; but possessive pronouns agree with the nouns which they qualify in gender, number and case, like adjectives.

Sua mater, *His mother.* Suus pater, *Her father.*

63. **Demonstrative Pronouns** are used to point out some person or thing.

In Cl. L. *hic, haec, hoc* denotes that which is near to the speaker and is generally translated *this.*

Ille, illa, illud denotes that which is more remote, and is generally translated *that.*

Iste, ista, istud denotes that which belongs to the person spoken to; it is sometimes used contemptuously and translated *that of yours.*

Is, ea, id is an unemphatic word, generally used as a personal pronoun of the third person and translated *he, she, it.*

Ipse, ipsa, ipsum is emphatic, and may be translated *himself, herself, itself.*

It is often used in speaking of a famous person, and so it is often used of God and Christ in the Vg.: it is used with other pronouns to give emphasis and also to show that they are reflexive. See examples below.

Idem, eadem, idem means *the same.*

64. In Ecc. L. the demonstrative pronouns are not strictly used in the senses given above: *iste* is often used where *hic* or *ille* would be used in Cl. L.

Ipsi scitis: quoniam ad ea quae mihi opus erant, et his qui mecum sunt, ministraverunt manus istae. *Ye yourselves know that these hands have ministered to those things that were needful for me and for those that were with me.* Acts xx, 34.

Omnes vos scandalum patiemini in me in ista nocte. *All ye shall be caused to stumble because of me this night.* Mt. xxvi, 31.

For an example of *hic* and *iste* used in exactly parallel senses:

Vos ascendite ad diem festum hunc: ego non ascendo ad diem festum istum. *Go ye up to this feast: I go not up to this feast.* Jn. vii, 8.

See also Rom. xi, 30, 31.

Hic, ille and even *ipse* are used to translate the Greek definite article.

Respondit ille homo (ὁ ἄνθρωπος). *The man replied.* Jn. ix, 30.

Ex hoc nunc (ἀπὸ τοῦ νῦν). *From henceforth.* Ps. cxii, 2.

In the titles to the psalms Ipsi David is a translation of τῷ Δαυείδ. See also Jn. xx. 3, 4; II Pet. ii. 22.

The following are examples of the use of *ipse.*

Emphatic use.

Omnia per ipsum facta sunt. *All things were made through him.* Jn. i, 3.

Johannes testimonium perhibet de ipso. *John bears witness about him.* Jn. i, 15.

Deus ipse Dominus; ipse fecit nos, et non ipsi nos. *God Himself is the Lord; He has made us, and not we ourselves.* Ps. xcix, 3.

Ego scio eum, quia ab ipso sum, et ipse misit me. *I know him, because I am from him, and he sent me.* Jn. vii, 29.

Reflexive use.

Tu de te ipso testimonium perhibes. *Thou bearest witness of thyself.* Jn. viii, 13, 28; Rom. xii, 16.

Ipse is also used in the sense of *the same*:

Ex ipso ore procedit benedictio et maledictio. *Out of the same mouth proceedeth blessing and cursing.* Jas. iii, 10.

See also Heb. xiii, 8.

Idipsum is used in the sense of *the same* to translate Gk. τὸ αὐτό.

Idipsum autem latrones improperaverunt ei. *But the robbers cast the same reproach at him.* Mt. xxvii, 44; I Cor. i, 10; Heb. iv, 11.

In idipsum is used in the sense of *together* to translate Gk. ἐπὶ τὸ αὐτό.

Dominus autem augebat, qui salvi fierent quotidie in idipsum. *But the Lord increased daily those who should be saved into one body.* Acts ii, 47.

Et iterum revertimini in idipsum. *And come together again.* I Cor. vii, 5.

Magnificate Dominum mecum: et exaltemus nomen ejus in idipsum. *O magnify the Lord with me: and let us exalt his name together.* Ps. xxxiii, 4.

Hierusalem quae aedificatur ut civitas, cujus participatio ejus in idipsum. *Jerusalem which is built as a city that is at unity in itself.* Ps. cxxi, 3.

See also Pss. lxi, 10, lxxiii, 6.

65. **The Relative Pronoun** is used like a conjunction to connect two clauses in a sentence: the second of the two connected clauses may be either subordinate to, or co-ordinate with the first.

The relative pronoun always refers back to some noun or pronoun (expressed or implied) in the clause which it connects to the clause in which it stands. This noun or pronoun is called its Antecedent. In Latin, relative pronouns agree with their antecedent in gender, number and person, but not in case.

The case of a relative pronoun depends on the function which it performs in the clause in which it stands.

The relative pronoun can never be omitted in Latin as it often is in Eng.

Examples:

Accepistis illud...sicut verbum Dei, qui operatur in vobis, qui credidistis. *You received it...as the word of God who works in you who believe.* I Thess. ii, 13.

Discedite a me, qui operamini iniquitatem. *Depart from me ye that work iniquity.* Mt. vii, 23.

66. A relative pronoun often stands at the beginning of a sentence and must then be translated into English by a personal pronoun[1].

It is often used in the Vg. to translate the Gk. ὁ δέ.

[1] An unsuccessful attempt to introduce this construction into English is to be noted in several places in the A.V., especially in Acts. See Acts xiv, 14.

Qui cum recessissent, ecce angelus Domini apparuit in somnis Joseph...qui consurgens accepit puerum. *And when they had departed, behold an angel of the Lord appeared to Joseph in a dream...and he arose and took the child.* Matt. ii, 13.

Quorum fidem ut videt, dixit.... *And when he saw their faith, he said....* Lk. v, 20.

A very harsh example is found in Acts xvii, 11:

Hi autem erant nobiliores eorum qui sunt Thessalonicae, qui susceperunt verbum cum omni aviditate.... *But these were more noble than those who are at Thessalonica, for they received the word with all eagerness....*

See also Mt. xv, 23; Jn. i, 38; Acts vii, 2.

67. Attraction of the Antecedent. The antecedent may be attracted into the case of the relative (inverse attraction) and at the same time be transferred from its own clause into the relative clause.

When this happens, a personal pronoun of the case that the antecedent would have been in, if it had not been attracted into the relative clause, may take its place in the main clause.

Et sermonem, quem audistis, non est meus: sed ejus, qui misit me, Patris. *And the word which ye hear is not mine, but the Father's which sent me.* Jn. xiv, 24.

Quem ego decollavi Johannem, hic a mortuis resurrexit. *John whom I beheaded is risen from the dead.* Mk. vi, 16.

See also Mt. xii, 36, xxi, 42; Dan. iv, 17.

An example of the relative being attracted into the case of the antecedent is found in Ps. ix, 23: *Comprehenduntur in consiliis quibus cogitant.*

68. A Demonstrative Pronoun in the same number, gender and case as the relative pronoun may be inserted in a relative clause in imitation of the Heb. The Heb. relative אשׁר is invariable in form and has a personal pronoun in apposition to it to show its relationship to the sentence.

Beatus vir, cujus est nomen Domini spes ejus.... *Blessed is the man whose hope is in the name of the Lord....* Ps. xxxix, 5.

Quem Dominus Jesus interficiet spiritu oris sui, et destruet illustratione adventus sui eum. *Whom the Lord Jesus will slay with the breath of his mouth, and destroy with the brightness of his coming.* II Thess. ii, 8.

See also Pss. xviii, 4, xxxii, 12, lxxiii, 2, cxlv, 5.

69. The Interrogative Pronoun *quis* may take the place of either a noun or an adjective.

When it is a true pronoun it has the form *quis* (*qui*), *quae*, *quid*.

When it is a pronominal adjective it has the form *qui* (*quis*), *quae*, *quod*.

In the Vg. it may be used in place of the Interrogative *uter*= which of two.

Quem vultis vobis de duobus dimitti? *Which of the two do ye wish to be released for you?* Mt. xxvii, 21.

See also Mt. ix, 5, xxi, 31; I Cor. iv, 21; Lucan, *Pharsalia* i, 126. *Quid* may be used like the Gk. τί to ask a question.

Quid hic statis tota die otiosi? *Why do ye stand here idle all the day?* Mt. xx, 6.

Ut quid is used to translate the Gk. ἵνα τί or εἰς τί.

Ut quid enim libertas mea judicatur ab aliena conscientia? *For why is my liberty judged of another man's conscience?* I Cor. x, 29.

See also Mt. ix, 4, xxvi, 8.

69*a*. **The Indefinite Pronoun** *quis*, *quae* or *qua*, *quid* may be used to take the place of either a noun or an adjective.

It is used by itself in the Vg. to translate the Gk. τις.

Infirmatur quis in vobis? *Is any among you sick?* Jas. v, 14.

See also Acts x, 47, xxvi, 31; Rom. v, 7; I Cor. iv, 2.

The Relative pronoun is used instead of the Indefinite *quisquis* in imitation of Gk. ὃς ἄν.

Qui ergo solverit unum de mandatis istis minimis, et docuerit sic homines, minimus vocabitur in regno caelorum. *Whosoever shall break one of these least commandments and shall teach men so, shall be called least in the kingdom of heaven.* Mt. v, 19.

70. **The Reciprocal Pronoun** which is expressed in Eng. by *one another*, and in Cl. L. by *alius alium*, *alter alterum*, *inter se* is generally expressed in the Vg. by *invicem* which is treated as an indeclinable pronoun.

It may also be expressed by *alterutrum*.

Estote autem invicem benigni, misericordes, donantes invicem. *But be ye kind to one another, pitiful, forgiving one another.* Eph. iv, 32.

Nolite murmurare in invicem. *Do not murmur one to another.* Jn. vi, 43.

Orate pro invicem. *Pray for one another.* Jas. v, 16.

Non ergo amplius invicem judicemus. *Let us not therefore judge one another any longer.* Rom. xiv, 13.

See also Jn. xiii, 35, xv, 17; Acts, xv, 39; Rom. xii, 16, xvi,16.

Confitemini ergo alterutrum peccata vestra. *Confess your sins one to another.* Jas. v, 16.

Dicebant ad alterutrum. *They were saying one to another.* Mk. iv, 40.

Id ipsum sapere in alterutrum. *To think the same thing one with another.* Rom. xv, 5.

See also Mk. iv, 40; Acts vii, 26.

71. *Hujusmodi* and *ejusmodi* are used in the Vg. with an ellipse of the noun which they should qualify, which makes them almost equivalent to a pronoun.

Hujusmodi enim Christo Domino nostro non serviunt. *For such men do not serve Christ our Lord.* Rom. xvi, 18.

Pro hujusmodi gloriabor.... *For such a one will I glory....* II Cor. xii, 5.

Adversus hujusmodi non est lex. *Against such there is no law.* Gal. v, 23.

See also Jn. viii, 5; Acts xxii, 22; Rom. xvi, 18; I Cor. vii, 28.

Verbs.

Mood.

72. Moods are forms which verbs assume to show the way in which the action or state denoted by the verb is to be regarded, i.e., if it is to be regarded as a statement, a command, a desire, or a thought.

The **Indicative** Mood (generally) makes a statement or asks a direct question.

The **Imperative** Mood gives a command, or expresses a wish.

The **Subjunctive** Mood expresses a thought rather than a fact. It is used to give a command or express a wish directly in the first or third person and is often used in prohibitions and in hesitating or polite statements or wishes.

It is generally used in indirect commands and questions and in many kinds of subordinate clauses, especially those that express purpose or result.

The uses of the Subj. are so various and its use in Latin is often so different from its use in English, that it is inadvisable to learn any English equivalent for it such as *I may love*, or *I might love*.

Very often it is translated by the Eng. Ind. The student must learn to translate it by observing its use in Latin.

The **Infinitive** Mood is really the dative or locative case of a verbal noun. It gets its name, which means "un-bounded," from the fact that it is not bounded like other parts of the verb by number and person.

The **Participle** is a verbal adjective.

The **Gerund** and **Supine** are verbal nouns.

Tense.

73. The action denoted by a verb may be defined both as regards its time and as regards its **state** or progress.

Its time may be defined as past, present, or future.

Its state or progress may be regarded as

continuous or incomplete,
perfect or complete,
simple or indefinite.

The combination of these ideas of time and state should produce nine different tenses.

Past	continuous	*I was loving.*	Present	continuous	*I am loving.*
	perfect	*I had loved.*		perfect	*I have loved.*
	simple	*I loved.*		simple	*I love.*
Future	continuous	*I shall be loving.*			
	perfect	*I shall have loved.*			
	simple	*I shall love.*			

Different forms to express all these combinations exist in Eng., but not in Latin.

The Latin tenses are arranged below in the same order as the Eng. tenses in the table above. The names commonly given to them in grammars are printed in capitals.

IMPERFECT	*amabam.*	(missing)	
PLUPERFECT	*amaveram.*	PERFECT	*amavi.*
PERFECT	*amavi.*	PRESENT	*amo.*
(missing)			
FUTURE PERFECT	*amavero.*		
FUTURE	*amabo.*		

It should be noticed that the tense called the Perfect in Latin has to do the work of two dissimilar tenses:—the Past Simple and the Present Perfect.

If continuous action in present or future time has to be expressed in Cl. L. the Simple Present or Future must be used.

In Ecc. L. we see the development of tenses formed by a participle and part of the verb *esse* which are very similar in meaning and form to the Eng. Present Continuous and Future Continuous. See section 90.

74. The Present tense denotes either an action or state in progress in present time, or customary or repeated action in present time.

Filius hominis traditur in manus peccatorum. *The Son of man is being betrayed into the hands of sinners.* Mt. xxvi, 45.

Domine, salva nos, perimus. *Lord, save us, we are perishing.* Mt. viii, 25.

Lampades nostrae extinguuntur. *Our lamps are going out.* Mt. xxv, 8.

Corrumpunt mores bonos conloquia mala. *Evil communications corrupt good manners.* I Cor. xv, 33.

Omnis arbor, quae non facit fructum bonum, exciditur et in ignem mittitur. *Every tree that bringeth not forth good fruit is hewn down and cast into the fire.* Mt. vii, 19.

See also Mt. ix, 17.

75. Conative Present. As the Present tense denotes action in progress which is not necessarily complete, it may be used to denote action which is attempted or desired, but not performed.

Multa bona opera ostendi vobis ex Patre meo: propter quod eorum opus me lapidatis? *I have shown you many good works from my Father: because of which of these do ye desire to stone me?* Jn. x, 32.

Evacuati estis a Christo, qui in lege justificamini; a gratia excidistis. *Ye are separated from Christ, ye who desire to be justified by the law: ye have fallen from grace.* Gal. v, 4.

See also I Cor. vii, 28.

76. Historic Present. The Present tense is used in narrative to denote events in past time for the sake of vividness.

Et veniunt rursus Hierosolyma. *And they come again to Jerusalem.* Mk. xi, 27.

77. The Present used for the Future. The Present is sometimes used colloquially in a Future sense.

Tempus meum prope est: apud te facio Pascha cum discipulis meis. *My time is at hand: I will eat the Passover at thy house with my disciples.* Mt. xxvi, 18.

Descendat nunc de cruce, et credimus ei. *Let him now come down from the cross, and we will believe him.* Mt. xxvii, 42.

See also Lk. xix, 8; Jn. xxi, 23.

78. The Present of ἔρχεσθαι which is used in a Future sense in the N.T. with reference to the Messiah, especially in the participle, is sometimes translated by the Future in the Vg. or even by the Perfect. It may also be translated by a Present.

See Mt. xi, 3; Jn. vi, 14, xi, 27, xiv, 3.

A very curious use of the Present among several Futures is found in Acts xxviii, 6. There is nothing to suggest it in the Gk.

79. The Imperfect tense denotes an action or state in progress in past time, or customary or repeated action in past time.

The Imperfect is a descriptive tense and denotes an action in progress or a state of things actually observed. Hence in many instances it does not differ in meaning from the Perfect. This is especially the case with the verb *esse*:

Dux erat and *Dux fuit* may mean practically the same thing, the former describes the condition, the latter only states it.

Et multi divites jactabant multa. *And many rich men were casting in much.* Mk. xii, 41.

Ecce quomodo amabat eum. *Behold how much he loved him.* Jn. xi, 36.

Petrus autem et Johannes ascendebant in templum ad horam orationis nonam. *But Peter and John used to go up to the temple at the hour of prayer, the ninth hour.* Acts iii, 1.

In Acts xii, 4–7 there are several examples of the use of the Imperfect tense and the contrasted use of the Perfect tense.

See also Mt. viii, 2; Lk. iii, 10, xv, 16; Eph. iv, 28.

80. Conative Imperfect. The Imperfect is sometimes used to denote an action in past time which was attempted or desired, but not performed.

Et vocabant eum nomine patris ejus Zachariam. *And they wished to call him by the name of his father Zacharias.* Lk. i, 59.

See Acts vii, 26, xxvi, 11.

81. The Imperfect is also used to express a polite or hesitating wish which the speaker does not like to express directly.

Volebam et ipse hominem audire. *I should like to hear the man myself.* Acts xxv, 22.

Optabam enim ipse ego anathema esse a Christo pro fratribus meis. *I could wish myself accursed from Christ for the sake of my brethren.* Rom. ix, 3.

82. **The Future tense** denotes an action or state which is expected to take place in future time.

The context decides whether the action denoted by the verb is simple or continuous.

Pariet autem filium: et vocabis nomen ejus Jesum. *For she shall bring forth a son: and thou shalt call his name Jesus.* Mt. i, 21.

Et in hoc gaudeo, sed et gaudebo. *And in this I rejoice, yea I will continue to rejoice.* Phil. i, 18.

83. The Future may have the force of an **Imperative.**

Relinque ibi munus tuum ante altare, et vade prius reconciliare fratri tuo: et tunc veniens offeres munus tuum. *Leave there thy gift before the altar, and go first to be reconciled to thy brother, and then come and offer thy gift.* Mt. v, 24

Et cum oratis, non eritis sicut hypocritae. *And when ye pray, be not as the hypocrites.* Mt. vi, 5.

See also Mk. xii, 31.

84. **The Perfect tense** in Latin performs the functions of two tenses which are quite distinct in Eng. and Gk. These are the tenses which are commonly called the **Past Simple** (or Preterite) and the **Perfect** (or Present Perfect) in Eng., and the **Aorist** and **Perfect** in Gk.

The translation of the tenses in the Vg. is generally very careful: the Imperfect represents the Gk. Imperfect and the Perfect the Gk. Aorist or Perfect in the Ind. mood.

The Aorist is used in Gk. far more frequently than the Perfect. The Perfect in Gk. denotes completed action. The Aorist Indicative generally denotes action in past time, but must often be translated into English by the form which is called the Perfect (the tense form made with the auxiliary verb *have*).

It would be impossible and confusing to go into the reasons for this here. Those who wish for further information on the point will find it in the author's *Syntax of N.T. Greek.*

The point to be remembered by the Latin student is that the Latin Perfect may be translated by either the English Past Simple or by the **Perfect.**

The most suitable form to use is decided by the context in all cases. The Gk. original is not a safe guide.

Example of the Latin Perfect denoting simple action in past time.

Et veniens ad discipulos suos, vidit turbam magnam circa eos. *And when he came to his disciples he saw a great crowd round them.* Mk. ix, 14.

Examples of the Latin Perfect denoting that the action of the verb is regarded as complete[1] at the time of speaking, and that its results are regarded as still existing.

Bonum certamen certavi, cursum consummavi, fidem servavi. *I have fought the good fight, I have finished the course, I have kept the faith.* II Tim. iv, 7.

Sed potius ite ad oves quae perierunt domus Israel. *But rather go to the sheep that have perished* (*or the lost sheep*) *of the house of Israel.* Mt. x, 6.

Omnium autem finis appropinquavit. *But the end of all things is at hand.* I Pet. iv, 7.

85. The Perfect is used to translate the **Greek Timeless Aorist** and expresses a general truth, an habitual action, or action at a time not defined. When so used it must be translated by the Present tense in English.

Exortus est enim sol cum ardore, et arefecit faenum, et flos ejus decidit, et decor vultus ejus deperiit. *For the sun arises with its burning heat, and dries up the grass, and its flower falls, and the beauty of its shape perishes.* Jas. i, 11.

See also I Pet. i, 24 and the curious imitation of the Gk. in Wordsworth and White's text in Jn. xv, 6.

Tu es filius meus dilectus, in te complacui. *Thou art my beloved son, in thee I am well pleased.* Mk. i, 11.

Calendas vestras, et sollemnitates vestras, odivit anima mea: facta sunt mihi molesta, laboravi sustinens. *Your festivals and feasts my soul hateth: they are a trouble to me, I am weary to bear them.* Isa. i, 14.

[1] When it is said that the action is regarded as *complete* this does not mean that it is regarded as ended, but only that it is regarded as brought to its appropriate conclusion in such a way that its effects still remain in action The tense when used in this sense has as much to do with present as with past time, as it describes the present result of a past action. It may sometimes be translated by an Eng. Present.

86. The Pluperfect tense denotes an action or state completed in past time, or an action which took place before some point in past time referred to in the context, or which the speaker has in mind.

Et descendit pluvia, et venerunt flumina, et flaverunt venti, et irruerunt in domum illam, et non cecidit: fundata enim erat super petram. *And the rain descended, and the floods came, and the winds blew, and they fell upon that house, and it fell not: for it had been founded upon a rock.* Mt. vii, 25.

Venit enim filius hominis salvare quod perierat. *For the Son of man came to save that which had been lost.* Mt. xviii, 11.

The force of the Perfect, Pluperfect and Imperfect tenses is seen in the following example:

Et vidit duas naves stantes secus stagnum: piscatores autem descenderant, et lavabant retia. *And he saw two ships standing by the lake: but the fishermen had come down out of them, and were washing their nets.* Lk. v, 2.

87. The Future Perfect tense denotes an action or state which is regarded as completed at some point in future time which the speaker has in mind or which is referred to in the context.

It is used very frequently in Latin where in Eng. we use a Simple Future, a Present, or a Perfect.

His autem expletis, proposuit Paulus in Spiritu, transita Macedonia et Achaia, ire Hierosolymam, dicens: Quoniam postquam fuero ibi, oportet me et Romam videre. *When this was ended Paul purposed in the Spirit, after he had passed through Macedonia and Achaia, to go to Jerusalem, saying: "After I have been there I must also see Rome."* Acts xix, 21.

Nisi abundaverit justitia vestra plus quam Scribarum et Pharisaeorum, non intrabitis in regnum caelorum. *Unless your righteousness exceed that of the Scribes and Pharisees, ye shall not enter into the kingdom of heaven.* Mt. v, 20.

Si fuerint alicui centum oves, et erraverit una ex eis, nonne relinquet nonaginta novem in montibus...? *If any man has a hundred sheep and one of them goes astray, will he not leave the ninety and nine in the mountains...?* Mt. xviii, 12.

88. It is used in indefinite relative clauses and in indefinite clauses of time and place, referring to future time. See sections 154, 155.

Et in quamcumque domum intraveritis, ibi manete, et inde ne exeatis. *And into whatever house ye enter, there remain, and go not forth from thence.* Lk. ix, 4.

Qui enim voluerit animam suam salvam facere, perdet illam: nam qui perdiderit animam suam propter me, salvam faciet illam. *For whoso wishes to save his soul shall lose it: but whoso shall lose his soul for my sake shall save it.* Lk. ix, 24.

Et beatus est qui non fuerit scandalizatus in me. *And blessed is he who is not offended in me.* Mt. xi, 6.

See also Mt. xxvi, 13; Rom. xv, 24.

89. It is also used like the Future with the force of an **Imperative.**

Nihil tuleritis in via. *Take nothing for the way.* Lk. ix, 3.

See also Mt. xxvii, 4; Acts xviii, 15.

90. **Periphrastic forms of tenses** are formed in Ecc. L. as in Eng., by joining the appropriate tense of *esse* to the present participle.

Periphrastic **Present** formed from the Present tense of *esse* and the Present Participle.

Non enim sumus sicut plurimi adulterantes verbum Dei. *For we are not as many adulterating the word of God.* II Cor. ii, 17.

Esto consentiens adversario tuo cito dum es in via cum eo. *Agree with thine adversary quickly while thou art in the way with him.* Mt. v, 25.

Periphrastic **Imperfect.**

Et erat plebs expectans Zachariam. *And the people was expecting Zacharias.* Lk. i, 21.

Et erat tribus diebus non videns, et non manducavit neque bibit. *And he was three days without sight, and did neither eat nor drink.* Acts ix, 9.

Periphrastic **Future.**

Noli timere: ex hoc jam homines eris capiens. *Fear not: from henceforth thou shalt be catching men.* Lk. v, 10.

91. A Future tense is also formed from the **Future Participle** of *esse* with a clause introduced by *ut* as its subject.

Futurum est enim ut Herodes quaerat puerum ad perdendum eum. *For Herod will seek the young child to destroy him.* Mt. ii, 13.

A Future Subj. is formed from the Future Participle and the Present Subj. of *esse*.

Nolite putare quia ego accusaturus sim vos apud Patrem. *Do not think that I shall accuse you to the Father.* Jn. v, 45.

92. Periphrastic tenses formed with *habere* and *facere*.

The beginning of the periphrastic formation of tenses which resulted in the forms now used for the **Future** tenses in French and Italian is to be discerned in Ecc. L.

The use began in the employment of the verb *habere* in its ordinary sense with an explanatory Inf. This is found in the Classics.

Adhuc multa habeo vobis dicere. *I have yet many things to say to you.* Jn. xvi, 12.

Quia non habent retribuere tibi. *Because they have not* (*anything*) *whence to pay you back.* Lk. xiv, 14.

Hence arises a sense of future necessity:

Baptisma autem habeo baptizari. *But I have a baptism with which I must be baptised*[1]. Lk. xii, 50.

Habes, homo, imprimis aetatem venerare aquarum, quod antiqua substantia. *First, O man, you must venerate the age of water; because it is an ancient substance.* Tert. *de Bapt.* iii.

Aquas video quas videbam quotidie: istae me habent mundare in quas saepe descendi, et nunquam sanatus sum. *I see water which I was used to see every day: it has got to cleanse me, though I have often gone down into it, and I have never been cleansed.* Ambrose, *de Mysteriis*, iv, 19.

93. The Imperfect tense of *habere* is also found as an auxiliary verb with a **past participle**—a construction which became the normal way of expressing the pluperfect tense in Italian and French.

Tantum autem auditum habebant.... *Only they had heard....* Gal. i, 23.

94. The Infinitive is used with the verb *facere* to denote causation.

Et adduxerunt asinam et pullum, et imposuerunt super eos vestimenta sua, et eum desuper sedere fecerunt. *And they brought the ass and the colt and put on them their clothes, and they made him sit thereon.* Mt. xxi, 7.

[1] Plater and White state that the following use of this const. in a future sense is found in the Old Latin: "Omnes vos scandalizari habetis." Mt. xiv, 27. See also Cypr. Test. 1, 4.

95. The sequence of tenses. The Present, Future, Future Perfect and Perfect (when translated by the English Perfect formed with the auxiliary *have*) are called **Primary** tenses.

The Imperfect, Pluperfect and Perfect (when translated by the English Past) are called **Secondary** tenses.

When the verb in a principal clause is in a Primary tense, a verb in the Subj. mood in a subordinate clause is in a Primary tense in certain kinds of clauses.

When the verb in a principal clause is in a Secondary tense, a verb in the Subj. mood in a subordinate clause is in a Secondary tense in certain kinds of clauses. This rule is not strictly observed in Ecc. L.

VOICE.

96. The **Active** voice is used when the subject of the verb is spoken of as acting or doing something.

The **Passive** voice is used when the subject of the verb is spoken of as suffering or being acted upon. Only Transitive verbs can have a passive voice.

There are certain verbs such as *to fall* and *to die* which do not speak of the subject as acting, but which are regarded as being in the active voice because they are Intransitive.

97. Certain verbs in Latin are passive in form, but active in meaning. These are called **Deponent** verbs because the old grammarians thought that they had laid aside a passive and assumed an active meaning.

A few verbs such as *gaudeo, -ere, gavisus sum* have the deponent form only in the Perfect, Pluperfect and Future Perfect tenses. These are called Semi-deponent verbs.

THE USE OF THE IMPERATIVE MOOD. THE SUBJUNCTIVE MOOD IN PRINCIPAL CLAUSES.

98. The Imperative Mood is used to express commands and entreaties in the second person singular or plural, and has forms which may be used to express a command given in the third person.

Sed, si quid potes, adjuva nos. *But, if thou canst do anything, help us.* Mk. ix, 22.

Dixit ergo Jesus: Facite homines discumbere. *Therefore Jesus said: Make the men sit down.* Jn. vi, 10.

In Ecc. L. the second person of the Present Subj. is used to express a command or entreaty.

Nec doleas, quod talem amiseris, sed gaudeas, quod talem habueris. *Do not grieve because you have lost such a man, but rejoice because you had him.* Jerome, *Ep.* 60.

The Present Subjunctive is generally used to express a command or entreaty in the first or third person. This use of the Subj. is called the **Jussive Subjunctive.**

Nam Deus dixit: Honora patrem et matrem; et: Qui maledixerit patri vel matri morte moriatur. *For God said: Honour thy father and mother; and: If any curse his father or his mother, let him surely die.* Mt. xv, 4.

Sometimes *sine* or *sinite* = *allow* is prefixed to the Subj.

Sine ejiciam festucam de oculo tuo. *Let me cast out the mote out of thine eye.* Mt. vii, 4.

99. Prohibitions are negative commands or entreaties. The Imperative is not used in prohibitions, except in poetry.

Prohibitions are expressed in prose:

(1) By *noli* or *nolite* followed by an Inf.

(2) By *ne* (or *non* in Ecc. L.) followed by the Perfect Subj.

(3) By *ne* or *non* followed by the Present Subj.

(4) By *vide* followed by a negative and the Present or Perfect Subj.

The first two methods are regularly used in Cl. prose. The last two are often found in Ecc. L.

(1) Noli vexare illum. *Trouble him not.* Lk. viii, 49.

Nolite dare sanctum canibus, neque mittatis margaritas vestras ante porcos. *Do not give that which is holy to the dogs, and do not cast your pearls before swine.* Mt. vii, 6.

(2) In viam gentium ne abieritis, et in civitates Samaritanorum ne intraveritis. *Go not into the way of the Gentiles, and into the cities of the Samaritans enter ye not.* Mt. x, 5.

Nihil feceris tibi mali. *Do thyself no harm.* Acts xvi, 28.

(3) Nec vocemini magistri. *Be not ye called masters.* Mt. xxiii, 10.

Non mireris quia dixi tibi: Oportet vos nasci denuo. *Marvel not that I said to thee: Ye must be born again.* Jn. iii, 7.

Qui furabatur, jam non furetur, magis autem laboret. *Let him that stole steal no more, but rather let him labour.* Eph. iv, 28.

(4) Videte ne contemnatis unum ex his pusillis. *See that ye despise not one of these little ones.* Mt. xviii, 10.

Vide nemini dixeris. *See thou tell no man.* Mt. viii, 4.

100. An emphatic and absolute prohibition may be expressed by *omnis* and a verb in the Present Subj. negatived by *non* in imitation of Heb.

Omnis sermo malus ex ore vestro non procedat. *Let no corrupt speech proceed out of your mouth.* Eph. iv, 29.

101. **Hortatory Subjunctive.** Besides expressing commands the Subj. may express an exhortation or a wish.

Transeamus usque Bethleem, et videamus hoc verbum quod factum est. *Let us go to Bethlehem and see this thing which has come to pass.* Lk. ii, 15.

In expressing a wish the Present Subj. denotes that the wish is still possible, the Imperfect Subj. or Pluperfect Subj. that it is unaccomplished in present time, or in certain cases that it is impossible. *Utinam* is often used before the Past tenses of the Subj. when they express an unaccomplished wish.

Sanctificetur nomen tuum: adveniat regnum tuum. *Hallowed be thy name: thy kingdom come.* Mt. vi, 9.

Utinam fuisset dominus meus ad prophetam, qui est in Samaria. *Would that my master were with the prophet who is in Samaria.* II Kings v, 2.

Utinam frigidus esses aut calidus. *Would that thou wert cold or hot.* Rev. iii, 15; I Cor. iv, 8.

102. **Deliberative Subjunctive.** In Cl. L. the Subj. is used in deliberative questions when a person asks himself or another what he is to do.

In Ecc. L. the Future or the Present Ind. is also often used in this sense.

Subj. Euntes emamus denariis ducentis panes? *Are we to go and buy two hundred pennyworth of bread?* Mk. vi, 37.

Fut. Quid faciemus et nos? *What shall we do?* Lk. iii, 14.

Pres. Ind. Tu es qui venturus es, an alium expectamus? *Art thou he that should come, or are we to look for another?* Mt. xi, 3.

103. Potential Subjunctive. The Subj. is used to express an action which is not regarded as actual, but only as possible or conceivable. Expressions of this kind may be regarded as the apodoses[1] of conditional sentences where the condition is not expressed. The Subj. is rarely used in this sense in the Vg.

Profecto curasset eum a lepra, quam habet. *Surely he would have cured him of his leprosy.* II Kings, v, 2.

Vix enim pro justo quis moritur: nam pro bono forsitan quis audeat mori. *For scarcely for a just man does one die, but perhaps for a good man one would dare to die.* Rom. v, 7.

Vellem autem esse apud vos modo, et mutare vocem meam. *But I should like to be among you now and to change my tone.* Gal. iv, 20.

See also Mt. xxv, 27.

The above uses of the Subj. are the only ones which occur in independent sentences and principal clauses.

NOUN CLAUSES.

The importance of distinguishing between different senses of the same word.

104. Many of the difficulties that beginners find in mastering a foreign language arise from the fact that they do not consider the meaning of some of the words that most frequently occur, but look only at their form.

Some of these words which are in common use are employed in several totally different senses.

Take for example the Eng. word *that.* It may be

(1) A Demonstrative Pronoun or Adjective trans. by the Latin *ille*, etc.

Give me that. *Da mihi illud.*

I see that woman. *Illam mulierem video.*

(2) A Relative Pronoun trans. by Latin *qui*, etc.

I have the book that you bought. *Librum, quem emisti, habeo.*

I see the man that sent for me. *Virum, qui me arcessivit, video.*

(3) A Conjunction introducing a clause of purpose trans. by Latin *ut.*

I came that I might see you. *Ut te viderem, veni.*

(4) A Conjunction introducing a clause of consequence trans. by Latin *ut* or *ita ut.*

[1] See section 167.

The storm was so great that the ship was wrecked. *Tanta erat procella, ut navis demergeretur.*

(5) A Conjunction introducing a noun clause which is trans. either by the Acc. and Inf. construction, or by a clause introduced by *ut*, or in Ecc. L. by *quod, quia* or *quoniam*.

He said that my brother had come. *Fratrem meum venisse dixit.*

It is expedient that I should do this. *Expedit ut hoc faciam.*

He prayed that the Lord would send labourers into the harvest. *Rogavit ut Dominus operarios in messem ejiceret.*

We know that you speak the truth. *Scimus quia vera dicis.*

The constructions mentioned in sub-section 5 are explained in the following pages. The object of the above paragraph is to warn the student not to confuse the noun clauses, now to be described, with the adverbial clauses described in sections 157–165.

As the Eng. word *that* is used in so many entirely distinct senses, it is obviously most essential to be certain of its meaning before trying to translate it into Latin.

Take for example the sentences:

I know that that that that man says is true. *Vera esse scio ea, quae ille dicat.*

He told me that he went to Rome that he might see Caesar. *Dixit mihi se Romam adivisse, ut Caesarem videret.*

The great difference between Eng. and Latin is obvious from these examples.

105. While this question of words with similar forms having widely different meanings is being discussed, it will be well to refer to the Latin words which present a similar difficulty.

These are *ut, cum, quod.*

Ut when it introduces a clause with the verb in the **Indicative** mood means either *as, when* or *where* according to the context.

The clause that it introduces is either a clause of comparison, a clause of time, or a clause of place. See sections 153–155, 175.

When *ut* introduces a clause with the verb in the **Subjunctive** mood the clause may be:

(1) A clause of purpose. See sections 157, 158.

(2) A clause of consequence. See section 163.

(3) A noun clause. See sections 116–127, 142, 145.

In all these cases *ut* is translated by *that* in Eng.

Example:

Et factum est, ut discesserunt ab eis angeli in caelum, pastores loquebantur ad invicem.... *And it came to pass when the angels were gone away from them into heaven, the shepherds were saying one to another....* Lk. ii, 15.

In the following example *ut* is first used to introduce a clause of purpose and secondly a clause of comparison.

Non ut confundam vos haec scribo, sed ut filios meos carissimos moneo. *I do not write these things that I may confound you, but as my beloved sons I warn you.* I Cor. iv, 14.

In the following example *ut* is used first to introduce a noun clause, in the second place to introduce a clause of consequence, in the third place to introduce a clause of comparison.

Orantes simul et pro nobis, ut Deus aperiat nobis ostium sermonis ad loquendum mysterium Christi, propter quod etiam vinctus sum, ut manifestem illud ita ut oportet me loqui. *Praying at the same time for us also, that God would open to us a door of utterance to speak the mystery of Christ, for which also I am bound, that I may make it manifest as I ought to speak.* Col. iv, 3.

Cum may be either a preposition meaning *together with* or a conjunction introducing a clause of time, a clause of cause, or a clause of concession and trans. *when, since, although.* See sections 153, 154, 156, 166, 210.

In old Latin books *cum* when used as a conjunction is generally spelt *quum.* In books recently printed it is spelt *cum* or *quom.*

Quod may be either the neuter singular of the relative pronoun or a conjunction introducing a clause of cause and trans. *because,* or (in Ecc. and late Latin only) a conjunction introducing a noun clause. See section 156. A careful study of the context is often needed to find out whether *quod* is a relative pronoun or a conjunction.

The Infinitive Mood and its equivalents.

106. The so-called **Infinitive Mood** had its origin in the Dat. or Loc. case of a verbal noun. *Habere* meant originally *for having* or *in having.* In early Latin the Dat. sense of the Inf. was still obvious, for it was used to express purpose.

Reddere hoc, non perdere, erus me misit. *My master sent me to return (for returning) this, not to lose it.* Plautus, *Ps.* 642.

Nec dulces occurrent oscula nati
Praeripere. *Nor will your sweet children run to you to snatch your kisses.* Lucretius, iii, 895.

This usage apparently held its ground in vernacular Latin, and appears occasionally in the Augustan poets who would be encouraged to use it by the analogy of the use of the Inf. in Gk. to express purpose.

Nos numerus sumus, et fruges consumere nati. *We are a mere collection of nonentities, born to devour the fruits of the earth.* Horace, *Ep.* I, ii, 27.

This use of the Infinitive never occurs in Classical Latin prose. Its place is taken by a clause introduced by *ut*, or by one of the other const. mentioned in sections 157–162.

In Ecc. L. the Inf. is frequently used to express purpose.

107. In Cl. L. the Inf. is treated as the Nom. or Acc. case of a verbal noun. Its Dat. sense is generally ignored.

In the same way, although the Eng. Inf. is generally found with the preposition *to* in front of it, this preposition is no part of the Inf., and is omitted after certain verbs such as *may, can, shall, bid, let, make.*

Examples: *I can do this. Let me go. Make him stay. I will say what I like. I bid you come here.*

Contrast these with: *I am able to do this. Allow me to go. Force him to stay. I intend to say what I like. I command you to come here.*

The omission or insertion of the preposition *to* before the Inf. is quite arbitrary: it contributes nothing to the meaning of the phrase.

In such a sentence as: *To err is human, to forgive divine,* the Infs. are treated exactly as if they were verbal nouns standing as the subjects of the clauses: the preposition *to* is absolutely without meaning.

The preposition only has its proper force when the Inf. is used to express purpose or result, or is used in an explanatory sense. Examples: *I came here to fish. I am tall enough to look over your head. It is time to go home.* Even in this use the force of the preposition is so little felt that another preposition may be inserted in front of it. Example: *What went ye out for to see?*

108. **The Infinitive** partakes of the nature both of a verb and a noun.

As a verb it has a subject, expressed or understood; if it is the infinitive of a transitive verb, it has an object: it governs the same case as the verb from which it is derived; it is qualified by adverbs: it has tense and voice.

As a noun it can be used as the subject or object of a sentence, or it may stand in apposition to another noun: but in Latin it cannot be governed by a preposition.

The subject of an Inf. is in the **Accusative Case**. The reason for this will be explained later.

The fact that the Inf. is a verbal noun caused it to be used in noun clauses.

109. In Cl. L. the Inf. with its subject in the Acc. (called the **Accusative and Infinitive Construction**) is regularly used in object clauses standing as objects of verbs denoting saying and thinking.

There are however two other constructions that are in some sense equivalent to the Acc. Inf. construction in noun clauses.

These are

(1) A clause introduced by *ut* with the verb in the Subj. (called **ut with the Subjunctive construction**).

(2) A clause introduced by *quod, quia, quoniam* with the verb in the Ind. or Subj. (called **quod, quia, quoniam construction**).

This latter construction only occurs in Ecc. L. with very few exceptions mentioned below.

The use of these constructions is described in the following sections. A few words may be said here about their origin.

110. The *ut with the Subjunctive* construction is most frequently found in object clauses depending on verbs meaning to command, to request, to bring about, etc.

Examples:

Ut hoc facias tibi impero.
Te rogo ut mihi subvenias.
Effecit ut ex urbe exirent.

It is easy to see that there is something of a sense of *purpose* or *desired result* in the clauses introduced by *ut*.

The meaning of these sentences might be expressed as follows:

I give a command to you *in order that* you may do this.

I make a request to you *in order that* you may help me.

He brought it about *with the result that* they went out of the city.

As is explained in sections 157, 163, clauses introduced by *ut* with a verb in the Subj. mood denote both purpose and result.

111. The *ut with the Subjunctive* construction is however found in other noun clauses, especially in clauses which are the subjects of impersonal verbs or of the verb *to be*.

In some of these no sense of purpose or result can be discovered. It seems as if this construction were used as a substitute for the Inf., just as the "ἵνα with a Subjunctive" construction is used in later Gk.

Example:

Expedit vobis ut ego vadam. *It is expedient for you that I go away.* Jn. xvi, 7.

συμφέρει ὑμῖν ἵνα ἐγὼ ἀπέλθω.

This construction is quite Cl., and goes back to the beginning of the language, as far as we know it.

112. The *quod, quia, quoniam* construction however is not Cl. It seems to have become prevalent during the decadence of the language, and it is especially common in the Latin Bible where it was used to translate literally certain Greek constructions.

From the frequent use which Ecclesiastical writers made of the Latin Bible it was natural that they should employ this construction to an ever increasing extent.

It is so common in Ecc. L., and so characteristic of it, that its origin must be treated at length.

113. Clauses introduced by the neuter relative *quod* referring to a noun or pronoun (expressed or understood) in the main clause, are used in Cl. L. in a sense approximating to that of a noun clause in apposition.

Haec res mihi curae est, quidnam hoc sit negoti, quod filia repente expetit ex me, ut ad se irem. *This is what worries me, what can be the reason that my daughter suddenly asks me to go to her.* Plaut. *Men.* 762.

Accidit perincommode, quod eum nusquam vidisti. *It happens most awkwardly that you have never seen him.* Cic. *Ep. ad Att.* i, 17.

Hoc scio quod scribit nulla puella tibi. *This I do know that no girl writes to you.* Mart. xi, 64.

Hoc uno praestamus vel maxime feris, quod exprimere dicendo sensa possumus. *In this one thing we surpass the beasts most of all, namely that we can express our thoughts in speech.* Cic. *Or.* i, 8.

There are two examples in early Latin where a clause introduced by *quod* stands as the object of a verb of saying or feeling. The verb is in the Subj.

Equidem scio jam filius quod amet meus istanc meretricem. *Truly I know now that my son loves that harlot.* Plaut. *As.* 52.

The other example is in Cato the Elder.

This construction also occurs in the book on the Spanish war, written by a follower of Caesar in an uncultivated style, in Suetonius, Apuleius and Tacitus, but only very rarely.

In later writers it becomes more and more common.

Examples:

Renuntiaverunt quod Pompeium in potestate haberent. *They announced that they had Pompey in their power.* *Bell. Hisp.* 36.

Titus, recordatus quondam super cenam quod nihil cuiquam toto die praestitisset.... *Titus, remembering once during supper that he had given nothing to anyone during the whole day....* Suetonius, *Titus.*

Qui puellae nuntiaret quod eam juvenis vocaret ad se.... *Who was to tell the girl that the young man called her to him....* Apuleius x.

See also Tacitus, *Ann.* xiv, 6.

The usual opinion about this construction is that it is a vernacular idiom, ignored by the Cl. writers, which came into common use during the decay of the language.

Madvig[1] however thinks that, if this had been a vernacular idiom, it would have occurred more frequently in Plautus. He prefers to connect it with the use of *quod* in apposition mentioned above, and regards the passages in Plautus and Cato as possibly corrupt.

114. However this may be, the use of this construction received a great extension in the Old Latin version of the Bible and is quite common there as well as in the Ecclesiastical writers who were

[1] Madvig, *Opusc. Acad.* ii, p. 232.

naturally much influenced in their style by the version of the Bible which they used.

In the Bible and in these writers both the Ind. and Subj. moods are used indifferently in this construction.

The reason why the translators of the Bible made so much use of this construction is that there is in Gk. an alternative construction to the Acc. and Inf. construction used after verbs of saying or thinking. This consists of a clause introduced by ὅτι with the verb in the Ind. mood. In certain of its uses ὅτι corresponds to the Latin *quod*, and the translators, who strove to translate the Gk. as literally as possible, eagerly seized upon the construction with *quod* which was coming into use in Latin to translate clauses introduced by ὅτι.

They also kept the mood of the Gk. original in some cases, although this was quite contrary to Latin usage.

They did even more than this. ὅτι also means *because* in Gk., and there are two Latin words that can be used to translate it literally in this sense, namely *quia* and *quoniam*.

These words were therefore used to translate ὅτι when introducing an object clause after a verb of saying or thinking exactly as *quod* was used.

There seems to be a certain approximation to this use in the lines of Catullus:

Id gratumst mihi, me quoniam tibi dicis amicum,
Muneraque et Musarum hinc petis et Veneris.

This is pleasing to me, that you call me your friend and seek the gifts of Venus and the Muses from me. lxviii, 8.

where *quoniam* picks up and explains *id* just as *quod* did in the examples in section 113.

Some usage of this kind in familiar speech may have served to help the introduction of this form of expression; but it must have made the early versions of the Bible sound very strangely to educated ears.

However this usage spread from these versions to all Ecclesiastical writers, even to Tertullian and Cyprian, although they employ it sparingly. Generally speaking this construction is employed by the early Fathers in those parts of their writings which were intended for partly educated people, or which deal directly with the Bible.

Jerome retained it in his revised version of the Bible, which we call the Vulgate, even in the O.T. which he translated anew from the Hebrew, although he modified some of the extreme literalness of the old versions.

115. The use of clauses introduced by *quod* was widely extended in later Latin to cover most of the senses that had been expressed in Cl. L., and even in the early Fathers, by an Acc. Inf. or a clause introduced by *ut*.

From these uses descend the many uses of *que* in French and *che* in Italian.

It should be noticed how much nearer the general construction of Eng. is to the style of Ecc. L. than to that of Cl. L.

Eng. is not derived from Latin except in respect of a great part of its vocabulary; but there is no doubt that the general structure of Eng. has been largely modified by the style of the English Bible of 1611, the style of which was in its turn influenced by the Vg.

Examples of noun clauses introduced by *quod, quia, quoniam* are given in section 135.

The Infinitive or its equivalents used as the subject or complement of a verb.

116. The Simple Inf., an Acc. and Inf., a clause introduced by *ut*, or (in Ecc. L. only) a clause introduced by *quod, quia, quoniam* is used as the subject of impersonal verbs and in many expressions containing the verb *esse*.

The usage varies with different periods of the language and with different writers; the student must learn the construction of the various verbs by experience.

In Eng. the syntax of sentences of this kind is confused by the fact that they are written in the following forms:

It is more blessed to give than to receive.

It is expedient that one man should die for the people.

The real subject of the first of these sentences is *to give than to receive*.

The real subject of the second sentence is *that one man should die for the people*.

The word *it* in each sentence is the Preparatory Subject, and the sentences are written in this way in Eng., because, in that language, the subject is nearly always put first in the sentence.

Indeed, this is the only way in which the subject can be distinguished from the object in Eng. owing to the absence of case endings. The Preparatory Subject serves to give notice that the real subject is coming afterwards.

In many Latin grammars impersonal verbs are said *to take an Infinitive, or a clause with* ut *and the Subj. after them.*

This confuses the student who may think that these clauses come after the verbs as objects, whereas they are really subjects.

117. A Simple Inf. may be used in Latin, as in Eng., as the subject of a verb, especially of the verb *to be*.

As Subject:

Beatius est magis dare quam accipere. *It is more blessed to give than to receive.* Acts xx, 35.

Mihi vivere Christus est, et mori lucrum. *To me to live is Christ, and to die is gain.* Phil. i, 21.

117*a*. A Simple Inf. may be used in Latin as in Eng. as the complement of a verb, especially of the verb *to be*.

Hoc est praeceptum Dei facere, hoc est voluntatem Patris adimplere. *This is to perform the commandment of God: this is to fulfil the will of the Father.* Cyprian.

See the whole selection *Quid est voluntas Dei* in the Appendix, p. 119, for examples of the use of the Simple Inf.

118. The verb *oportet* generally has an Acc. and Inf. clause as its subject (see Section 130).

Illum oportet crescere, me autem minui. *He must increase, but I must decrease.* Jn. iii, 30.

Oportet Deo obedire magis quam hominibus. *It is necessary for us to obey God, rather than men.* Acts v, 29.

But it may take a clause introduced by *quod* in Ecc. L.

Oportet quod verbum Dei in nobis manens continue meditemur. *We ought continually to meditate on the word of God which abides in us.* T. Aq. *de Symb. Ap.*

119. We may here notice a peculiar idiom which is also found in Cl. L., namely to use a Past tense of the verb *oportere* with a Present Inf.

as its subject to express an unfulfilled duty. This is expressed in Eng. by the use of a Past Inf.

Haec oportuit facere, et illa non omittere. *These ye ought to have done, and not to have left the other undone.* Mt. xxiii, 23.

Oportuit ergo te mittere pecuniam meam nummulariis, et veniens ego recepissem utique quod meum est cum usura. *Thou oughtest to have put my money to the bankers, and then at my coming I should have received my own with usury.* Mt. xxv, 27.

See Acts xxiv, 20.

A Past tense of *oportere* may have however simply a past sense without any idea of unfulfilled duty.

Oportebat autem eum transire per Samariam. *But he had to go through Samaria.* Jn. iv, 4; Lk. xv, 32.

120. Other impersonal verbs may have either a clause introduced by *ut* or an Acc. Inf. for subject. In some cases *ut* is omitted and a Simple Subj. with its subject, etc. forms the noun clause. The use of Ecc. writers varies much from that of Cl. writers and no exact rule can be laid down.

121. The expression *factum est* to represent the Gk. ἐγένετο, which in its turn represents the Heb. וַיְהִי, is very frequent in the Vg. and is generally translated *it came to pass*. It is not Cl.

It generally has for its subject a clause introduced by *ut*, but it may have an Acc. and Inf. or even a clause with the verb in the Ind. and no connecting particle.

Factum est autem et in alio Sabbato, ut intraret in synagogam, et doceret. *And it came to pass on another Sabbath that he entered into a synagogue and taught.* Lk. vi, 6.

Factum est autem revertenti mihi in Hierusalem, et oranti in templo, fieri me in stupore mentis. *And it came to pass that when I had returned to Jerusalem and was praying in the temple, I was in a trance.* Acts xxii, 17.

See Acts xvi, 16.

Factum est autem in illis diebus, exiit in montem orare. *And it came to pass in those days that he went out into a mountain to pray.* Lk. vi, 12.

122. *Accidit, contigit, expedit, pertinet* have for their subject a clause introduced by *ut* in Cl. L.

In the Vg. the Acc. and Inf. construction is sometimes used, or even a subjunctive without *ut*. Very rarely the subject clause is introduced by *quia*. Mk. iv, 36.

Accidit autem ut sacerdos quidam descenderet eadem via. *But it happened that a certain priest was going down by the same way.* Lk. x, 31.

Et cum iter faceret contingit ut adpropinquaret Damasco. *And when he was travelling it happened that he drew near to Damascus.* Acts ix, 3.

Expedit vobis ut ego vadam. *It is expedient for you that I go away.* Jn. xvi, 7.

Contigit autem patrem Publii...jacere. *But it happened that the father of Publius lay sick.* Acts xxviii, 8.

Et contigit, dum iret, a turbis comprimebatur. *And it happened that while he went he was pressed by the crowds.* Lk. viii, 42.

123. *Necesse est, decet.* The subject clause is constructed either with the Acc. and Inf. or with *ut*.

Unde necesse est et hunc habere aliquid quod offerat. *Whence it is necessary that he should have something to offer.* Heb. viii, 3.

Necesse est enim ut veniant scandala. *It must needs be that offences come.* Mt. xviii, 7.

I Thess. i, 8; Heb. vii, 12; Heb.ix, 16: (*ut* omitted).

Sine modo, sic enim decet nos implere omnem justitiam. *Suffer it to be so now, for thus it becomes us to fulfil all righteousness.* Mt. iii, 16.

Talis enim decebat ut esset nobis pontifex. *For it was befitting that there should be such a high priest for us.* Heb. vii, 26.

124. *Licet* and *placet* have a Simple Inf. for subject with a dative of the person to whom the action is allowable or pleasing. The *ut* clause is also used.

Non licet mittere eos in corbonan. *It is not lawful to put them into the treasury.* Mt. xxvii, 6.

See also Mt. xxii, 17.

Placuit nobis remanere Athenis solis. *It pleased us to remain in Athens alone.* I Thess. iii, 1.

Cum placuit ei...ut revelaret Filium suum in me. *When it pleased him...to reveal his Son in me.* Gal. i, 15.

125. *Interest* is only used once in the N.T. and has its peculiar construction of an Abl. feminine of the possessive pronoun to express the person in whose interest the action takes place.

Quales aliquando fuerint, nihil mea interest. *Whosoever they were makes no matter to me.* Gal. ii, 6.

The following are examples of the use of *quod* and *quia* in subject clauses:

Non ad te pertinet quia perimus? *Doth it not matter to thee that we perish?* Mk. iv, 38.

Latet enim eos hoc volentes, quod caeli erant prius. *For this they are willingly ignorant of, that the heavens were of old.* II Pet. iii, 5.

126. An impersonal predicate made up of a neuter adjective and the verb *esse* may have either a Simple Inf. or Acc. and Inf. or a clause introduced by *ut* (or in Ecc. L. by *quod*, etc.) as its subject.

Non est vestrum nosse tempora vel momenta, quae Pater posuit in potestate sua. *It is not yours to know times and seasons which the Father put in his own power.* Acts i, 7.

Facilius est enim camelum per foramen acus transire, quam divitem intrare in regnum Dei. *For it is easier for a camel to go through the eye of a needle than for a rich man to enter into the kingdom of God.* Lk. xviii, 25.

Bonum est enim mihi magis mori, quam ut gloriam meam quis evacuet. *For it is better for me to die than that anyone should make my glory vain.* I Cor. ix, 15.

Reliquum est, ut et qui habent uxores, tanquam non habentes sint. *It remains that those that have wives should be as if they had none.* I Cor. vii, 29.

Manifestum est enim quod ex Juda ortus sit Dominus noster. *For it is manifest that our Lord sprang out of Juda.* Heb. vii, 14.

127. A clause introduced by *ut* (or in Ecc. L. by *quod*, etc.) may form the subject of any verb used impersonally whether in the Active or the Passive voice.

Ascendit in cor ejus ut visitaret fratres suos, filios Israel. *It came into his heart to visit his brothers the children of Israel.* Acts vii, 23.

Hic jam quaeritur...ut fidelis quis inveniatur. *Here it is expected that a man be found faithful.* I Cor. iv, 2.

Sic ergo patet quod multum utile est habere fidem. *So then it is plain that it is very profitable to have faith.*

Thos. Aq. *Symb. Ap.* i.

The Infinitive or its equivalents used to complete the meaning of certain verbs.

128. In Latin as in English an Infinitive is used as a complement of the predicate with certain verbs. These are called **Modal verbs** because they add new modes of expression or moods to the verbs which are used with them.

The most important are *possum, volo, nolo, malo,* and also verbs denoting beginning or ceasing, habit, continuance, desire, purpose, aim or duty.

If the subject of the principal verb is the same as that of the Inf. the subject of the Inf. is often not expressed, it is however generally speaking in the Nominative case and any adjectives that agree with it must be in that case; see example 2.

If the subject of the Inf. is not the same as the subject of the principal verb, the subject of the Inf. is in the Acc. case; see example 3.

In Ecc. L. a clause introduced by *ut* with the Subj., or a Subj. without *ut*, or even an Ind. may take the place of the Inf. after *volo*.

Quomodo potest homo nasci, cum senex sit? *How can a man be born when he is old?* Jn. iii, 4.

Si vis perfectus esse, vade, vende quae habes. *If thou wishest to be perfect, go and sell what thou hast.* Mt. xix, 21.

Volo ergo viros orare in omni loco. *I wish therefore men to pray in every place.* I Tim. ii, 8.

Omnia ergo quaecumque vultis ut faciant vobis homines, et vos facite eis. *Whatsoever things therefore that ye wish men should do unto you, do ye also unto them.* Mt. vii, 12.

See also Jn. xvii, 24; Mt. xx, 32.

Ubi vis paremus tibi comedere Pascha? *Where dost thou wish us to prepare for thee to eat the Passover?* Mt. xxvi, 17.

Vis imus et colligimus ea? *Dost thou wish us to go and gather them up?* Mt. xiii, 28.

Et iterum coepit docere ad mare. *And he began again to teach by the sea.* Mk. iv, 1.

Ut cessavit loqui, dixit ad Simonem.... *When he ceased to speak, he said to Simon....* Lk. v, 4.

Per diem autem festum dimittere solebat illis unum ex vinctis. *On the feast day he was wont to release to them one of the prisoners.* Mk. xv, 6.

THE INFINITIVE OR ITS EQUIVALENTS USED AS THE OBJECT OF A VERB.

129. The Simple Inf. may be used as the object of a verb, just like a noun.

Perficere autem non invenio. *But how to perform it I find not.* Rom. vii, 18.

129*a*. The Inf. may be used as one of two objects after certain verbs such as *docere, jubere*, and in Ecc. L. *rogare*.

Docuerunt enim linguam suam loqui mendacium. *For they taught their tongue to speak a lie.* Jer. ix, 5.

Jussit milites descendere et rapere eum de medio eorum. *He commanded the soldiers to go down and to take him from the midst of them.* Acts xxiii, 10.

Propter quod rogo vos accipere cibum pro salute vestra. *Wherefore I ask you to take food for your health's sake.* Acts xxvii, 34.

The Inf. may be retained as object after a passive verb of this kind.

Ubi inventis fratribus rogati sumus manere apud eos dies septem. *Where having found brethren, we were asked to remain with them seven days.* Acts xxviii, 14.

See also II Cor. x, 2, 9.

130. Out of this construction there arose a usage of the greatest importance in Latin. The Acc. and Inf., instead of being regarded as two separate objects of the main verb, combined together so as to form a single object clause in which the Inf. acquired a predicative sense and the Acc. was regarded as its subject.

This usage is called the Acc. with the Inf. construction, because the Acc. goes with the Inf. as its subject and not with the main verb as its object[1].

[1] This definition was suggested by Professor Sonnenschein's *New Latin Grammar*, p. 125.

Example:

Jussit eum duci in castra. *He commanded him to be led to the camp.* Acts xxi, 34.

This sentence does not state that the order was given to Paul: the whole clause *duci eum in castra* is the object of the main verb.

This construction is very common in Cl. L. in object clauses depending on verbs denoting saying or thinking (*verba declarandi vel sentiendi*).

Whole speeches are commonly reported in this way and are then given not in the words in which they were actually delivered, but in the words of a reporter. When applied to speeches this construction is called the **Oratio Obliqua.** It is very uncommon in the Vg., for in the Heb. original of the O.T. speeches are given in the words of the original speaker and not reported. In the N.T. the influence of Heb. methods of expression causes the Oratio Obliqua to be equally rare and it is not common in Ecc. writers.

It seems unnecessary to go into a long description of this complicated construction in a book intended as an introduction to Ecc. L.

It may suffice to say that in this construction all main verbs are in the Inf. mood, and all verbs in subordinate clauses in the Subj. mood. The latter half of this rule is not universally observed in Ecc. L.

131. Noun clauses standing as objects of verbs are of three kinds.

1. **Dependent statements,** or object clauses depending on verbs denoting saying or thinking (*verba declarandi vel sentiendi*).

2. **Dependent commands,** or object clauses depending on verbs denoting entreaty, command, exhortation, or bringing about (*verba imperandi vel efficiendi*).

3. **Dependent questions,** or object clauses depending on verbs denoting questioning, or clauses introduced by an interrogative word depending on verbs of various meanings.

132. Dependent statements. In Eng. these nearly always take the form of a clause introduced by *that* with the verb in the Ind. mood. The tense of the verb in these clauses is always one stage further in the past than the tense used by the original speaker, if the verb on which the clause depends is in a past tense.

Thus:

He said that he was pleased to be in London.

The original words used by the speaker were:

I am pleased to be in London.

He said that he had seen his brother.

The original words used by the speaker were:

I have seen my brother.

He said that he would go to London on Friday.

The original words used by the speaker were:

I will go to London on Friday.

N.B. In modern Grammars the tense formed with *would* and *should* is called the *Future in the past.*

This, as has been said, is the usual construction; but there are a few verbs in Eng. that are followed by an Acc. Inf. construction.

The judge declared him to be a criminal.
I believe them to be safe.
I consider you to be incompetent.

But even in the case of these verbs a clause introduced by *that* may also be used.

The judge declared that he was a criminal. (Notice the change of tense.)
I believe that they are safe.
I consider that you are incompetent.

133. In Cl. L. the only construction that is used in object clauses after verbs of *sentiendi vel declarandi* is the Acc. and Inf.

As has already been explained a clause introduced by *quod, quia* or *quoniam* can be used in Ecc. L. instead of the Acc. and Inf. The verb in these clauses may be either Subj. or Ind.

If the main verb is in the third person singular or plural and the subject of the Inf. in the subordinate clause is the same as that of the main verb, the reflexive pronoun *se* is always used. Otherwise a demonstrative pronoun is used.

The use of the tenses of the Inf. is not very exact in Ecc. L., but, generally speaking, if the time of the action denoted by the main verb and that of the action denoted by the Inf. is the same, the Present Inf. is used.

Dicitis in Beelzebub ejicere me daemonia. *You say that I cast out devils in Beelzebub.* Lk. xi, 18.

If the time denoted by the Inf. is prior to that of the main verb the Perfect Inf. is used.

Aestimantes eum mortuum esse. *Thinking he was dead.*
Acts xiv, 19, xvi, 27; Phil. iii, 13.

If the time denoted by the Inf. is future to that of the main verb the Fut. Inf. is used.

Et responsum acceperat a Spiritu Sancto non visurum se mortem.... *And he had received a reply from the Holy Ghost that he should not see death....* Lk. ii, 26.

134. The tenses of verbs in subordinate clauses in dependent statements should follow the rule of the sequence of tenses; but sometimes the tense used when the words were actually spoken or the thought framed is retained, in imitation of Gk.

Dicentes se visionem angelorum vidisse, qui dicunt eum vivere. *Saying that they saw a vision of angels, who say that he is alive.* Lk. xxiv, 23.

Notice the use of *se* and *eum* in this example and also the use of an Ind. in a subordinate clause.

Huic omnes prophetae testimonium perhibent, remissionem peccatorum accipere per nomen ejus omnes qui credunt in eum. *To him all the prophets bear witness that all who believe in him receive remission of sins through his name.* Acts x, 43.

The normal Cl. construction is seen in the example below:

Et respondebant se nescire unde esset. *And they answered that they did not know whence he was.* Lk. xx, 7.

135. The following are examples of the construction of object clauses with *quod, quia* and *quoniam,* the origin of which is explained in sections 113–115.

The verb may be in the Ind. or Subj. mood without any difference in meaning.

De escis autem quae idolis immolantur, scimus quia nihil est idolum in mundo, et quod nullus Deus nisi unus. *With regard to meats offered to idols, we know that an idol is nothing in the world, and that there is no God but one.* I Cor. viii, 4.

Credere enim oportet accedentem ad Deum quia est, et inquirentibus se remunerator fit. *For one that cometh to God ought to believe that he is, and that he becomes a rewarder of those that seek him.* Heb. xi, 6.

Sometimes the tense of the original thought is retained as in Greek.

Et nesciebat quia verum est, quod fiebat per angelum. *And he did not know that what was done by the angel was true.*

Acts xii, 9.

The following is an example of the use of the *quod, quia, quoniam* construction from Tertullian, showing how soon this construction was adopted even by an educated writer:

Adeo postea in Actis Apostolorum invenimus, quoniam, qui Johannis baptismum habebant, non accepissent Spiritum Sanctum. *De Bapt.* 10.

136. Here may be noticed the very peculiar imitation of the Gk. idiom found in the N.T. and the LXX by which ὅτι is used to introduce the actual words of a speaker. *Quod, quia* or *quoniam* are employed to translate ὅτι in this sense quite indifferently. They must not be translated into Eng. The only Eng. equivalent to them when used in this way is the use of inverted commas. The punctuation of the Vg. is sometimes peculiar, as will be seen from the examples below. The introductory word is printed with a capital letter after a colon, as if it were part of the speech.

Et mulieri dicebant: Quia jam non propter tuam loquellam credimus; ipsi enim audivimus, et scimus quia hic est vere salvator mundi. *And they kept saying to the woman, "We believe, not because of your talking; for we have heard him ourselves, and we know that this is truly the saviour of the world."*

Jn. iv, 42.

Scriptum est enim quod Angelis suis mandabit de te, ut conservent te: et quia In manibus tollent te.... *For it is written "He shall give his angels charge concerning thee, that they may preserve thee": and "In their hands they shall bear thee up...."* Lk. iv, 10, 11.

Si quis dixerit quoniam diligo Deum, et fratrem suum oderit, mendax est. *If any man say "I love God," and hateth his brother, he is a liar.* I Jn. iv, 20.

For the use of *quod, quia,* etc. see Jn. iv, 46–54.

137. Special forms of dependent statements.

In Cl. L. verbs denoting *to promise, to hope, to swear,* and similar verbs which relate to the future are followed by the Acc. with a Future Inf.

In Ecc. L. a Present Inf. may be used, or a clause introduced by *quia*, etc. or *ut*.

Devotione devovimus nos nihil gustaturos, donec occidamus Paulum. *We have bound ourselves by a great curse that we will eat nothing until we have killed Paul.* Acts xxiii, 14.

Spero autem in Domino Jesu, Timotheum cito me mittere ad vos. *But I hope in the Lord Jesus that I may send Timothy to you shortly.* Phil. ii, 19.

Quibus autem juravit non introire in requiem ipsius, nisi illis qui increduli fuerunt? *But to whom did he swear that they should not enter into his rest, except to those that were unbelieving?* Heb. iii, 18; Acts ii, 30.

Simul et sperans quia pecunia daretur a Paulo. *At the same time hoping that money would be given by Paul.* Acts xxiv, 26.

Juravit ut non transirem Jordanem. *He swore that I should not pass over Jordan.* Deut. iv, 21 and i, 8.

137 *a*. In imitation of Heb. the verb *jurare* may be followed by *si* to express a strong negative, and by *nisi* to express a strong affirmative.

Sicut juravi in ira mea: Si introibunt in requiem meam. *As I sware in my wrath: "They shall not enter into my rest."* Heb. iii, 11.

Juravit per semetipsum, dicens: Nisi benedicens benedicam te, et multiplicans multiplicabo te. *He sware by himself, saying: "Surely I will bless thee and multiply thee exceedingly."* Heb. vi, 13.

In Mk. viii, 12, a construction of the same character is found after *dicere*.

Amen dico vobis, si dabitur generationi isti signum. *Verily I say to you, no sign shall be given to this generation.*

The Hebraic form of adjuration *Vivo ego, dicit Dominus* is followed by *quoniam* or *quia*.

Vivo ego, dicit Dominus, quoniam mihi flectet omne genu. Rom. XIV, 11, cited from Is. xlv, 23.

138. The verbs *audire* and *videre* may be followed by an Acc. and a participle in imitation of Gk., if they refer to something that was actually heard or seen when it was taking place.

Et vidit omnis populus eum ambulantem et laudantem Deum. *And all the people saw him walking and praising God.* Acts iii, 9.

Et cadens in terram audit vocem dicentem sibi.... *And falling to the earth he heard a voice saying to him....* Acts ix, 4.

Contrast with this:

Audierunt autem de te quia discessionem doceas a Mose. *For they have heard of thee that thou teachest departure from Moses.* Acts xxi, 21.

See also Mt. vi, 16; Lk. iv, 23; Acts ii, 6.

139. Verbs meaning *to fear* are generally followed in Cl. L. by a clause introduced by *ne* (which is equivalent to *lest* or *that* in Eng.) when the subordinate clause is affirmative, and by a clause introduced by *ut* when the subordinate clause is negative.

Vereor ne veniat. *I fear that he will come.*

Vereor ut veniat. *I fear that he will not come.*

Examples from the Vg.:

Timens tribunus ne discerperetur Paulus ab ipsis.... *The tribune fearing that Paul would be torn in pieces by them....* Acts xxiii, 10.

In the Vg. an Inf. is found after *timere*:

Timuit illuc ire. *He was afraid to go there.* Mt. ii, 22.

140. In Cl. L. object clauses after verbs meaning *to refuse, to prevent,* etc. are introduced by *quominus* or *quin* and have the verb in the Subj. *Quominus* and *quin* are rare in the Vg. A Simple Inf. is found after verbs of this kind.

Non enim subterfugi quominus adnuntiarem.... *For I have not shrunk from announcing....* Acts xx, 27.

Propter quod et impediebar...venire ad vos. *On account of which I was hindered...from coming to you.* Rom. xv, 22.

See also Acts xxiv, 24; I Cor. xiv, 39.

141. *Mirari* and *admirari* are followed by a clause introduced by *quia* or *quod* and occasionally by *si* in imitation of Gk.

Non mireris quia dixi tibi: Oportet vos nasci denuo. *Wonder not that I said to you: Ye must be born again.* Jn. iii, 7.

Nolite mirari, fratres, si odit vos mundus. *Do not wonder, brethren, if the world hates you.* I Jn. iii, 13.

See also Mk. xv, 44.

142. **Dependent commands.** In Eng. object clauses after verbs meaning to entreat, to command, to exhort, to bring about, etc., are generally expressed by the Acc. and Inf. construction.

In Cl. L. they are nearly always expressed by a clause introduced by *ut* with its verb in the Subj.

This causes a great deal of difficulty to beginners unless they get the fact clearly in their minds that where Cl. L. uses an Inf., Eng. generally uses a clause introduced by *that*, and where Cl. L. uses a clause introduced by *ut*, Eng. generally uses the Inf.

The verb *jubere, to command*[1], is followed by the Acc. Inf. construction in Cl. L.

[1] N.B. *Dicere* often means *to command* in Ecc. L. It is then followed by a clause introduced by *ut* or by an Inf.

Et dixit discipulis suis ut navicula sibi deserviret. *And he commanded his disciples that a little ship should wait on him.* Mk. iii, 9.

See also Mt. v, 39; Mk. v, 43; Rom. xii, 3.

In Ecc. L. object clauses after verbs of commanding, etc., are generally expressed by a clause introduced by *ut*. Sometimes *ut* is omitted. An Acc. and Inf. construction may also be used after these verbs in imitation of Gk., or even a simple Imperative.

Rogate ergo Dominum messis ut ejiciat operarios in messem. *Pray ye therefore the Lord of the harvest to thrust out labourers into his harvest.* Mt. ix, 38.

Statuerunt ut ascenderent Paulus et Barnabas. *They determined that Paul and Barnabas should go up.* Acts xv, 2.

Ecce faciam illos ut veniant, et adorent ante pedes tuos. *Behold I will make them come and worship before thy feet.* Rev. iii, 9.

Propter quod obsecro patienter me audias. *Wherefore I beseech thee to hear me patiently.* Acts xxvi, 3.

The following are examples of the use of the Inf.

Ascendens autem in unam navem, quae erat Simonis, rogavit eum a terra reducere pusillum. *And going into one ship which was Simon's, he asked him to push out a little from the land.* Lk. v, 3.

Petistis virum homicidam donari vobis. *Ye asked for a murderer to be granted to you.* Acts iii, 14.

Admone illos principibus et potestatibus subditos esse. *Warn them to be in subjection to princes and powers.* Tit. iii, 1.

Itaque, fratres, aemulamini prophetare. *And so, brethren, desire earnestly to prophesy.* I Cor. xiv, 19.

Progenies viperarum, quis demonstravit vobis fugere a futura ira? *Offspring of vipers, who warned you to flee from the wrath to come?* Mt. iii, 7.

See also Acts iii, 12, xi, 24, xxvi, 29; I Cor. v, 11, vii, 10; Phil. iv, 2; Heb. xiii, 19; I Pet. ii, 11.

The following is an example of the use of the Imperative:

Obsecro te respice in filium meum. *I beseech thee look at my son.* Lk. ix, 38.

An independent command may even be introduced by *quod* in late writers.

Sed nos desideramus quod, sicut voluntas Dei completa est in beatis, ita compleatur in nobis. *But we pray that as the will of God is fulfilled among the blessed so it may be fulfilled among us.* Thomas Aquinas.

A clause introduced by *si* may be used after a verb denoting requesting, to denote a request that seems unlikely to be fulfilled.

Obsecrans si quomodo tandem aliquando prosperum iter habeam in voluntate Dei veniendi ad vos. *Praying if by any means yet sometime I may have a prosperous journey by the will of God to come to you.* Rom. i, 10.

143. Dependent questions. Object clauses after verbs meaning *to ask a question* or clauses introduced by an interrogative word after other verbs are called Dependent Questions in Latin grammar. In Eng. such clauses have the verb in the Ind. and present no difficulty; but in Cl. L. the verb is nearly always in the Subj. in these clauses.

In Ecc. L. the verb in a Dependent Question is often in the Ind[1].

Examples of the ordinary Classical construction:

Et interrogabat quis esset, et quid fecisset. *And he asked who he was, and what he had done.* Acts xxi, 33.

Nescimus quid factum sit ei. *We know not what has happened to him.* Acts vii, 40.

Et annuntiaverunt eis quanta ad eos principes sacerdotum et seniores dixissent. *And they announced to them all that the chief priests and elders had said to them.* Acts iv, 23.

Et quaerebant summi sacerdotes et scribae quomodo eum cum dolo tenerent et occiderent. *And the chief priests and scribes sought how they might take him with guile and kill him.* Mk. xiv, 1.

Cognoscet de doctrina utrum ex Deo sit, an ego a me ipso loquar. *He shall know of the doctrine whether it is of God, or whether I speak of myself.* Jn. vii, 17.

144. Examples of dependent questions with the verb in the Ind.:

[1] This usage is also found in early and late Latin. Compare Lucan, *Pharsalia*, i, 126, ix, 563.

Domine, nescimus quo vadis. *Lord, we know not whither thou goest.* Jn. xiv, 5.

Redi domum tuam, et narra quanta tibi fecit Deus. *Return to thy home, and tell all that God has done for thee.* Lk. viii, 39.

Quomodo autem nunc videat, nescimus: aut quis ejus aperuit oculos nos nescimus. *We know not how he now sees, nor do we know who opened his eyes.* Jn. ix, 21.

NOUN CLAUSES IN APPOSITION TO A NOUN OR PRONOUN.

145. A noun clause is sometimes used in apposition to a noun or pronoun to explain the meaning of the noun or pronoun.

These clauses are generally expressed by *ut* with the Subj. or by an Inf. In Ecc. L. they may be expressed by a clause introduced by *quod, quia, quoniam.*

Meus cibus est ut faciam voluntatem ejus, qui misit me. *My meat is to do the will of him that sent me.* Jn. iv, 34.

Visum est Spiritui Sancto et nobis nihil ultra imponere vobis oneris quam haec necessario: ut abstineatis vos ab immolatis.... *It seemed good to the Holy Spirit and to us to lay no further burden on you than these things necessarily: that you should abstain from things sacrificed....* Acts xv, 28.

Quandoquidem recte mihi vivere puero id proponebatur, obtemperare monentibus. *Since this was set before me as the ideal of a boy's existence, namely to obey those that instructed me.* Augustine.

See also II Cor. vii, 11; Eph. iii, 8.

Hoc est autem judicium: quia lux venit in mundum, et dilexerunt homines magis tenebras quam lucem.... *But this is the judgement: that light came into the world, and men loved darkness rather than light....* Jn. iii, 19.

Omnia ostendi vobis, quoniam sic laborantes oportet suscipere infirmos. *I have shown you all things, that so labouring ye ought to support the weak.* Acts xx, 35.

See also Phil. i, 6.

146. The Infinitive used as an Imperative. The Pres. Inf. is very rarely used in the sense of an Imperative in imitation of a rare use in N.T. Gk. This idiom is found in French and Italian, rarely in Eng.

Gaudere cum gaudentibus, flere cum flentibus. *Rejoice with them that do rejoice and weep with those that weep.* Rom. xii, 15.

The Inf. in Mt. v, 34, 39 may possibly be an Imperative Inf.

147. Explanatory Infinitive. The Inf. (retaining somewhat of its original Dat. sense) is used with certain adjectives and nouns, generally such as denote power, capacity, merit, fitness, in an explanatory sense.

Scio cui credidi, et certus sum quia potens est depositum meum servare in illum diem. *I know in whom I have believed and I am certain that he is able to keep that which I have deposited with him until that day.* II Tim. i, 12.

See also Lk. v, 24; II Cor. ix, 8; Rev. xiii, 5.

Qui idonei erunt et alios docere. *Who shall be fit to teach others also.* II Tim. ii, 2.

Non habent necesse ire. *They have no need to go away.* Mt. xiv, 16.

But we also find:

Et non necesse habetis ut aliquis doceat vos. *And ye have no need that anyone should teach you.* I Jn. ii, 27.

Et jam non sum dignus vocari filius tuus. *And I am no longer worthy to be called thy son.* Lk. xv, 19, xxi, 36.

A clause introduced by *ut* is also used with *dignus* in imitation of the Gk. Jn. i, 27. See also Mt. viii, 8.

Et hoc scientes tempus: quia hora est jam nos de somno surgere. *And that knowing the time, that it is now the hour for us to awake out of sleep.* Rom. xiii, 11; Rev. xi, 18.

Bonam voluntatem habemus magis peregrinari a corpore, et praesentes esse ad Dominum. *We have a good will rather to be absent from the body and to be present with the Lord.* II Cor. v, 8.

In Cl. L. prose such words would be followed by a Gerund or Gerundive with *ad*, by a Relative clause, or by a Gen. of the Gerund or Gerundive, as in this example:

Et hic habet potestatem a principibus sacerdotum alligandi omnes, qui invocant nomen tuum. *And here he has power from the chief priests to bind all that call on thy name.* Acts ix, 14.

148. The Inf. is used in an explanatory sense after verbs: sometimes it describes the purpose and sometimes the consequence of the verb on which it depends.

It is used in imitation of Gk., and would not be so used in Cl. prose.

Esurivi enim et dedistis me manducare. *I was hungry and ye gave me to eat.* Mt. xxv, 35.

Quomodo tu, Judaeus cum sis, bibere a me poscis, quae sum mulier Samaritana? *How is it that thou, although thou art a Jew, askest to drink of me who am a Samaritan woman?* Jn. iv, 9.

Observabant autem scribae et Pharisaei, si sabbato curaret, ut invenirent accusare illum. *And the scribes and the Pharisees watched him, whether he would heal on the Sabbath; that they might find how to accuse him.* Lk. vi, 7.

Moram facit Dominus meus venire. *My lord delays to come.* Mt. xxiv, 49.

Elegit Deus per os meum audire gentes verbum evangelii. *God chose that the Gentiles should hear through my mouth the word of the gospel.* Acts xv, 7.

Nunc ergo quid temptatis Deum imponere jugum super cervicem discipulorum? *Now therefore why do ye tempt God to put a yoke upon the neck of the disciples?* Acts xv, 10.

See also Mt. vii, 5; Acts xvi, 14; Heb. xi, 8.

The Vg. is not at all consistent in this usage. *Ut* is used in Heb. v, 5, vi, 10, and Col. iv, 6, where an Inf. is used in Gk.

ADJECTIVAL CLAUSES.

149. An **Adjectival Clause** qualifies a noun or pronoun, which is called its antecedent, in the same way as an adjective.

Adjectival clauses are introduced by the relative pronouns *qui*, *quicumque*, or by the relative adverbs *quo*, *unde*, *quomodo*, etc.

When an adjectival or relative clause, as it is generally called, refers to an actual event or fact, it is called a Definite Relative Clause.

The verb in a definite relative clause is in the Ind. mood, as it is in Eng.; unless the clause comes under one of the classes specified below which have their verb in the Subj.

Example:

Nonne ecce omnes isti qui loquuntur Galilaei sunt? *Are not all these who speak Galilaeans?* Acts ii, 7.

150. The verb in a definite relative clause is in the Subj. mood:

(1) To indicate that the person or thing denoted by the antecedent is capable of performing, or is of such a character as to be likely to perform or to suffer the action denoted by the relative clause.

Such clauses may be called Characterising Relative Clauses.

Viri Ephesii, quis enim est hominum, qui nesciat Ephesiorum civitatem cultricem esse magnae Dianae? *Men of Ephesus, what man is there that does not know that the city of the Ephesians is a worshipper of great Diana?* Acts xix, 35.

Quia adversarius vester diabolus tamquam leo rugiens circuit, quaerens quem devoret. *Because your adversary the devil goeth about like a roaring lion seeking whom he may devour.* I Pet. v, 8.

Neminem enim habeo tam unanimem, qui sincera affectione pro vobis sollicitus sit. *For I have no one so like minded who with sincere affection is likely to care for you.* Phil. ii, 20.

Filius autem hominis non habet ubi caput reclinet. *For the Son of man hath not where to lay his head.* Mt. viii, 20.

See also Acts xi, 17, xiii, 11; Jn. xii, 48; I Kings xviii, 26.

The following uses are akin to the above:

(*a*) A Subj. is sometimes found in a relative clause when the principal clause has for its predication the idea of existence.

Ego autem non quaero gloriam meam: est qui quaerat et judicet[1]. *But I do not seek my own glory: there is one that seeks and judges.* Jn. viii, 50.

Omnes declinaverunt, simul inutiles facti sunt, non est qui faciat bonum, non est usque ad unum. *They have all gone out of the way, they have all together become profitless, there is not one that doeth good, no not one.* Rom. iii, 12.

(*b*) A relative clause with the verb in the Subj. is sometimes found after the adjectives *dignus* and *indignus*.

Et si in vobis judicabitur mundus, indigni estis, qui de minimis judicetis? *And if the world shall be judged by you, are you unworthy to judge the smallest matters?* I Cor. vi, 2.

(2) The Subj. is used in a relative clause if the clause expresses purpose, consequence, or cause.

[1] This is tne reading of SC. WW. had Ind. in both verbs.

Purpose:

Et observantes miserunt insidiatores, qui se justos simularent. *And observing him they sent forth spies who should feign themselves to be just men.* Lk. xx, 20.

Consequence:

Quis enim novit sensum Domini, qui instruat eum? *For who knows the mind of the Lord, so as to instruct him?* I Cor. ii, 16.

Nam et Pater tales quaerit, qui adorent eum. *For the Father looks for such to worship him.* Jn. iv, 23.

(3) When a relative clause forms part of an indirect statement or question the verb in the relative clause is put in the Subj. in Cl. L. The Ind. is generally used in the Vg.

Venerunt dicentes se etiam visionem angelorum vidisse qui dicunt eum vivere. *They came saying that they had seen a vision of angels who say that he is alive.* Lk. xxiv, 23.

Generally speaking, if a relative clause depends on a clause with its verb in the Subj. the verb in the relative clause is also in the Subj. in Cl. L. The following is an example from the Vg.

Et dum intra se haesitaret Petrus quidnam esset visio quam vidisset.... *And while Peter doubted in himself what the vision was which he had seen....* Acts x, 17.

In Mt. xxvii, 15 there is an example of what is known as *Virtual Oratio Obliqua* because the relative clause expresses the thought of the people not as expressed by themselves, but as conceived by Pilate.

151. When a relative clause refers to a supposed event or instance and hence implies a condition, it is called an Indefinite Relative Clause. The Future Perfect tense is generally used in indefinite relative clauses referring to future time.

Non occides: qui autem occiderit reus erit judicio. *Thou shalt not kill: but whosoever shall kill shall be guilty so as to be in danger of the judgement.* Mt. v, 21.

ADVERBIAL CLAUSES.

152. **Adverbial Clauses** are clauses that stand in **relationship** of an adverb to some verb in another clause.

Adverbial clauses may be divided into eight classes:

(1)	Clauses of Time.	(Temporal Clauses.)
(2)	Clauses of Place.	(Local Clauses.)
(3)	Clauses of Cause.	(Causal Clauses.)
(4)	Clauses of Purpose.	(Final Clauses.)
(5)	Clauses of Consequence.	(Consecutive Clauses.)
(6)	Clauses of Concession.	(Concessive Clauses.)
(7)	Clauses of Condition.	(Conditional Clauses.)
(8)	Clauses of Comparison.	(Comparative Clauses.)

The names given in brackets are those given to these clauses in most grammars. They are not very satisfactory, as the words *temporal, final, consecutive* have quite a different sense in ordinary use to that which they have when used as grammatical terms. These names should however be known, as they are so commonly used.

The names given first are those suggested by the Committee on Grammatical Terminology.

153. (1) **Clauses of Time** denote the time at which the action of the verb in the clause on which they depend is said to happen.

They are introduced by the conjunctions

cum, ut[1], quando, ubi[2]	= *when*;
antequam, priusquam	= *before*;
postquam	= *after*;
dum	= *while, until*;
donec, quoad	= *until*.

The Ind. mood is used in clauses of time introduced by *ut, quando, ubi* and *postquam*. (In Ecc. L. the Subj. is rarely found after *postquam*. Lk. xv, 14; Rev. xxii, 8.)

[1] This use of *ut* must be carefully distinguished from the uses mentioned in sections 157, 158, 163.

[2] *ubi* nearly always means *where* in the Vg., but see Gal. iv, 4.

Venit nox, quando nemo potest operari. *The night cometh, when no man can work.* Jn. ix, 4.

Et ut cognovit vocem Petri, prae gaudio non aperuit januam. *And when she knew the voice of Peter, she did not open the door for joy.* Acts xii, 14.

Postquam autem resurrexero, praecedam vos in Galilaeam. *But after I am risen, I will go before you into Galilee.* Mt. xxvi, 32.

153*a*. A clause introduced by *cum* has the verb in the Ind., if the clause only indicates the time of the action of the verb which it qualifies. If the clause introduced by *cum* denotes the circumstances that lead up to the condition or action of the verb which it qualifies, the verb in the clause introduced by *cum* is in the Subj. mood.

In Ecc. L. the verb in a clause introd. by *cum* is sometimes put in the Subj. mood without any apparent reason.

In the following examples the clause introduced by *cum* only indicates the time of the action of the verb which it qualifies.

In the first three the verb is in the Ind. mood in accordance with Cl. usage: in the fourth the Subj. is used.

In veritate dico vobis, multae viduae erant in diebus Heliae in Israel, quando clausum est caelum annis tribus et mensibus sex, cum facta est fames magna in omni terra. *I tell you in truth there were many widows in the days of Elias in Israel, when the heaven was shut up for three years and six months, when a great famine took place in all the earth.* Lk. iv, 25.

Et spiritus immundi, cum eum videbant, procidebant ei. *And the unclean spirits, when they saw him, used to fall down before him.* Mk. iii, 11.

Cum ergo venerit, ille nobis annuntiabit omnia. *Whenever therefore he shall come, he will tell us all things.* Jn. iv, 25.

Cum autem adpropinquaret portae civitatis, ecce defunctus efferebatur. *But when he was drawing near to the gate of the city, behold a dead man was being borne out.* Lk. vii, 12.

In the following examples the clause introduced by *cum* denotes not only the time of the action of the main verb, but also the attendant circumstances which explain it, or seem likely tc hinder it.

Quod cum videret Simon Petrus, procidit ad genua Jesu *And when Simon Peter saw it, he fell down at Jesus' knees.*

Lk. v, 8.

(The clause explains why he fell down.)

Quomodo potest homo nasci cum senex sit? *How can a man be born when he is old?* Jn. iii, 4.

(His age is likely to prevent his being born.)

Ne forte, cum aliis praedicaverim, ipse reprobus efficiar. *Lest perchance, when I have preached to others, I myself may become reprobate.* I Cor. ix, 27.

(The fact that he has preached to others ought to save him from becoming reprobate; but will it?)

154. In clauses introduced by *antequam, priusquam, dum, donec, quoad*, either the Ind. or the Subj. mood may be used.

The Ind. mood is used in Cl. L. if the clause merely denotes the **time** of the action of the verb which it qualifies.

The Subj. mood is used if the clause refers to an action which is only in prospect and explains the **purpose** of the action of the verb which it qualifies.

Examples:

Clause simply denoting time.

Antequam abiit, hoc dixit. *He said this before he went away.*

Dum apud me es, ille in Hispaniam properavit. *While you were with me, he hastened into Spain.*

Clause denoting expectation and purpose.

Num expectas donec testimonium dicat? *Are you waiting until he gives his evidence?* (i.e. *with a view to hearing him*).

Impetum hostium sustinuit donec ceteri scalas ad muros ponerent. *He sustained the attack of the enemy until the others could set ladders to the walls.*

Ad oppidum, antequam milites a terrore se reciperent, properavit. *He hastened to the town* (*so as to be there*) *before the soldiers should recover themselves from their terror.*

In Ecc. L. either the Ind. or the Subj. is used in clauses introduced by *antequam, priusquam, dum, donec,* without any distinction of meaning. The Subj. is more frequently used than the Ind.

Examples from the Vg.:

Priusquam te Philippus vocaret, cum esses sub ficu, vidi te. *Before Philip called thee, when thou wast under the fig tree, I saw thee.* Jn. i, 48.

Dum autem irent emere, venit sponsus. *But while they went to buy, the bridegroom came.* Mt. xxv, 10.

Simile est regnum caelorum fermento, quod acceptum mulier abscondit in farinae satis tribus, donec fermentatum est totum. *The kingdom of heaven is like leaven which a woman took and hid in three measures of meal, until the whole was leavened.* Mt. xiii, 33.

Dico tibi, Petre, non cantabit hodie gallus, donec ter abneges nosse me. *I say to thee, Peter, the cock shall not crow this day until thou hast denied three times that thou knowest me.* Lk. xxii, 34.

See also Mt. xviii, 30; Lk. viii, 42, ix, 27, 29; Acts xxi, 26, 27.

Clauses of time may also be expressed by the Abl. Absolute or by a Participle: see sections 51, 183.

155. (2) **Clauses of Place** denote the place where the action of the verb in the clause on which they depend is said to happen.

They are introduced by the conjunctions

ubi, quo = *where, whither*;
unde = *whence*.

Mood: Ind., as in Eng.

If the clause of place refers to an action which will take place in some indefinite place in future time, the verb is generally in the Future Perfect tense.

Nolite thesaurizare vobis thesauros in terra, ubi erugo et tinea demolitur. *Lay not up for yourselves treasures on the earth, where rust and moth doth corrupt.* Mt. vi, 19.

Ego semper docui in synagoga et in templo, quo omnes Judaei conveniunt.... *I always taught in the synagogue and in the temple, whither all the Jews come together....* Jn. xviii, 20.

Amen dico vobis, ubicumque praedicatum fuerit hoc evangelium in toto mundo, dicetur et quod haec fecit in memoriam ejus. *Verily I say to you, wherever this gospel shall be preached in the whole world, this which she hath done shall be told for a memorial of her.* Mt. xxvi, 13.

156. (3) **Clauses of Cause** denote the reason (real or alleged) given for the action of the verb in the clause on which they depend.

They are introduced by *quia, quoniam, quod, eo quod, cum,=since, because,* etc.

In Cl. L. the Ind. is generally used in clauses introduced by *quia, quoniam, quod,* if the clause states what was the real cause of the action of the main verb in the opinion of the speaker or writer.

If however the clause denotes the cause of the action of the main verb in the opinion of some one other than the speaker or writer, or gives an opinion as to its cause which the speaker or writer once held, but which he now does not hold, the Subj. is used.

Examples:

Judaei Apostolos, quod legem violaverant, persecuti sunt. *The Jews persecuted the Apostles because they had* (in point of fact) *broken the law.*

Judaei Apostolos, quod legem violavissent, persecuti sunt. *The Jews persecuted the Apostles, because* (in the opinion of the Jews) *they had broken the law.*

In the first example the writer states that the Apostles were persecuted because they had actually broken the law. In the second example the writer leaves it an open question as to whether the Apostles had broken the law, or not; but he states that the Jews persecuted them, because they thought the Apostles had broken the law.

In Ecc. L. clauses introduced by *quia, quoniam, quod, eo quod* may have the verb in the Subj. even when they imply that the cause given for the action of the main verb is the real cause in the opinion of the speaker or writer.

Exi a me, quia homo peccator sum, Domine. *Depart from me, for I am a sinful man, O Lord.* Lk. v, 8.

Serve nequam, omne debitum dimisi tibi, quoniam rogasti me. *Thou worthless slave, I forgave thee all thy debt because thou didst ask me.* Mt. xviii, 32.

Non quod ipse esset Pater et Filius...sed quod tam similes sint Pater et Filius, ut qui unum noverit, ambos noverit. *Not because the Father and the Son were the same...but because the Father and the Son are so much alike, that he who knows one, knows both.* Aug. *Tract. in Joh. lxx.*

Ipse autem Jesus non credebat semetipsum eis, eo quod ipse nosset omnes. *But Jesus himself did not trust himself to them, because he knew all men.* Jn. ii, 24.

N.B. These clauses should be carefully distinguished from the noun clauses introduced by *quia, quoniam* and *quod* dealt with in sections 112 sq.

156*a*. Clauses of cause introduced by *cum* have the verb in the Subj. both in Cl. and Ecc. L.

De omnibus quibus accusor a Judaeis, rex Agrippa, aestimo me beatum apud te cum sim defensurus me hodie. *I think that I am fortunate, king Agrippa, because I am going to defend myself before thee to-day about all the things whereof I am accused by the Jews.* Acts xxvi, 2.

Hi homines conturbant civitatem nostram, cum sint Judaei. *These men disturb our state, because they are Jews.* Acts xvi, 20.

Rarely an Ind. is found in these clauses:

Ut, cum circa servos talis est Dominus, exemplo suo doceret, qualis circa compares et aequales debeat esse conservus. *That he might teach by his example what a fellow-servant ought to be with respect to his companions and equals, since he himself is such a Lord to his servants.* Cypr. *De bono patientiae.*

Clauses of cause may also be expressed by a Participle or by the Abl. Absolute. See sections 51, 183.

157. (4) **Clauses of Purpose** denote the purpose of the action of the verb in the clause on which they depend.

Clauses of purpose are generally introduced by

ut when affirmative = *that, in order that,*
ne when negative (*ut non* may occur in Ecc. L.),
quo when comparative.

Mood: Subj. always.

These clauses may also be expressed by

1. A relative clause with the verb in the Subj.
2. The Gerund or Gerundive Participle with *ad* or *causa.*
3. A Future Participle. (In Ecc. L. a Present Participle may be used in this sense.)
4. A Supine. (This is rare.)

157*a*. In Ecc. L. an Inf. is often used to express purpose as in Eng. and Gk.

This construction is found in the Latin poets, but not in Cl. prose. It seems to have been a vernacular idiom which came into literary use at a late period.

158. Purpose expressed by *ut*, etc.

Paenitemini igitur et convertimini, ut deleantur vestra peccata. *Repent therefore and be converted that your sins may be blotted out.* Acts iii, 19.

Hic venit in testimonium, ut testimonium perhiberet de lumine. *He came for a testimony in order that he might bear witness about the light.* Jn. i, 7.

Et in manibus tollent te, ne forte offendas ad lapidem. *And they shall bear thee in their hands, that thou dash not thy foot against a stone.* Mt. iv, 6.

Nolite judicare ut non judicemini. *Judge not that ye be not judged.* Mt. vii, 1.

159. Purpose expressed by a relative clause.

Considerate ergo, fratres, viros ex vobis boni testimonii septem,...quos constituamus super hoc opus. *Look out therefore from among yourselves, brethren, seven men of good report that we may set them over this work.* Acts vi, 3.

Tunc summiserunt viros, qui dicerent se audisse eum dicentem verba blasphemiae in Mosen et Deum. *Then they suborned men to say that they had heard him speaking blasphemous words against Moses and God.* Acts vi, 11.

160. Purpose expressed by the Gerundive Participle with *ad*.

Propterea et ego amplius non sustinens, misi ad cognoscendam fidem vestram. *Wherefore I also, since I could no longer forbear, sent to know your faith.* I Thess. iii, 5.

See also Rom. xv, 8.

161. Purpose expressed by the Future or the Present Participle.

Post annos autem plures eleemosynas facturus in gentem meam veni. *But after many years I came to give alms to my nation.* Acts xxiv, 17.

Vobis primum Deus suscitans Filium suum, misit eum benedicentem vobis. *For you first God, having raised up his Son, sent Him to bless you.* Acts iii, 26.

See also Jn. vi, 6.

162. Purpose expressed by the Inf.

Venisti huc ante tempus torquere nos? *Hast thou come here before the time to torment us?* Mt. viii, 29.

Et circumspiciebat videre eam quae hoc fecerat. *And he looked about to see her that had done this.* Mk. v, 32.

Non enim misit me Christus baptizare, sed evangelizare. *For Christ sent me not to baptize, but to preach the gospel.* I Cor. i, 17.

163. (5) **Clauses of Consequence** denote the consequence or result of the action of the verb in the clause on which they depend. They are introduced by *ut* or *ita ut, so that,* when affirmative and are negatived by *non.*

Mood: Subj. always.

Sic enim dilexit Deus mundum, ut Filium suum unigenitum daret. *For God so loved the world, that he gave his only begotten Son.* Jn. iii, 16.

Et convenerunt multi, ita ut non caperet neque ad januam. *And many came together, so that there was no room for them even at the door.* Mk. ii, 2.

Numquid aquam quis prohibere potest, ut non baptizentur hi qui Spiritum Sanctum acceperunt sicut et nos? *Can any forbid water, that these should be baptized who have received the Holy Ghost as well as we?* Acts x, 47.

Si confiteamur peccata nostra fidelis est et justus ut remittat nobis peccata nostra. *If we confess our sins, he is faithful and just to forgive us our sins.* I Jn. i, 9.

These clauses should be observed with special care as the construction of them is so very unlike Eng.

164. The Inf. may be used (in the Vg.) to denote consequence in imitation of the Gk.

O insensati Galatae quis vos fascinavit non obedire veritati? *O foolish Galatians, who has bewitched you that you should not*[1] *obey the truth?* Gal. iii, 1.

Et quomodo conversi estis ad Deum a simulacris, servire

[1] This is reading of SC text.

Deo vivo et vero. *And how ye were turned to God from idols, to serve the living and true God.* I Thess. i, 9.

Anania, cur tentavit Satanas cor tuum, mentiri te Spiritui Sancto? *Ananias, why hath Satan tempted thine heart that thou shouldest lie to the Holy Spirit?* Acts v, 3.

In Rom. i, 10 a Gk. Inf. denoting consequence is trans. by the Gen. of the Gerund.

165. Very rarely clauses of consequence are introduced by *quia*, and once, in a quotation from the O.T., by *quod* and *quoniam*.

Quo hic iturus est, quia non inveniemus eum? *Where does he intend to go that we shall not find him?* Jn. vii, 35.

See also Mt. viii, 27; Mk. iv, 40.

Quid est homo quod memor es ejus, aut filius hominis quoniam visitas eum? *What is man that thou art mindful of him, or the son of man that thou visitest him?* Heb. ii, 6, cited from Ps. viii, 5.

166. (6) **Clauses of Concession** denote some fact which is regarded as likely to prevent or to have prevented the occurrence of the action of the verb in the clause on which they depend.

They are introduced by *cum, quamvis, etsi, licet* = *although*. In the Vg. the principal clause may be introduced by *sed* or *sed tamen*: see examples below.

In clauses introduced by *cum* in this sense, the verb is always in the Subj. In Cl. L. *quamquam* is followed by a verb in the Ind. and *quamvis* is followed by a verb in the Subj. In Ecc. L. the Subj. is found after both these words. Clauses introduced by *etsi* are similar in construction to clauses of condition. Clauses introduced by *licet* have the verb in the Subj. (Ind. also in Vg.).

The tense is the same as that which is used in the English. Negative *non*.

Ecce et naves, cum magnae sint, et a ventis validis minentur, circumferuntur a modico gubernaculo. *Behold also the ships, although they are so big and although they are threatened by strong winds, are turned about by a small helm.* Jas. iii, 4.

See also Mt. xxvi, 60.

Unum scio, quia, caecus cum essem, modo video. *One thing I know, that, although I was blind, now I see.* Jn. ix, 25.

Nam cum liber essem ex omnibus, omnium me servum feci. *For although I was free from all men, I made myself a slave of all.* I Cor. ix, 19.

Quamvis non longe sit ab unoquoque nostrum. *Although he is not far from each one of us.* Acts xvii, 27.

Quamquam Jesus non baptizaret, sed discipuli ejus. *Although Jesus did not baptize, but his disciples.* Jn. iv, 2.

See also Phil. iii, 4; Heb. vii, 5.

Cum possemus vobis oneri esse...sed facti sumus parvuli in medio vestrum. *Although we might have been burdensome to you...we made ourselves like little children in the midst of you.* I Thess. ii, 7.

Etsi omnes scandalizati fuerint: sed non ego. *Although all shall be offended in thee: yet will I never be offended.* Mk. xiv, 29.

See also Col. ii, 5.

Sed licet nos, aut angelus de caelo evangelizet vobis praeterquam quod evangelizavimus vobis, anathema sit. *But although we, or an angel from heaven preach to you any other gospel than that which we have preached to you, let him be accursed.* Gal. i, 8.

Sed licet is qui foris est noster homo corrumpitur.... *But although our outward man decays....* II Cor. iv, 16.

A clause of concession may also be expressed by a participle or by the Abl. Absolute. See sections 51, 183.

167. (7) **Clauses of Condition** state the condition on which the action of the verb in the clause on which they depend would take place.

A clause of condition and the clause on which it depends make up a sentence which is called a **Conditional Sentence**. In such a sentence the clause of condition states a supposition, and the principal clause states the result of the fulfilment of the supposition.

The clause of condition is called the **Protasis** and the principal clause is called the **Apodosis** of the conditional sentence.

Clauses of condition are introduced by *si*, if, *nisi*, unless. Negative *non*.

In Cl. L. if the verb in the principal clause is in the Ind. mood, the verb in the clause of condition is also in the Ind. mood. If the verb in the principal clause is in the Subj. mood, the verb in the clause of condition is also in the Subj. mood. There are exceptions to this rule; but they are rare and generally due to a desire to produce a rhetorical effect. In Ecc. L. the rule given above is not strictly observed.

The construction of conditional sentences varies according as the time of the supposition is **Past**, **Present**, or **Future**, and according as the condition is regarded as **fulfilled**, or **unfulfilled**.

It is obvious that a condition is never regarded as fulfilled at the time contemplated by the clause on which it depends. It may however be stated in such a way as to imply that it has not been fulfilled.

Consider the sentences

If you are ill I shall send for the doctor.

If you were ill I should send for the doctor.

If you had been ill I should have sent for the doctor.

In the first of these sentences it is left an open question whether the condition will be fulfilled, or not. In the other two sentences it is implied that the condition has not been fulfilled. The first of the two relates to illness extending up to the present time: the second of the two refers to illness in the past.

The two latter sentences illustrate what is meant by an **unfulfilled conditional sentence.**

168. Present or past suppositions implying nothing as to the fulfilment of the condition.

A Present or Past tense of the Ind. is used in the clause of condition. Almost any part of the verb may be used in the principal clause.

Si judico ego, judicium meum verum est. *If I judge, my judgment is true.* Jn. viii, 16.

Si Filius Dei es, dic ut lapides isti panes fiant. *If thou art the Son of God, command these stones to become loaves....* Mt. iv, 3.

Si Abraham ex operibus justificatus est, habet gloriam. *If Abraham was justified by works, he has whereof to glory.* Rom. iv, 2.

Si vero ex Deo est, non poteritis dissolvere eos. *If it is really of God, you will not be able to break them up.* Acts v, 39.

169. Present or Past suppositions implying that the condition has not been fulfilled.

The Imperfect or Pluperfect Subj. is used both in the clause of condition and in the principal clause. The Imperfect Subj. denotes continued action in past time, or action extending up to the present moment. The Pluperfect Subj. denotes action in past time.

Si adhuc hominibus placerem, Christi servus non essem. *If I were still pleasing men, I should not be the slave of Christ.* Gal. i, 10.

Si diligeretis me, gauderetis utique. *If ye loved me, ye would certainly rejoice.* Jn. xiv, 28.

Non haberes potestatem adversum me ullam, nisi tibi datum esset de super. *Thou wouldst have no power at all against me unless it had been given thee from above.* Jn. xix, 11.

Si non esset hic malefactor, non tibi tradidissemus eum. *If this man were not a malefactor, we would not have given him up to thee.* Jn. xviii, 30.

Si opera non fecissem in eis, quae nemo alius fecit, peccatum non haberent. *If I had not done among them the works that no man else did, they would not have sin.* Jn. xv, 24.

Domine, si fuisses hic, frater meus non fuisset mortuus. *Lord, if thou hadst been here, my brother would not have died.* Jn. xi, 21.

170. If one of the **Modal verbs** such as *possum, debeo, oportet* or a **Periphrastic** tense made up of the Future Participle or the Gerund or Gerundive with part of *esse* stands in the principal clause of a conditional sentence in which there is a Subj. in the clause of condition, the **Indicative** mood of such verbs is used instead of the Subj.

Nisi esset hic a Deo, non poterat facere quicquam. *If this man were not of God, he could do nothing.* Jn. ix, 33.

Dimitti poterat homo hic, si non appellasset Caesarem. *This man might have been let go, if he had not appealed to Caesar.* Acts xxvi, 32.

171. The following are examples of sentences in which the rule that, if there is an Ind. in the principal clause, there should be an Ind. in the clause of condition is not observed.

Bonum erat ei, si natus non fuisset homo ille. *It was good for that man, if he had not been born.* Mt. xxvi, 24.

Nam concupiscentiam nesciebam, nisi lex diceret: Non concupisces. *For I did not know covetousness, if the law had not said: Thou shalt not covet.* Rom. vii, 7.

172. Future Suppositions. There are two forms of future suppositions.

1. The more vivid form.
2. The less vivid form.

The Future or Future Perfect Indicative is used in the more vivid form. The Present Subj. is used in the less vivid form.

In Eng. the Present Ind. is often used in the Protasis of these conditional sentences. This use is really incorrect: the Latin is much more accurate in its use of tenses: consider the force of the Latin Future and Future Perfect tenses in the examples given below.

If the action expressed in the Protasis of the conditional sentence is represented as taking place before the action denoted by the verb in the principal clause, the Future Perfect is properly used, because the action denoted by the principal clause is itself still future. Strictly speaking the Future should only be used in the Protasis when the time denoted by the Protasis and Apodosis is identical. For example:

Dum hic ero, te amabo. *As long as I am here, I shall love you.*

It will be noticed however that this principle is not strictly observed.

Si quis autem templum Dei violaverit, disperdet eum Deus. *But if any man defile the temple of God, him will God destroy.* I Cor. iii, 17.

Si omnes scandalizati fuerint in te, ego numquam scandalizabor. *If all men shall be offended in thee, yet will I never be offended.* Mt. xxvi, 33.

Haec tibi omnia dabo, si cadens adoraveris me. *All these things will I give thee, if thou wilt fall down and worship me.* Mt. iv, 9.

Fidelis sermo: nam si commortui sumus, et convivemus: si sustinebimus, et conregnabimus: si negabimus, et ille negabit nos. *Faithful is the saying: for if we have died with him, we shall also live with him: if we endure, we shall also reign with him: if we deny him, he also will deny us.* II Tim. ii, 11.

173. The use of the less vivid form is rare.

Quid enim proficit homo, si lucretur universum mundum, se autem ipsum perdat, et detrimentum sui faciat? *For what does it profit a man if he should gain the whole world, but lose himself, and work his own destruction?* Lk. ix, 25.

Sic est regnum Dei, quemadmodum si homo jaciat sementem in terram.... *So is the kingdom of God as if a man should cast a seed into the earth....* Mk. iv, 26.

See also I Cor. vii, 8.

174. In accordance with Heb. usage, sentences similar in meaning to Conditional Sentences are found in the Vg. where the conditional clause is expressed by (*a*) an inversion, (*b*) an Imperative.

(*a*) Tristatur aliquis vestrum? oret aequo animo et psallat. Infirmatur quis in vobis? inducat presbyteros Ecclesiae. *Is any sad among you? let him pray with a calm mind and let him sing psalms. Is any sick among you? let him send for the elders of the Church.* Jas. v, 13.

(*b*) Petite, et dabitur vobis: quaerite, et invenietis: pulsate, et aperietur vobis. *Ask, and it shall be given to you: seek, and ye shall find: knock, and it shall be opened to you.* Mt. vii, 7.

175. (8) **Clauses of Comparison** compare the action or state denoted by the verb in the clause on which they depend to the action or state denoted by the verb in the clause of comparison.

They are introduced by *ut, sicut, prout, quomodo, tanquam, quasi,* etc., *as, as if.* Negative *non.*

The verb in clauses of comparison is in the **Indicative**, if it is implied that the comparison is in accordance with fact.

If it is implied that the comparison involves a condition improbable or contrary to fact, the verb may be in the **Subjunctive.**

Sometimes only a Participle is used and sometimes the verb is omitted altogether in the clause of comparison.

Ita et viri debent diligere uxores ut corpora sua. *So men ought to love their wives as their own bodies.* Eph. v, 28.

Non ergo oportuit et te misereri conservi tui, sicut et ego tui misertus sum? *Oughtest thou not therefore to have had pity on thy fellow slave, even as I had pity on thee?* Mt. xviii, 33.

Ut quomodo Christus surrexit a mortuis...ita et nos in novitate vitae ambulemus. *That as Christ rose from the dead ...so we also may walk in newness of life.* Rom. vi, 4.

Consilium autem do tanquam misericordiam consecutus a Domino. *But I give my advice as one that has received mercy from the Lord.* I Cor. vii, 25.

Ostendens se tanquam sit Deus. *Showing himself as if he were God.* II Thess. ii, 4.

Diliges proximum tuum tanquam te ipsum. *Thou shalt love thy neighbour as thyself.* Mk. xii, 31.

Iis qui sub lege sunt, quasi sub lege essem, cum ipse non essem sub lege, ut eos, qui sub lege erant, lucri facerem. *To those that are under the law as if I were under the law, although I was not under the law, that I might gain them that were under the law.* I Cor. ix, 20.

Carissimi, nolite peregrinari in fervore qui ad temptationem vobis fit, quasi novi aliquid vobis contingat. *Beloved, do not be disturbed at the fiery trial which has come upon you to test you, as if some new thing were happening to you.* I Pet. iv, 12.

Optulistis mihi hunc hominem, quasi avertentem populum. *Ye have brought to me this man as one that is turning away the people....* Lk. xxiii, 14.

Sic curro, non quasi in incertum: sic pugno, non quasi aerem verberans. *So run I not as uncertainly: so fight I not as one that beateth the air.* I Cor. ix, 7.

Sometimes a clause of comparison is expressed by *sicut* or *sic* followed by *et.*

Fiat voluntas tua sicut in caelo et in terra. *Thy will be done in earth as it is in heaven.* Mt. vi, 10.

PARTICIPLES.

176. A Participle is a verbal adjective sharing the characteristics of both verbs and adjectives.

As a verb it has a subject, and, if it is the Participle of a transitive verb, it has an object. It governs the same case as the verb from which it is derived. It has also tense and voice.

As an adjective it agrees with the noun which it qualifies in number, gender and case.

The Latin language is very short of Participles: it only has:

A Present Participle Active.
A Future Participle Active.
A Past Participle Passive.

In the case of deponent verbs the Past Participle is used in an active sense, as well as a passive.

The time denoted by the tense of a Participle is relative to the time of the main verb, and not to the time of speaking, or writing.

177. Properly speaking the **Present Participle** denotes action going on at the **same time** as the action of the main verb, but in Ecc. L. the Present Participle is continually used to represent the Aorist Participle in Gk. and to denote action which took place before the action of the main verb. See examples.

The **Future Participle** denotes action which is expected to take place.

The **Past Participle** is also a **Perfect Participle** and so denotes past action complete and so continuing to have its effect at the time of the action of the main verb as well as simple past action.

178. Examples of the use of the tenses of the Participle:

Present Participle in the sense of action contemporaneous **with** that of the main verb.

Igitur qui dispersi erant pertransibant evangelizantes verbum. *Those therefore that were scattered went everywhere preaching the word.* Acts viii, 4.

Viri autem illi qui comitabantur cum eo, stabant stupefacti, audientes quidem vocem, neminem autem videntes. *But the men who were travelling with him stood amazed, hearing the voice, but seeing no man.* Acts ix, 7.

Notice the use of the Past Participle *stupefacti* in a Perfect sense.

Present Participle in the sense of action previous to that of the main verb.

Ascendens autem, frangensque panem et gustans, satisque allocutus usque ad lucem, sic profectus est. *But having gone up and having broken bread and eaten, and having addressed them a long time even until dawn, so he departed.* Acts xx, 11.

Notice that the Present Participle and the Past Participle are used in exactly the same sense in this passage.

See also Mk. iii, 13; Eph. ii, 14, 15.

179. **Future Participle** in the sense of expected action.

Genimina viperarum, quis ostendit vobis fugere a ventura ira? *O generation of vipers, who hath warned you to flee from the wrath to come?* Lk. iii, 7.

180. Past Participle in sense of past or perfect action.

Demoratus autem inter eos dies non amplius quam octo aut decem, descendit Caesaream. *And having remained among them not more than eight or ten days he descended to Caesarea.* Acts xxv, 6.

181. A Participle may be used either **adjectivally** or **adverbially**.

When it is used adjectivally it limits the meaning of the noun which it qualifies just like an adjective. A participle may also be used by itself in this sense, the noun with which it agrees being understood. Adjectival Participles are generally best translated by an adjectival clause, an adjective or a noun.

When it is used adverbially it is equivalent to an adverbial clause modifying some verb in the sentence. Adverbial Participles are generally best translated by a suitable adverbial clause.

The context must decide which kind of adverbial clause the Participle in question is equivalent to. The Participle itself does not denote time, purpose, cause, concession, or condition, but the context implies one of these ideas, and the Participle admits it.

Participles are used much more frequently in Latin than in Eng., and this is the reason why it is so often advisable to translate a Participle by a clause.

182. Adjectival Participles. These are generally best translated by a relative clause, or by a noun.

Nolumus autem vos ignorare, fratres, de dormientibus. *But we do not wish you to be ignorant, brethren, concerning those that are asleep.* I Thess. iv, 13.

Quam pius es petentibus, sed quid invenientibus? *How good thou art to those that seek, but what to those that find?* St Bernard.

Qua cessabunt persequentes, et regnabunt patientes. *Where the persecutors shall cease, and the patient shall reign.* Hym. Lat.

The use of participles as nouns is characteristic of Late Latin.

Credentes = *believers.* Diffidentes = *unbelievers.*
Discentes = *disciples.*

183. Adverbial Participles.

Equivalent to a clause of Time.

Orantes autem, nolite multum loqui. *But when ye pray, do not say much.* Mt. vi, 7.

Oportuit ergo te mittere pecuniam meam nummulariis, et veniens ego recepissem utique quod meum est cum usura. *You ought to have put out my money to the bankers, and then, when I came, I should have received my own with usury.* Mt. xxv, 27.

Equivalent to a clause of Cause.

Peccavi tradens sanguinem justum. *I have sinned, because I have betrayed righteous blood.* Mt. xxvii, 4.

See also Acts iv, 21, xii, 3; II Pet. i, 19.

Equivalent to a clause of Concession.

Et nullam causam mortis invenientes in eum, petierunt a Pilato ut interficerent eum. *And although they found no cause of death in him, yet they asked Pilate that they might slay him.* Acts xiii, 28.

See also II Pet. i, 12; Jude, 5.

Equivalent to a clause of Purpose.

The future participle is generally used in this sense; but in Ecc. L. a present participle may be so used.

Post autem annos plures eleemosynas facturus in gentem meam veni. *But after many years I came to make offerings to my nation.* Acts xxiv, 17.

Sine videamus an veniat Helias liberans eum. *Let us see if Elias will come to save him.* Mt. xxvii, 49.

Vobis primum Deus suscitans Filium suum, misit eum benedicentem vobis. *To you first God, having raised up his Son, sent him to bless you.* Acts iii, 26.

Equivalent to a clause of Condition.

Tempore enim suo metemus, non deficientes. *For in his own time we shall reap, if we faint not.* Gal. vi, 9.

A quibus custodientes vos, bene agetis. *If ye keep yourselves from these, ye shall do well.* Acts xv, 29.

See also Rom. ii, 27, xii, 20.

184. After verbs denoting ceasing, continuing, making an end or failing a participle is used to complete the sense, as in Gk.

Et factum est cum consummasset Jesus praecipiens duodecim discipulis suis.... *And it came to pass when Jesus had made an end of giving commands to his twelve disciples....* Mt. xi, 1.

Vos autem, fratres, nolite deficere bene facientes.... *But you, brethren, do not cease to do well....* II Thess. iii, 13.

Petrus autem perseveravit pulsans. *But Peter continued knocking.* Acts xii, 16.

See also Acts v, 42; Eph. i, 16; Col. i, 9.

185. A peculiar use of the Present Participle which is an attempt to reproduce the Heb. Inf. Absolute is found in the Vg.

The Pres. Part. is used with a mood of the same verb to make a strong or positive statement.

Conterens non conteram domum Jacob. *I will not utterly destroy the house of Jacob.* Amos ix, 8.

Videns vidi afflictionem populi mei. *I have surely seen the affliction of my people.* Acts vii, 34.

See also Heb. vi, 14; Mt. xiii, 14.

The same sense may also be expressed by an Abl. of the Gerund or by the Abl. of a noun of kindred meaning to the verb.

Praecipiendo praecepimus vobis ne doceretis in nomine isto. *We have strictly charged you that ye should not teach in this name.* Acts v, 28.

Qui maledixerit patri vel matri, morte moriatur. *Whosoever curses father or mother, let him surely die.* Mt. xv, 4.

Desiderio desideravi hoc pascha manducare vobiscum antequam patiar. *I have greatly desired to eat this Passover with you before I suffer.* Lk. xxii, 15.

A Pres. Part. may also be used in the sense of the Abl. of the gerund.

Quis autem vestrum cogitans potest adjicere ad staturam suam cubitum unum? *Which of you by thinking can add one cubit to his stature?* Mt. vi, 27.

THE GERUND, GERUNDIVE PARTICIPLE AND SUPINE.

186. These parts of the Latin verb have no exact equivalents in Eng., although the Eng. verbal noun ending in *ing* is equivalent to some uses of the Gerund.

The Gerund and Supine are verbal nouns and the Gerundive is a verbal adjective.

The Nom. case of the verbal noun is expressed in Latin by the

Inf. and so is the Acc. case, except in uses where the verbal noun stands after a preposition.

The Gen., Dat. and Abl. cases of the verbal noun and the Acc. case, when standing after a preposition, are expressed by the Gerund.

The Gerund is not used very often in the Vg.

For the sake of clearness some simple examples of each case of the verbal noun are given first and then some examples from the Vg. etc.

Nominative. Edere jucundum est. *To eat (or eating) is pleasant.*

Accusative. Dicit edere jucundum esse. *He says that eating is pleasant.*

Accusative (with a prep.). Omnia ad edendum parata sunt. *All things are prepared for eating.*

Genitive. Amor edendi magnum malum est. *The love of eating is a great evil.*

Dative. Dat operam edendo. *He gives attention to eating.*

Ablative. Vivimus edendo. *We live by eating.*

187. Examples of the use of the Gerund in the Vg.:

Et dedit illis potestatem curandi infirmitates. *And he gave them the power of curing diseases.* Mk. iii, 15; Mt. xi, 15.

Deus autem spei repleat vos omni gaudio et pace in credendo. *But may the God of hope fill you with all joy and peace in believing.* Rom. xv, 13.

Quae quaestum magnum praestabat dominis suis divinando. *Who brought much gain to her masters by soothsaying.* Acts xvi, 16.

See also Acts x, 33; I Cor. xii, 24; I Tim. v, 21.

188. A peculiar use of the Abl. of the Gerund which is employed to translate a Present or Aorist Participle in the Gk. is found in the Vg. This is generally best translated by a present participle in Eng.

Qui pertransivit bene faciendo et sanando omnes oppressos a diabolo. *Who went about doing good and healing all that were oppressed by the devil.* Acts x, 38.

Hodie, in David dicendo, post tantum temporis.... *Saying in David: "To-day, after so long a time...."* Heb. iv, 7.

In casulis habitando cum Isaac.... *Dwelling in tents with Isaac....* Heb. xi, 9.

In quo et laboro, certando secundum operationem ejus, quam operatur in me in virtute. *In which I also labour, working according to his operation which he works in me with power.* Col. i, 29.

A similar use is found in the "Stabat Mater."

Vidit suum dulcem Natum
Moriendo desolatum.

And in Augustine:

Nec jam ingemiscebam orando ut subvenires mihi.

Confess. vi, 3.

189. In the Vg. translation of the Psalms (which is not Jerome's direct translation from the Heb., but a revised form of the Old Latin) the Abl. of the Gerund with *in* is found in a sense which is best translated into Eng. by a clause of time.

This is also found in Augustine.

Example:

In convertendo inimicum meum retrorsum.... *When mine enemy is turned back....* Ps. ix, 4.

In deficiendo ex me spiritum meum, et tu cognovisti semitas meas. *When my spirit failed within me, thou knewest my paths.* Ps. cxli, 4.

See also ci, 23, cxxv, 1.

190. In Cl. L. if the verb is transitive and the object expressed the **Gerundive Participle** is generally used instead of the Gerund.

As the Gerundive Participle is in the passive voice in Latin and the verbal noun ending in "ing" is in the active voice in English (as also is the Latin Gerund), some re-arrangement of the syntax of the sentence is necessary. The word which is the object of the verbal noun in English (or the Gerund in Latin) is the word with which the Gerundive is made to agree in gender, number and case. The case of this noun depends on the function that it performs in the sentence.

Thus, instead of the Gerund construction

Miserunt legatos ad petendum pacem,
They sent ambassadors to seek for peace,

where "pacem" is the object of the Gerund "petendum," one writes

Miserunt legatos ad petendam pacem,

where "pacem" is governed by "ad" and the Gerundive agrees with it. So one writes not Legionem opprimendi causa, but Legionis opprimendae causa as a translation of the English phrase

For the sake of destroying the legion: instead of Opprimendo legiones one writes Opprimendis legionibus to translate the Eng. phrase *By destroying the legions.*

This Gerundive construction is nearly always used in the Acc. and Dat. and generally in the Gen. and Abl. The Gen. Pl. is avoided.

Examples of the Gerundive construction from the Vg.:

Ad dandam scientiam salutis plebi ejus . . . . *To give the knowledge of salvation to his people* . . . . Lk. i, 77.

Dico enim Christum Jesum ministrum fuisse circumcisionis, propter veritatem Dei, ad confirmandas promissiones patrum. *For I say that Christ Jesus was a minister of the circumcision, on account of the truth of God, to confirm the promises of the fathers.* Rom. xv, 8.

See also Mt. xxvi, 12; I Thess. iii, 5.

191. The following are examples of the Gerund governing a direct object.

Hoc autem ipse de se, non profecto jactando virtutem, sed deflendo potius defectum, quem sibi per curam pastoralem incucurrisse videbatur, referre consueverat. *This he used to say about himself, not certainly by way of boasting of his virtue, but rather by way of lamenting his shortcomings, which he seemed to have incurred through the pastoral office.* Bede, *Hist. Ecc.*

Ego autem dico vobis: quoniam omnis, qui viderit mulierem ad concupiscendum eam, jam moechatus est eam in corde suo. *But I say to you that every one who looketh on a woman to lust after her hath already committed adultery with her in his heart.* Mt. v, 28.

See also Mk. iii, 15, quoted above, and Rom. i, 5.

192. In the Nominative and Accusative case the Gerundive has a meaning quite different from those mentioned above.

It expresses duty or obligation. The name of the person on whom the duty lies is put in the Dative case. But if the verb governs a Dative case, the Ablative with *a* used is to avoid ambiguity. Since the Gerundive is a participle, it agrees in number gender and case with the word which it qualifies, but if the verb used governs a Dative case an impersonal construction is used (seeparagraph 39).

Examples:

Mater tua tibi amanda est. *Your mother must be loved by you,* or *You must love your mother.*

Parentibus nostris a nobis parendum est. *We must obey our parents.*

The Gerundive may also be used impersonally without any obvious reference to any particular subject.

Currendum est mihi. *I must run.*

Examples from the Vulgate:

Filius hominis tradendus est in manus hostium. *The Son of man must be betrayed into the hands of men.* Mt. xvii, 22.

Horrendum est incidere in manus Dei viventis. *It is a thing to be feared to fall into the hands of a living God.* Heb. x, 31.

Qui praedicas non furandum furaris? *Thou who preachest that a man should not steal, dost thou steal?* Rom. ii, 21.

The Gerundive used in the sense of an parallel with the Future Participle:

At illi existimabant eum in tumorem convertendum et subito casurum et mori. *But they thought that he would swell up and suddenly fall down and that he was dying.* Acts xxviii, 6.

The Supine.

193. The Supine ending in *um* expresses purpose. It is rare in Ecclesiastical Latin.

Et quicumque potum dederit uni ex minimis istis calicem aquae frigidae tantum . . . non perdet mercedem suam. *And whosoever shall give only a cup of cold water to one of the least of these to drink . . . he shall not lose his reward.* Mt. x, 42.

METHODS OF ASKING QUESTIONS.

194. In Cl. L. direct questions which may be answered by either *yes* or *no* are expressed by adding the particle *ne* to an emphatic word at the beginning of the sentence.

In the Vg. there is often nothing but the context to show if a sentence is a question or not.

Pilatus vocavit Jesum et dixit ei: Tu es rex Judaeorum? *Pilate called Jesus and said to him: Art thou the king of the Jews?* Jn. xviii, 33.

195. If an affirmative answer is expected to the question it is introduced by *nonne* and in the Vg. by *an*.

Domine, Domine, nonne in nomine tuo prophetavimus? *Lord, Lord, did we not prophesy in thy name?* Mt. vii, 22.

An nescitis quoniam sancti de mundo judicabunt? *Do ye not know that the saints shall judge concerning the world?* I Cor. vi, 2.

See also Mt. xxvi, 53; Rom. iii, 29, vi, 3.

Numquid non is also found in the Vg. in this sense: Rom. x, 18.

196. If a negative answer is expected to the question it is introduced by *num* in Cl. L. and by *numquid* in the Vg.

Respondit Pilatus: Numquid ego Judaeus sum? *Pilate answered: Am I a Jew?* Jn. xviii, 35.

Num is apparently not found in the Vg. N.T. It is found in the O.T.

Num custos fratris mei ego sum? *Am I my brother's keeper?* Gen. iv, 9.

Both methods of asking a question are seen in this example:

Alii dicebant: Hic est Christus. Quidam autem dicebant: Numquid a Galilaea venit Christus? Nonne scriptura dicit: Quia ex semine David...venit Christus? *Others said: This is Christ. But certain said: Does Christ come out of Galilee? Does not the scripture say that Christ comes of the seed of David?* Jn. vii, 41.

See also Mk iv, 21.

197. In the Vg. *si* is often used in imitation of Gk. to introduce both direct and indirect questions.

Dixitque ad eos: Si Spiritum Sanctum accepistis credentes? At illi dixerunt ad eum: Sed neque si Spiritus Sanctus est, audivimus. *And he said to them: Did you receive the Holy Spirit when ye believed? But they said to him: We have not even heard whether there is a Holy Spirit.* Acts xix, 2.

See also Acts x, 18, xxi, 37.

198. Questions may be introduced by the interrogative pronoun *quis* or by expressions compounded with it such as *quomodo* or *ut quid*, which is an imitation of the Gk. *ἵνα τί* or *εἰς τί*.

See Mt. ix, 4, xxvi, 8; Acts vii, 26; I Cor. x, 29.

Quid is used in the sense of *cur* = *why* in Mt. xx, 6.

Alternative or double questions are expressed by *utrum...an*, see Jn. vii, 17, or by *an* alone in the second member of the question. The latter is the usual method in the Vg.

Tu es qui venturus es, an alium expectamus? *Art thou he that should come, or are we to look for another?* Mt. xi, 3.

Quem vultis dimittam vobis: Barabbam, an Jesum qui dicitur Christus? *Which do you wish that I should release for you: Barabbas, or Jesus who is called Christ?* Mt. xxvii, 17.

Notice the use of the interrogative pronoun *quem* here where *utrum* would have been used in Cl. L.

See also Jn. xviii, 34.

ADJECTIVES.

199. An adjective whether used as an attribute of a noun or to complete a predicate agrees with the noun which it qualifies in number, gender and case.

Sometimes, however, if the noun is a collective noun, the adjective agrees rather with the idea that is signified by the noun than with the grammatical number and gender of the noun (*constructio ad sensum*).

Sed turba haec, quae non novit legem, maledicti sunt. *But this crowd which knows not the law are cursed.* Jn. vii, 49.

See also Jas. iii, 8; Rev. vii, 9.

Multitudo militiae caelestis laudantium Deum et dicentium.... *A multitude of the heavenly host (of angels) praising God and saying....* Lk. ii, 13.

200. Adjectives are often used as equivalent to nouns, the masculine denoting men, or people in general of the kind described by the adjective, the feminine women, the neuter things.

Resurrectio justorum et iniquorum. *A resurrection of the just and the unjust.* Acts xxiv, 15.

Invisibilia enim ipsius...per ea quae facta sunt intellecta conspiciuntur. *For the invisible things of him...being understood by the things that are made, are perceived.* Rom. i, 20.

The neuter of the adjective may be used in the sense of an abstract noun. *Salutare* = salvation, Lk ii, 30.

201. The adjective *unus* is used in the Vg. in the sense of the indefinite article. This use became general in the Romance languages.

Et accessit ad eum una ancilla dicens: Et tu cum Jesu Galilaeo eras. *And there came to him a maid and said: Thou also wert with Jesus the Galilaean.* Mt. xxvi, 69.

See also Mt. xxi, 19.

202. The adjective *omnis* is used with a negative to express a strong negative statement or command in imitation of Heb.

Et nisi breviati fuissent dies illi, non fieret salva omnis caro.... *And unless those days had been shortened, no living thing would be saved.* Mt. xxiv, 22.

Omnis sermo malus ex ore vestro non procedat. *Let no corrupt speech proceed out of your mouth.* Eph. iv, 29.

See also Rom. iii, 20; I Cor. i, 29; Rev. xviii, 22.

Comparison of Adjectives.

203. The positive degree of an adjective may be used in the Vg. in the sense of a comparative.

Bonum est tibi...in vitam intrare...quam mitti in gehennam. *It is better for thee to enter into life than to be cast into Gehenna.* Mt. xviii, 9.

The comparative may be used in the sense of a superlative.

Major autem horum est charitas. *But the greatest of these is love.* I Cor. xiii, 13.

The superlative may be used in the sense of the comparative.

Quod minimum quidem est omnibus seminibus. *Which indeed is less than all seeds.* Mt. xiii, 32; Heb. xi, 4.

204. The ordinary const. after an adj. in the comparative degree in Cl. L. to express the object with which the comparison is made is to put the word which denotes this object in the Abl. case, or to use *quam*.

Amen dico vobis, non surrexit inter natos mulierum major Johanne Baptista. *Verily I say to you, there has not arisen any one greater than John the Baptist among those born of women.* Mt. xi, 11.

Qui amat patrem aut matrem plus quam me, non est me dignus. *He who loves father or mother more than me is not worthy of me.* Mt. x, 37.

In the Vg. in imitation of Heb. the preps. *a*, *ex*, *prae*, *super* may be used after an adjective in the comparative degree, or even a Gen. case, in imitation of Gk.

See Lk. xiii, 2, xviii, 14; II Cor. xii, 11; Heb. ii, 7, iii, 3; Ps. xviii, 11, cxxxviii, 6, and section 33 of this book.

PREPOSITIONS.

205. The use of prepositions in Ecc. L. differs somewhat from their use in Cl. L.

This is due in the first place to the natural development of the language. Prepositions are used with increasing frequency in the place of simple cases, until, in the Romance languages, they have replaced the cases altogether.

In the Vg. the influence of Heb., felt through the LXX and also in the direct translation of the O.T. by Jerome, has given rise to some very peculiar methods of expressing comparison and the instrument, by means of prepositions.

Greek is rich in prepositions and in delicate shades of meaning expressed by using the same preposition with different cases.

The Latin translators have on the whole been very successful in rendering these Gk. prepositions into Latin; but, in so doing, they have somewhat deviated from normal Latin usage.

It has been thought well to give the Gk. originals of which the usages of the Latin prepositions given below are translations.

Prepositions governing an Ablative case.

206. A, Ab, Abs. Usual meaning *from*, or *by* (of the agent).

Representing Gk. ἀπό, ὑπό with gen., rarely ἐκ, and in comparisons παρά with accusative or genitive, or simple genitive.

Discedite a me qui operamini iniquitatem. (ἀπό.) Mt. vii, 23.

Omnia mihi tradita sunt a Patre meo. (ὑπό.) Mt. xi, 27.

In Late Latin *a* is used even with the names of towns etc.

Post haec egressus ab Athenis, venit Corinthum. (ἐκ, ἀπό.) Acts xviii, 1, xii, 25; Mk. vii, 1.

So it is used of the Instrument:

Ecce et naves...circumferuntur a modico gubernaculo. (ὑπό.) Jas. iii, 4.

Other uses to translate Gk. ἀπό and ἐκ.

Attendite a falsis prophetis.... (ἀπό.) Mt. vii, 15, x, 17.

Invenit...hominem...ab annis octo jacentem in grabato.... (ἐκ.) Acts ix, 33.

Jesum a Nazareth.... (ἀπό.) Acts x, 38; Mk. xv, 43; Jn. i, 44.

Perdidisti omnes qui fornicantur abs te. (ἀπό.) Ps. lxxii, 27.

A is used in comparisons even where there is no adjective or adverb in the comparative degree in imitation of Heb. מִן.

Nihil enim minus fui ab iis.... (Gen.) II Cor. xii, 11.

Descendit hic justificatus in domum suam ab illo. (παρά, acc.) Lk. xviii, 14.

Minuisti eum paulominus ab angelis. (παρά, acc.) Heb. ii, 7, from Ps. viii, 6.

Et a te quid volui super terram? (παρά, gen.) Ps. lxxii, 25.

In the Psalms *a* is used in the sense of *because of*.

A voce gemitus mei adhaesit os meum carni meae. (ἀπό.) Ps. cii, 6, 11, xxxvii, 6; xliii, 17.

207. Absque. Not used in Cl. L. In Early and Late Latin used in sense of *sine* = *without*.

Represents Gk. χωρίς, privative ἀ and ἀπό in composition.

Tentatum autem per omnia pro similitudine absque peccato. (χωρίς.) Heb. iv, 15.

Absque foedere.... (ἀσπόνδους.) Rom. i, 31.

Absque synagogis facient vos. (ἀποσυναγώγους.) Jn. xvi, 2.

208. Coram. Usual meaning *in the presence of, openly, before.*

Representing Gk. ἔμπροσθεν, ἐναντίον, ἐνώπιον.

Sic luceat lux vestra coram hominibus.... (ἔμπροσθεν.) Mt. v, 16.

Et placuit sermo coram omni multitudine.... (ἐναντίον.) Acts vi, 5, viii, 32.

Peccantes coram omnibus argue. (ἐνώπιον.) I Tim. v, 20.

209. Clam. Usual meaning *secretly*.

Not used as a preposition in the N.T. but as an adverb, to translate λάθρα, Mt. ii, 7.

Used as prep. in Gen. xxxi, 26, xlvii, 18.

210. Cum. Usual meaning *together with, in company with,* also used to express the manner in which an action is done.

Representing Gk. μετά with gen., σύν, ἐν, or the simple dative.

Filius enim hominis venturus est in gloria Patris sui cum angelis suis.... (μετά.) Mt. xvi, 27.

Et rogabat illum vir, a quo daemonia exierant, ut cum eo esset. (σύν.) Lk. viii, 38.

Et loquebantur verbum Dei cum fiducia. (μετά.) Acts iv, 31.

So it is used to express manner even with nouns qualified by an adjective where a simple ablative is generally used in Cl. L.

Regressus est cum magna voce magnificans Deum. (μετά.) Lk. xvii, 15.

Cum bona voluntate servientes, sicut Domino, et non hominibus. (μετά.) Eph. vi, 7.

Carcerem quidem invenimus clausum cum omni diligentia.... (ἐν.) Acts v, 23.

Instrumental use (very rare in Classics, see Verg. *Aen.* ix, 816).

Et redemptorem misit cum manu angeli, qui apparuit illi in rubo. (σύν.) Acts vii, 35.

Replebis me jucunditate cum facie tua. (μετά.) Acts ii, 28.

Cum impositione manuum presbyterii. (μετά.) I Tim. iv, 14.

In the following passages *cum* is used to trans. μετά.

Facere misericordiam cum patribus nostris. Lk. i, 72.

Rationem ponere cum servis.... Mt. xviii, 23.

211. De. Usual meaning *from, down from, concerning, made from.* The favourite preposition of Late Latin, used where Cl. L. would use *ex* or a simple Gen. Compare the use of *de* in French in the sense of *from* and also *of.*

Represents Gk. ἀπό, ἐκ, περί with Gen. or simple Gen.

From, down from.

Numquid colligunt de spinis uvas, aut de tribulis ficus? (ἀπό.) Mt. vii, 16.

Cum autem descendisset de monte.... (ἀπό.) Mt. viii, 1.

Facite vobis amicos de mamona iniquitatis. (ἐκ.) Lk. xvi, 9.

Concerning.

De his quae dicta sunt a pastoribus ad ipsos. (περί.) Lk. ii, 18.

De bono opere non lapidamus te.... (περί.) Jn. x, 33.

Deus filium suum mittens in similitudinem carnis peccati et de peccato, damnavit peccatum in carne. (περί.) Rom. viii, 3.

In the sense of *out of.*

Baptizatus autem Jesus confestim ascendit de aqua. (ἀπό.) Mt. iii, 16.

De corde enim exeunt cogitationes malae.... (ἐκ.) Mt. xv, 19.

In the sense of denoting the material of which a thing is made.

Et plectentes coronam de spinis.... (ἐκ.) Mt. xxvii, 29.

Regnum meum non est de hoc mundo. (ἐκ.) Jn. xviii, 36.

In a partitive sense representing Gk. gen.

Quamdiu non feceritis uni de minoribus his, nec mihi fecistis. Mt. xxv, 45.

Effundam de Spiritu meo.... Acts ii, 18.

212. **E, Ex.** Usual sense *out of, from within.*

Representing Gk. ἐκ or ἐξ.

In the Vg. and Late Latin *de* is used where *ex* would be used in Cl. L. *Ex* is generally used in a metaphorical sense.

Et diliges Dominum Deum tuum ex toto corde tuo. Mk. xii, 30.

Eis autem qui sunt ex contentione.... Rom. ii, 8.

Si enim qui ex lege heredes sunt, exinanita est fides.... Rom. iv, 14.

Justus ex fide vivet. Gal. iii, 11.

Ex may also be used in a partitive sense to translate the Gk. partitive gen.

Quamdiu fecistis uni ex his fratribus meis minimis, mihi fecistis. Mt. xxv, 40.

Compare the use of *de* in verse 45.

Ex may be used in comparison in imitation of Heb.

Mirabilis facta est scientia tua ex me. Ps. cxxxviii, 6.

213. **Pro.** Usual meaning *for, on behalf of, instead of, before.*

Representing Gk. ὑπέρ with gen., περί with gen., ἀντί, ἐπί with genitive.

Orate pro persequentibus et calumniatoribus vestris. (ὑπέρ.) Mt. v, 44.

Alioquin quid facient, qui baptizantur pro mortuis? (ὑπέρ.) I Cor. xv, 29.

Et panis, quem ego dabo, caro mea est pro mundi vita. (ὑπέρ.) Jn. vi, 52.

Gratias ago Deo meo semper pro vobis.... (περί.) I Cor. i, 4.

Archelaus regnabat in Judea pro Herode patre suo. (ἀντί.) Mt. ii, 22.

Statuto autem die Herodes vestitus veste regia sedit pro tribunali. (ἐπί.) Acts xii, 21.

Exceptional use.

Pro similitudine.... (καθ' ὁμοιότητα.) Heb. iv, 15.

214. Prae. Usual meaning *before, because of, compared with.*

Representing a number of Gk. prepositions in sense of *because of,* such as διά with accusative, ἀπό, ἐκ, ἐν.

When used in the sense of *compared with* is translated by Gk. παρά with accusative.

Et cum non possent offerre illum illi prae turba. (διά.) Mk. ii, 4.

Dormientes prae tristitia.... (ἀπό.) Lk. xxii, 45.

Et cum non viderem prae claritudine luminis.... (ἀπό.) Acts xxii, 11.

Prae confusione sonitus maris.... (ἐν.) Lk. xxi, 25.

Et blasphemaverunt Deum caeli prae doloribus et vulneribus suis. (ἐκ.) Rev. xvi, 11.

Putatis quod hi Galilaei prae omnibus Galilaeis peccatores fuerunt quia talia passi sunt? (παρά.) Lk. xiii, 2.

Amplioris enim gloriae iste prae Moyse dignus est habitus.... (παρά.) Heb. iii, 3.

215. Sine. Usual meaning *without.*

Representing Gk. χωρίς, ἄνευ or privative ἀ.

Arbitramur enim justificari hominem per fidem sine operibus legis. (χωρίς.) Rom. iii, 28; Jas. ii, 18.

Et unus ex illis non cadet super terram sine Patre vestro. (ἄνευ.) Mt. x, 29.

Adhuc et vos sine intellectu estis? (ἀσύνετοι.) Mt. xv, 16.

Prepositions governing the Accusative case.

216. Ad. Usual meaning *To, into (of motion to), at, near, according to.*

Generally represents the Gk. πρός with acc. or dat., or εἰς, sometimes κατά with acc.

It is used in the Vg. after verbs of speaking where the dat. would be used in Cl. L.

Dixerunt ergo ad eum.... (πρός.) Jn. vi, 28.

Disputabat igitur in synagoga cum Judaeis et colentibus et in foro per omnes dies ad eos, qui aderant. (πρός.) Acts xvii, 17.

The following uses, most of which may be parallelled from the Classics, may be noted.

With a view to, for, resulting in.

Cognoscebat autem illum, quod ipse erat, qui ad eleemosynam sedebat. (πρός.) Acts iii, 10; Col. ii, 23.

Ad victimam taurus ducitur. Cyp. *de Patientia.*

Corde enim creditur ad justitiam: ore autem confessio fit ad salutem. (εἰς.) Rom. x, 10.

At, near, by the side of, at the sight of.

Petrus autem stabat ad ostium foris. (πρός with dat.) Jn. xviii, 16.

Intrantes autem juvenes invenerunt illam mortuam: et extulerunt et sepelierunt ad virum suum. (πρός, acc.) Acts v, 10; II Cor. v, 8.

In Mt. xx, 21 to translate ἐξ.

Cum ad crucem Domini confundantur sidera. Cyp. *de Pat.*

Because of.

Ad duritiam cordis vestri.... (πρός.) Mt. xix, 8.

According to.

Sed ad desideria coacervabunt magistros.... (κατά.) II Tim. iv, 3.

Used to translate πρός in various senses (not Classical).

Ad horam. *For an hour.* Jn. v, 35; II Cor. vii, 8.

Ad ullum verbum. Mt. xxvii, 14.

Exceptional use:

Ad manus illum trahentes. (χειραγωγοῦντες.) Acts ix, 8.

217. Adversus. Usual meaning *against.*

Represents Gk. κατά with gen.

Nolite gloriari et mendaces esse adversus veritatem. Jas. iii, 14; I Cor. xv, 15.

218. Ante. Ordinary meaning *before* both of place and time.

Represents Gk. παρά with acc., ἔμπροσθεν, κατά with acc., πρό, ἀπό.

Et ponebant ante pedes apostolorum. (παρά.) Acts iv, 35.

Ita, Pater: quoniam sic fuit placitum ante te. (ἔμπροσθεν.) Mt. xi, 26.

Quod parasti ante faciem omnium populorum. (κατά.) Lk. ii, 31.

Scio hominem in Christo ante annos quattuordecim.... (πρό.) II Cor. xii, 2.

Exceptional use:

Erat velatum ante eos.... (ἀπό.) Lk. ix, 45.

219. **Apud.** Ordinary meaning *by, near, in the house of, in the presence of.*

Representing Gk. παρά with dat., πρός with acc. and dat., ἐπί with gen.

Apud quem hospitaremur.... (παρά, with dat.)
Acts xxi, 16; Col. iv, 16.

Et nunc clarifica me tu, Pater, apud temetipsum. (παρά, dat.)
Jn. xvii, 5.

Apud homines hoc impossibile est. (παρά, with dat.)
Mt. xix, 26.

Et verbum erat apud Deum. (πρός, acc.) Jn. i, 1.

Audet aliquis...judicari apud iniquos, et non apud sanctos? (ἐπί, gen.) I Cor. vi, 1.

220. **Circa.** Usual meaning *about, around, concerning.*

Representing Gk. κατά with acc., περί with acc.

Circa domos. (κατά.) Acts ii, 46.

Quae circa me sunt. (κατά.) Eph. vi, 21.

Circa frequens ministerium. (περί.) Lk. x, 40.

Habens fidem et bonam conscientiam, quam quidam repellentes circa fidem naufragaverunt. (περί.)
I Tim. i, 19.

In Mk. iv, 4 *circa* is used to translate παρά instead of *secus.*

221. **Contra.** Usual meaning *against, over against.*

Representing Gk. κατά with gen.

Non post multum misit se contra ipsam ventus Typhonicus...
Acts xxvii, 14.

222. **Erga.** Usual meaning *towards, with respect to.*

Representing Gk. περί with acc.

Sollicita es, et turbaris erga plurima.
Lk. x, 41; Phil. ii, 30.

223. **Inter.** Usual meaning *among, between.*

Represents Gk. ἐν.

Non ita erit inter vos. (ἐν.) Mt. xx, 26.

Inter vos = μετ' ἀλλήλων. Jn. xvi, 19.

Also used to express a superlative in accordance with Heb. usage.

Benedicta tu inter mulieres. (ἐν.) Lk. i, 42.

224. Juxta. Usual meaning *near, according to.*
Representing Gk. παρά with dat., ἐγγύς, πλησίον, κατά with acc.
Stabant autem juxta crucem Jesu mater ejus et soror matris ejus. (παρά.) Jn. xix, 25.
Erat enim Johannes baptizans in Aenon juxta Salim. (ἐγγύς.) Jn. iii, 23.
Quare non ambulant juxta traditionem seniorum? (κατά.) Mk. vii, 5.
Also in sense of *along.*
Ambulans autem Jesus juxta mare Galilaeae. (παρά, with acc.) Mt. iv, 18.

225. Penes. Usual meaning *in possession of.*
Represents Gk. κατά with acc.
Tu fidem habes? penes temetipsum habe coram Deo. Rom. xiv, 22.

226. Praeter. Usual meaning *besides, except, beyond.*
Representing Gk. παρά with acc., ἐκτός, πλήν, χωρίς, εἰ μή.
Fundamentum aliud nemo potest ponere praeter id quod positum est. (παρά.) I Cor. iii, 11.
Omnia subjecta sunt ei, sine dubio praeter eum, qui subjecit ei omnia. (ἐκτός.) I Cor. xv, 27.
Praeter illa, quae extrinsecus sunt, instantia mea quotidiana, sollicitudo omnium ecclesiarum. (χωρίς.) II Cor. xi, 28.
Nihil invenit praeter folia. (εἰ μή.) Mk. xi, 13.
In the sense of *contrary to.*
Rogo...ut observetis eos, qui dissensiones et offendicula praeter doctrinam, quam vos didicistis, faciunt.... (παρά.) Rom. xvi, 17.
Also Gal. i, 9.
In the sense of *more than.*
Putatis quia et ipsi debitores fuerunt praeter omnes homines habitantes in Jerusalem? (παρά.) Lk. xiii, 4.

227. Per. Usual meaning *through,* of place or time, *by means of, by* in oaths.
Representing Gk. διά with gen., κατά with acc. and gen.
Praeceptor, per totam noctem laborantes, nihil cepimus.... (διά.) Lk. v, 5.
Et ipse iter faciebat per civitates et castella. (κατά, acc.) Lk. viii, 1.

Distributively.

Et erunt terrae motus per loca. (κατά, acc.) Mk. xiii, 8.

Of repetition.

Per omnes annos. (κατ' ἔτος.) Lk. ii, 41.

Per omne sabbatum. Acts xv, 21.

Per omnia. Heb. iv, 15.

By means of.

Sic tamen quasi per ignem. (διά.) I Cor. iii, 15.

In oaths.

Adjuro te per Deum vivum. (κατά, gen.) Mt. xxvi, 63.

228. Propter. Usual meaning *on account of, because of.* Representing Gk. διά with acc., ἕνεκεν, εἰς.

Sabbatum propter hominem factum est, et non homo propter sabbatum. (διά.) Mk. ii, 27.

Quare et vos transgredimini mandatum Dei propter traditionem vestram? (διά.) Mt. xv, 3.

Beati, qui persecutionem patiuntur propter justitiam. (ἕνεκεν.) Mt. v, 10.

Cum venissem autem Troadem propter evangelium Christi.... (εἰς.) II Cor. ii, 12.

229. Post. Usual meaning *after, behind.* Represents Gk. μετά with acc., ὀπίσω, ὄπισθεν, κατά with acc.

Statim autem post tribulationem dierum illorum sol obscurabitur. (μετά.) Mt. xxiv, 29.

Post velamentum autem secundum, tabernaculum, quod dicitur Sancta Sanctorum. (μετά.) Heb. ix, 3.

Dimitte eam quia clamat post nos. (ὄπισθεν.) Mt. xv, 23.

Magis autem eos, qui post carnem in concupiscentia immunditiae ambulant. (ὀπίσω.) II Pet. ii, 10.

Unus post unum. (εἷς καθ' εἷς.) Jn. viii, 9.

230. Secundum. Usual meaning *after, according to.* Representing Gk. κατά with acc., πρός with acc.

Secundum opera vero eorum nolite facere. (κατά.) Mt. xxiii, 3.

Qui autem scrutatur corda, scit quid desideret Spiritus: quia secundum Deum postulat pro sanctis. (κατά.) Rom. viii, 27.

Ergo, fratres, debitores sumus non carni, ut secundum carnem vivamus. (κατά.) Rom. viii, 12.

Et non facit secundum voluntatem ejus.... (πρός.) Lk. xii, 47.

231. Secus. Usual meaning *otherwise*. In the Vg. and Late Latin it is used to represent the Gk. παρά with acc. or dat., κατά with acc., ἐπί with gen. or acc., πρός with acc., in the sense of *along*, *beside*[1], *at*.

In illo die exiens Jesus de domo sedebat secus mare. (παρά, acc.) Mt. xiii, 1.

Jesus...apprehendit puerum, et statuit illum secus se. (παρά, dat.) Lk. ix, 47.

Similiter et Levita cum esset secus locum.... (κατά, acc.) Lk. x, 32.

Et huic erat soror nomine Maria, quae etiam sedens secus pedes Domini, audiebat verbum illius. (πρός, acc.) Lk. x, 39.

Secus littus sedentes.... (ἐπί, acc.) Mt. xiii, 48.

Et videns fici arborem unam secus viam.... (ἐπί, gen.) Mt. xxi, 19.

For a very peculiar use see Lk. xx, 37.

Quia vero resurgant mortui, et Moyses ostendit secus rubum. *Moses showed in the place of the Scripture concerning the bush.* (ἐπί, gen.)

232. Supra. Usual meaning *on, upon, above, beyond*.

Representing Gk. ἐπάνω, ἐπί with acc. gen. dat., ὑπέρ with acc.

Non potest civitas abscondi supra montem posita. (ἐπάνω.) Mt. v, 14.

Invenit puellam jacentem supra lectum. (ἐπί, acc.) Mk. vii, 30.

Venit ad eos ambulans supra mare. (ἐπί, gen.) Mk. vi, 48.

Vere dico vobis quoniam supra omnia quae possidet, constituet illum. (ἐπί, dat.) Lk. xii, 44.

Et proficiebam in Judaismo supra multos coaetaneos meos. (ὑπέρ, acc.) Gal. i, 14.

[1] This seems to have been also a vulgar use of "secus"; it is found in Cato, *De re rustica*, and in inscriptions.

Prepositions governing both the Ablative and Accusative cases.

233. In with the Ablative. Usual meaning *in, at.*

Represents Gk. ἐν, ἐπί with dat., and even εἰς.

In Late Latin used with names of towns etc.

Quia si in Tyro et Sidone factae essent virtutes.... (ἐν.) Mt. xi, 21.

Viri astiterunt in domo. (ἐν.) Acts xi, 11.

Used to express the time when anything happens, where a simple Ablative would generally be used in Cl. L.

In diebus autem illis venit Johannes Baptista, praedicans in deserto Judaeae. (ἐν.) Mt. iii, 1.

Used in the Vg. of the Instrument or Agent in imitation of Heb. בּ, also to express manner.

Domine, si percutimus in gladio? (ἐν.) Lk. xxii, 49.

Hoc genus in nullo potest exire, nisi in oratione et jejunio. (ἐν.) Mk. ix, 28.

Quia in potestate et virtute imperat immundis spiritibus. (ἐν.) Lk. iv, 36.

Hic ejecit daemones in Beelzebub. (ἐν.) Mt. xii, 24.

In quo judicaturus est orbem in aequitate in viro, in quo statuit. (ἐν.) Acts xvii, 31.

In sense of *because of, at.*

Per totam noctem laborantes nihil cepimus: in verbo autem tuo laxabo rete. (ἐπί, with dat.) Lk. v, 5, 9.

Etsi omnes scandalizati fuerint in te, ego numquam scandalizabor. (ἐν.) Mt. xxvi, 33.

Putant quod in multiloquio exaudiantur. (ἐν.) Mt. vi, 7.

See also Ps. v, 8; Acts iii, 10, iv, 9, vii, 29; I Cor. i, 4; I Pet. iv, 14.

To express *accompaniment.*

Quoniam Dominus in jussu, et in voce archangeli, et in tuba Dei descendet de caelo. (ἐν.) I Thess. iv, 16.

Et ego cum venissem ad vos, fratres, veni non in sublimitate sermonis aut sapientiae.... (καθ' ὑπεροχήν.) I Cor. ii, 1.

Homo in spiritu immundo.... (ἐν.) Mk. i, 23.

In the sense of *concerning, with regard to* = εἰς.

Sacramentum hoc magnum est, ego autem dico in Christo et in ecclesia. Eph. v, 32.

See also Heb. vii, 14

Ut sim minister Christi in gentibus.... Rom. xv, 16.

In with the Ablative is used in certain passages, where *in* with the Accusative would have been expected. = εἰς.

(1) After verbs of motion:

Beatus homo qui non abiit in consilio impiorum.... Ps. i, 1.

(2) To express the object or end of an action:

Infirmum in fide assumite, non in disceptationibus cogitationum. Rom. xiv, 1.

An ignoratis quia quicumque baptizati sumus in Christo Jesu in morte ipsius baptizati sumus? Rom. vi, 3.

In is used to translate the Heb. בְּ in a passage which denotes the form under which anything appears (French *en*).

Qui apparui Abraham, Isaac et Jacob in Deo Omnipotente. Ex. vi, 3.

234. In with the Accusative. Usual meaning *into*.

Representing Gk. εἰς, also rarely ἐν.

Used in Late Latin with names of towns etc.

Mitte viros in Joppen. Acts x, 5.

Introivit in domum. Acts ix, 17; Lk. xxii, 10.

In a pregnant sense giving the result of the action of the verb.

Ecce viri, quos posuistis in carcerem, sunt in templo.... (ἐν.) Acts v, 25.

Qui exiit primo mane conducere operarios in vineam suam. (εἰς.) Mt. xx, 1.

Liberabit me Dominus ab omni opere malo et salvum faciet in regnum suum caeleste. (εἰς.) II Tim. iv, 18.

Used in a predicate to express result:

Lapidem, quem reprobaverunt aedificantes, hic factus est in caput anguli. (εἰς.) Mt. xxi, 42.

Et nutrivit eum sibi in filium. (εἰς.) Acts vii, 21.

Used to express purpose:

Emerunt ex illis agrum figuli in sepulturam peregrinorum. (εἰς.) Mt. xxvii, 7, 10.

Posui te in lucem gentium. (εἰς.) Acts xiii, 47.

Ego quidem baptizo vos in aqua in poenitentiam. (εἰς.) Mt. iii, 11.

Segregatus in evangelium Dei. (εἰς.) Rom. i, 1.

Ita et isti nunc non crediderunt in vestram misericordiam.... (Simple dat.) Rom. xi, 31.

In the sense of *concerning*.

David enim dicit in eum.... (εἰς.) Acts ii, 25.

Nolite ergo solliciti esse in crastinum. (εἰς.) Mt. vi, 34.

Used after *credere* in imitation of Gk. πιστεύειν εἰς.

Tu credis in Filium Dei? (εἰς.) Jn. ix, 35.

235. Sub. Usual meaning: *sub* with Abl. = *under, below,* in the sense of remaining under. *Sub* with Acc. = *up to* or *up under*.

In the Vg. *sub* is generally used with the Abl. in all senses.

Represents Gk. ὑπό with acc. and gen., ἐπί with gen. and dat.

Nam et ego sum homo sub potestate. (ὑπό, acc.) Mt. viii, 9.

With a verb of motion:

Omnia mihi licent, sed ego sub nullius redigar potestate. (ὑπό, gen.) I Cor. vi, 12.

In the sense of *in the time of*.

Et multi leprosi erant in Israel sub Elisaeo propheta.... (ἐπί, gen.) Lk. iv, 27.

See also Lk. iii, 2.

To translate ἐπί with gen. in the sense of *in the presence of*.

Adversus presbyterum accusationem noli recipere, nisi sub duobus aut tribus testibus. I Tim. v, 19; also vi, 13.

Exceptional use to translate ἐπί with dat. in sense of *concerning*.

A tribulatione, quae facta fuerat sub Stephano. Acts xi, 19.

236. Super. Usual meaning: *super* with Abl. = *concerning, about, because of,* rarely = *on*. *Super* with Acc. = *over, on the top of, beyond, above*.

(1) With the Abl. representing Gk. ἐπί with dat. or gen., ὑπέρ with gen., περί with gen.

Contristatus super caecitate cordis eorum.... (ἐπί, dat.) Mk. iii, 5.

Stupebant autem omnes, qui eum audiebant super prudentia et responsis ejus. (ἐπί, dat.) Lk. ii, 47.

Gentes autem super misericordia honorare Deum.... (ὑπέρ, gen.) Rom. xv, 9.

Attendite vobis super hominibus istis quid acturi sitis. (ἐπί, dat.) Acts v, 35.

Quia videbant signa, quae faciebat super his, qui infirmabantur. (ἐπί, with gen.) Jn. vi, 2.

In Acts xv, 2 *super* is used to trans. περί with gen.

(2) With the Acc. represents Gk. ἐπί with gen. acc. dat., ὑπέρ with acc.

Et duxerunt illum usque ad supercilium montis, super quem civitas illorum erat aedificata. (ἐπί, gen.) Lk. iv, 29.

Non est discipulus super magistrum, nec servus super dominum suum. (ὑπέρ, acc.) Mt. x, 24.

Nonne duo passeres asse veneunt? et unus ex illis non cadet super terram sine Patre vestro. (ἐπί, acc.) Mt. x, 29.

In the sense of *for*, *because of*, where the Abl. would be expected.

Quam cum vidisset Dominus, misericordia motus super eam. (ἐπί, dat.) Lk. vii, 13.

Nolite flere super me, sed super vos ipsas, et super filios vestros. (ἐπί, acc.) Lk. xxiii, 28.

Super is used after a comparative in Ps. xviii, 11.

EXTRACTS FROM ECCLESIASTICAL WRITERS

N.B. The numbers in the foot-notes refer to the sections in this book.

Visiones Perpetuae.

This is an extract from a unique document, namely the record of the imprisonment of a young Carthaginian matron Perpetua, written by herself. She was put to death in the persecution under Severus at the beginning of the third century. It is thought by some that these Acts were edited by Tertullian who refers to them in his treatise "De Anima."

Perpetua was arrested on the charge of being a Christian and cast into prison with four other catechumens. Her father, who was a pagan, did his best to persuade her to renounce Christ; but in vain. She was subsequently tried and condemned to the beasts and so suffered death with her companions.

The passages given below recount two visions which she saw in the prison.

The whole text of the Acts is given in one of the volumes of Hurter's series. A complete edition of all the Greek and Latin texts is published in "Texts and Studies," by J. A. Robinson, Cambridge.

Tunc dixit mihi frater meus: Domina soror, jam [1]in magnā dignitate es; [2]et tantā, ut postules visionem et ostendatur tibi, an passio sit, an [3]commeatus. Et ego, quae me sciebam [4]fabulari cum Domino, cujus beneficia [5]tanta experta eram, fidenter repromisi ei dicens: Crastinā die tibi renuntiabo. Et postulavi, et ostensum est mihi hoc: Video scalam auream [6]mirae magnitudinis [7]pertingentem usque ad caelum, et [8]ita angustam, per quam non nisi singuli ascendere possent: et in lateribus scalae omne genus [9]ferramentorum infixum. Erant ibi gladii, lanceae, [10]hami, machaerae, ut si quis negligenter, aut non sursum attendens ascenderet, [11]laniaretur, et carnes ejus inhaererent ferramentis. Et erat sub ipsā scalā draco cubans mirae magnitudinis, qui ascendentibus insidias parabat, et exterrebat ne ascenderent. Ascendit autem

[1] in magnā dignitate es = *you are held in great honour.* [2] et tantā, ut postules, 163. [3] commeatus = *release.* [4] fabulari = *to converse with*, a vernacular word found in the comic poets. [5] tanta, predicative, "whose loving-kindnesses I had found to be so many." [6] mirae magnitudinis, 26. [7] pertingentem = *reaching to.* [8] et ita angustam, per quam, for "ita angustam, ut per eam," 163. [9] ferramentorum = *iron instruments.* [10] hami, machaerae = *hooks and sabres* (μάχαιρα). [11] laniaretur = *he would be mangled.*

Saturus prior, et pervenit in caput scalae, et convertit se ad me, et dixit mihi: Perpetua, sustineo te: sed vide ne mordeat draco ille. Et dixi ego: Non [1]me nocebit in nomine Domini Jesu Christi. Et [2]de sub ipsā scalā quasi timens me, lente elevavit caput, et cum primum gradum [3]calcassem, calcavi illius caput. Et ascendi, et vidi spatium horti immensum, et in medio horti sedentem hominem [4]canum, in habitu pastoris, grandem, oves [5]mulgentem: et circumstantes [6]candidatos millia multa. Et levavit caput et adspexit me, et dixit mihi: [7]Bene venisti, tegnon. Et clamavit me, et de [8]caseo, quod mulgebat, dedit mihi quasi [9]bucellum, et ego accepi junctis manibus et [10]manducavi, et universi circumstantes dixerunt: Amen. Et ad sonitum vocis experrecta sum commanducans adhuc dulcis nescio quid. Et retuli statim fratri meo, et intelleximus passionem esse futuram, et coepimus nullam jam spem in [11]saeculo habere.

* * * * * *

Post dies paucos, dum universi oramus, subito mediā oratione profecta est mihi vox, et nominavi Dinocratem: et [12]obstupui quod nunquam mihi in mentem venisset nisi tunc, et dolui commemorata casūs ejus. Et cognovi me statim dignam esse, et pro eo petere debere. Et coepi pro ipso orationem facere multam, et ingemiscere ad Dominum. [13]Continuo ipsā nocte ostensum est hoc mihi in [14]oromate. Video Dinocratem exeuntem de loco tenebroso, ubi et complures erant aestuantem et sitientem valde, [15]sordido vultu, et colore pallido, et vulnus in facie ejus, quod, cum moreretur, habuit. Hic Dinocrates fuerat frater meus carnalis, annorum septem, [16]qui per infirmitatem facie canceratā male obiit, ita ut mors ejus [17]odio fuerit omnibus hominibus. Pro hoc ego orationem feceram: et inter me et illum grande erat [18]diastema, ita ut uterque [19]ad invicem accedere non possemus. Erat deinde in ipso loco, ubi Dinocrates erat, [20]piscina [21]plena aquā, altiorem marginem habens quam erat

[1] me. Many verbs which govern a dat. in Cl. L. do not always do so in Ecc. L., 37. [2] de sub (a double preposition) = *from below.* [3] calcassem = *I had trodden on.* [4] canum = *grey-haired.* [5] mulgentem = *milking.* [6] candidatos = *white-robed.* [7] Bene venisti, tegnon = *Welcome, child* (τέκνον). [8] caseo = *curd.* [9] bucellum = *a mouthful.* [10] manducavi = *I ate* (a vernacular verb, common in the Vg.). [11] saeculo = *this world*, as often in Vg. [12] obstupui quod, 135, 112–114. [13] Continuo = *straightway.* [14] oromate = *vision* (ὁράω). [15] sordido vultu = *unclean appearance*, 56. [16] qui per infirmitatem... = *who died miserably through a cancer in the face.* [17] odio = *disgusting*, 41. [18] diastema = *a gulf* (διά, ἵστημι). [19] ad invicem = *neither of us could go to the other*, 70. [20] piscina = *a basin.* [21] plena aquā, 49.

statura pueri, et extendebat se Dinocrates quasi bibiturus. Ego dolebam quod et piscina illa aquam habebat, et tamen propter altitudinem marginis bibiturus non [1]esset. Et experrecta sum et cognovi fratrem meum [2]laborare. Sed confidebam profuturam orationem meam [3]labori ejus, et orabam pro eo omnibus diebus quo usque transivimus in [4]carcerem castrensem. [5]Munere enim castrensi eramus [6]pugnaturi. [7]Natale tunc Getae Caesaris, et feci pro illo orationem die et nocte gemens et lacrimans, ut mihi [8]donaretur. Die autem quo in [9]nervo mansimus, ostensum est mihi hoc: Video locum illum, quem videram tenebrosum, esse lucidum: et Dinocratem mundo corpore, bene vestitum, [10]refrigerantem. Et ubi erat vulnus, video [11]cicatricem: et piscinam illam, quam retro videram, summisso margine usque ad [12]umbilicum pueri: et aquam de eā trahebat sine cessatione, et super margine [13]phiala erat plena aquā; et accessit Dinocrates, et de eā bibere coepit, quae phiala non deficiebat. Et satiatus abscessit de aquā [14]ludere more infantium gaudens, et experrecta sum. Tunc intellexi translatum eum esse de poena.

Cyprian, Bishop of Carthage (martyred 258), was converted to Christianity in middle life. He was a famous rhetorician in his early days; but after his conversion he laid his secular studies aside and devoted himself entirely to Christian literature. In the treatises intended for the ordinary members of his flock he did not shrink from occasionally using the expressions and even the solecisms which are found in the Old Latin version of the Bible. His numerous quotations are naturally derived from the same source, and often differ both in wording and in reading from the Vulgate.

He, in common with other writers of the period, abandons the periodic style of Classical prose for short sentences with frequent antitheses and rhetorical questions.

The signs of his rhetorical training are everywhere manifest. In the matter of his treatises he freely copies Tertullian; but popu-

[1] esset. This is subj. because it gives the thought of Perpetua, "he was not (as I thought) likely to drink." [2] laborare = *to be in torment.* [3] labori, 37. [4] carcerem castrensem = *the camp prison.* [5] Munere = *show.* [6] pugnaturi, i.e. with the beasts. [7] Natale tunc Getae Caesaris, understand "erat." [8] donaretur = *that he might be given to me*, i.e. *that he might be saved.* Compare Acts xxvii, 24, Et ecce donavit tibi Deus omnes qui navigant tecum. [9] nervo = *the stocks.* [10] refrigerantem = *refreshed* or *happy.* This is the word generally used in the inscriptions in the Catacombs to express the state of the blessed departed. REFRIGERET TIBI DEUS ET CHRISTUS ET DOMINI NOSTRI ADEODATUS ET FELIX (from the cemetery of Commodilla). See Proverbs xxix, 17. [11] cicatricem = *a scar.* [12] umbilicum = *waist.* [13] phiala = *a cup* (φιάλη). [14] ludere, 162.

larises and expands the materials that he borrows from him. In many respects, including the manner in which he uses quotations from Scripture, his treatises are curiously like some modern sermons. They are well worth the attention of the student on account of the simplicity of their style and their moral earnestness. The best modern edition of his works is in the Vienna Corpus by Hartel. Several of his treatises and a selection of letters are published in Hurter's SS. Patrum Opuscula Selecta.

Jerome excellently sums up the characteristics of Tertullian and Cyprian in his epistle to Paulinus:

Tertullianus creber est in sententiis; sed difficilis in loquendo. Beatus Cyprianus, instar fontis purissimi, dulcis incedit et placidus: et cum totus sit in exercitatione virtutum, occupatus persecutionum angustiis, de Scripturis divinis nequaquam disseruit.

Jesus Christus Patientiae Exemplar.

Atque ut plenius intelligere possimus, fratres dilectissimi, [1]quia patientia Dei [2]res est, et quisquis lenis et patiens et mitis est Dei Patris imitator est, Dominus ipse dixit in Evangelio suo: "Audistis quia dictum est: [3]Diliges proximum tuum et [4]odio habebis inimicum tuum. Ego autem dico vobis: Diligite inimicos vestros, et orate pro eis, qui vos persequuntur, ut sitis filii Patris vestri, qui in caelis est, qui solem suum oriri facit super bonos et malos, et pluit super justos et injustos. Si enim dilexeritis eos qui vos diligunt, quam mercedem habebitis? Nonne sic et Publicani faciunt? Et si salutaveritis fratres vestros tantum, quid amplius facitis? Nonne et ethnici [5]idipsum faciunt? [3]Eritis itaque vos perfecti, [6]quomodo Pater vester caelestis perfectus est."

Sic perfectos dixit fieri Dei filios si patientia Dei Patris [7]maneat in nobis. Nec hoc, fratres dilectissimi, Jesus Christus Dominus et Deus noster tantum verbis docuit sed implevit et factis. Et qui ad hoc descendisse se dixerat ut voluntatem Patris faceret, inter cetera mirabilia [8]virtutum suarum quibus indicia divinae majestatis expressit paternam quoque patientiam servavit. Omnes denique actūs ejus ab ipso statim adventu patientiā signantur, quod primum de illā sublimitate coelesti ad terrena descendens non aspernatur Dei Filius carnem hominis induere, et [9]cum peccator ipse non esset, aliena peccata portare.

[1] Quia. Observe the use of this barbarous construction even in Cyprian. 112-114. [2] res=*attribute.* [3] Diliges, 83. [4] odio, 41. [5] idipsum, 64. [6] quomodo, 175. [7] maneat, 167, 171. [8] virtutes=Gk. δυνάμεις, Mt. vii, 22, Heb. ii, 4. [9] cum, 166.

Immortalitate interim positā, fieri se et mortalem patitur, ut [1]innocens pro nocentium salute perimatur. Dominus baptizatur a servo, et [2]remissam peccatorum daturus, ipse non dedignatur [3]lavacro regenerationis corpus abluere. [4]Diebus quadraginta jejunat, per quem ceteri [5]saginantur: esurit et famem sentit, ut qui in [6]fame sermonis et gratiae fuerant, coelesti pane saturarentur. Discipulis non ut servis dominicā potestate praefuit, sed benignus et mitis fraternā eos caritate dilexit, dignatus etiam pedes apostolorum lavare, ut cum circa servos talis [7]est dominus, exemplo suo doceret, qualis circa compares et aequales debeat esse conservus. Sub ipsā autem passione et cruce, priusquam ad crudelitatem necis [8]veniret, quae contumeliarum toleravit ludibria. Coronatur spinis, qui martyres floribus coronat aeternis: palmis in faciem verberatur qui palmas veras vincentibus tribuit. Ille innocens, ille justus, immo innocentia ipsa et ipsa justitia, inter facinorosos [9]deputatur, et testimoniis falsis veritas premitur, judicatur judicaturus, et Dei Sermo [10]ad victimam tacens ducitur. Et cum [10]ad crucem Domini confundantur sidera, elementa turbentur, ille non loquitur, nec movetur. Usque ad finem perseveranter tolerantur omnia, ut consummetur in Christo plena et perfecta patientia. Et post ista omnia adhuc interfectores suos, si conversi ad eum veniunt, suscipit; et [11]patientiā salutari ad conservandum benignus et patiens Ecclesiam suam nemini claudit. Illos adversarios, illos blasphemos, illos nominis sui semper inimicos, si paenitentiam delicti agant, si admissum facinus agnoscant, non solum ad indulgentiam [12]criminis, sed et ad praemium [13]regni coelestis admittit. Quid potest patientius, quid benignius dici? Vivificatur Christi sanguine etiam qui fudit sanguinem Christi. Talis est Christi et tanta patientia; quae nisi talis ac tanta existeret, Paulum quoque apostolum Ecclesia non haberet.

Quod si et nos in Christo sumus, si ipsum induimus, si ipse est salutis nostrae via, qui Christum vestigiis salutaribus sequimur, per Christi exemplum gradiemur, sicut Johannes apostolus instruit dicens: "Qui dicit se in Christo manere, debet [14]quomodo ille ambulavit et ipse ambulare."

[1] innocens, 200. [2] remissam = *remissionem.* [3] lavacro, Titus iii, 5. [4] Diebus, 55. [5] saginare. In the Cl. this means *to stuff*; like many other words it has in Ecc. L. a more refined meaning = *fill.* [6] Amos viii, 11. [7] est. A very unusual Indicative in a clause of Cause, 156. [8] veniret, 154. [9] deputatur = *is reckoned*, Lk. xxii, 37. [10] ad, 216. [11] patientiā salutari, *with patience conducive to salvation.* [12] criminis, 24. [13] regni, 26. [14] quomodo, 175.

Item Petrus, super quem Ecclesia Domini dignatione fundata est, in epistolā suā ponit et dicit: "Christus passus est pro nobis, relinquens vobis exemplum ut sequamini vestigia ejus: qui peccatum non fecit, nec dolus inventus est in ore ejus, qui cum malediceretur non remaledicebat, cum pateretur non minabatur, tradebat autem se judicanti se [1]injuste."

De bono patientiae (adapted).

Quid est voluntas Dei?

Voluntas autem Dei est [2]quam Christus et fecit et docuit. Humilitas in [3]conversatione, stabilitas in fide, [4]verecundia in verbis, in factis justitia, in operibus misericordia, in moribus disciplina, injuriam facere non nosse et factam posse tolerare, cum fratribus pacem tenere, Deum toto corde diligere, amare in illo [5]quod Pater est, timere quod Deus est, Christo nihil omnino praeponere, quia nec nobis quidquam ille praeposuit, caritati ejus inseparabiliter adhaerere, cruci ejus fortiter ac fidenter [6]assistere quando de ejus nomine et honore certamen est, exhibere in sermone constantiam quā confitemur, in quaestione fiduciam quā [7]congredimur, in morte patientiam quā coronamur. Hoc est coheredem Christi esse velle, hoc est praeceptum Dei facere, hoc est voluntatem Patris adimplere.

De Oratione Dominica.

Notice the use of the infinitive as a verbal noun parallel with other nouns.

Quare justus cum Christo esse desiderat.

Scriptum est enim, justum fide vivere. Si justus es, et fide vivis, si vere in Christum credis, cur non cum Christo futurus et de Domini promisso [8]securus, [9]quod ad Christum voceris, amplecteris et quod diabolo careas, gratularis? Simeon denique ille justus, qui vere justus fuit, qui fide plenā Dei praecepta servavit, cum ei divinitus responsum fuisset, [10]quod non ante moreretur, quam Christum vidisset, agnovit in spiritu natum esse jam Christum, de quo sibi

[1] This reading differs from that of the received Gk. texts. [2] quam = *the will which.* [3] conversatione, ἀναστροφή = *manner of life*, Gal. i, 13. [4] verecundia = *modesty.* [5] quod Pater est = *the fact that he is Father.* [6] assistere, *to stand by.* [7] congredimur = *we agree together.* [8] securus = *free from care*, cf. Mt. xxviii, 14. [9] quod ad Christum... = *why do you not welcome the fact that you are being called to Christ, and rejoice that you are being freed from the devil?* [10] quod non ante moreretur, 112–114.

fuerat ante praedicatum; quo viso, scivit se cito esse moriturum. Laetus itaque de morte jam proximā, et de vicinā [1]accersitione securus, accepit in manus puerum, et benedicens Dominum exclamavit et dixit: "Nunc dimittis servum tuum, Domine, secundum verbum tuum in pace, quoniam viderunt oculi mei [2]salutare tuum." Probans scilicet atque contestans tunc esse servis Dei pacem, tunc liberam, tunc tranquillam quietatem, quando de istis mundi turbinibus extracti, [3]sedis et securitatis aeternae portum petimus, quando, [4]expunctā hac morte, ad immortalitatem venimus. Illa est enim vera pax, illa fida tranquillitas, illa stabilis et firma et perpetua securitas.

De Mortalitate.

De defectu fidei in tribulatione.

Hoc autem fit, fratres dilectissimi, quia fides deest, quia nemo credit vera esse, quae promittit Deus, qui [5]verax est, cujus sermo credentibus aeternus et firmus est.

Si tibi vir gravis et laudabilis aliquid polliceretur, haberes [6]utique pollicenti fidem, nec te falli aut decipi ab eo crederes, quem stare in sermonibus atque in actibus suis scires. Nunc Deus tecum loquitur; et tu mente incredulā perfidus fluctuas? Deus tibi de hoc mundo recedenti immortalitatem atque aeternitatem pollicetur, et tu dubitas? Hoc est Deum omnino non nosse: hoc est Christum credentium dominum et magistrum peccato incredulitatis offendere: hoc est in ecclesiā constitutam fidem in domo fidei non habere. Quantum prosit exire de saeculo Christus ipse salutis atque utilitatis nostrae magister ostendit, qui, cum discipuli ejus contristarentur quod dixit se jam recessurum, locutus est ad eos dicens, "Si me dilexistis, [7]gauderetis utique, quoniam vado ad Patrem": docens scilicet et ostendens, cum cari, quos diligimus, de saeculo exeunt, [8]gaudendum potius quam dolendum. Cujus rei memor beatus apostolus Paulus in epistolā suā ponit atque dicit: [9]"Mihi vivere Christus est, et mori lucrum": lucrum maximum computans jam saeculi [10]laqueis non teneri, jam nullis peccatis et vitiis carnis [11]obnoxium fieri, exemptum

[1] accersitione = *summons*. This word is often used in the inscriptions on graves. [2] salutare = Gk. σωτήριον, *salvation*, often used in the Psalms, cf. xii, 6. [3] sedis = *home*. [4] expunctā hac morte = *after this death has been destroyed*. [5] verax = *true*, Rom. iii, 4. [6] utique = *certainly*. [7] gauderetis, 167, 171. [8] gaudendum, 192. [9] Mihi vivere..., 117. [10] laqueum = *snare*. [11] obnoxium = *exposed to*.

[1]pressuris angentibus, et [2]venenatis diaboli faucibus liberatum ad laetitiam salutis aeternae Christo vocante proficisci.

At enim quosdam movet, quod aequaliter cum gentibus nostros morbi istius [3]valetudo corripiat; quasi ad hoc [4]crediderit Christianus, ut immunis a contactu malorum, mundo et saeculo feliciter perfruatur, et non omnia hic adversa perpessus ad futuram laetitiam reservetur. Movet quosdam quod sit nobis cum ceteris [5]mortalitas ista communis, quid enim nobis in hoc mundo non communis cum ceteris, quamdiu adhuc secundum legem primae nativitatis manet caro iste communis? [6]Quoadusque istic in mundo sumus, cum genere humano carnis aequalitate conjungimur, spiritu [7]separamur. Itaque donec corruptivum istud induat incorruptionem, et mortale hoc accipiat immortalitatem, et Christus nos perducat ad Deum Patrem, quaecumque sunt carnis incommoda, sunt nobis cum humano genere communia. Sic cum fetu sterili terra jejuna est, neminem fames [7]separat. Sic cum irruptione hostili civitas aliqua possessa est, omnes simul captivitas vastat. [8]Et quando imbrem nubila serena suspendunt, omnibus [9]siccitas una est. Et cum navem [10]scopulosa saxa [11]constringunt, navigantibus [12]naufragium sine exceptione commune est. Et oculorum dolor et impetus febrium et omnium valetudo membrorum cum ceteris communis est nobis, quamdiu portatur in saeculo caro ista communis.

De Mortalitate.

Quod filii Dei Patri similes esse debent.

Si hominibus laetum est et gloriosum filios [13]habere consimiles, et tunc magis [13]generasse delectat, si ad patrem lineamentis paribus [14]suboles subseciva respondeat, quanto major in Deo Patre laetitia est cum [15]quis sic spiritualiter nascitur, ut in actibus ejus et laudibus divina generositas praedicetur? Quae justitiae palma est, quae corona, esse se talem de quo Deus non [16]dicat "Filios generavi et exaltavi, ipsi autem spreverunt me." [17]Collaudet te potius Christus

[1] pressuris angentibus=*agonising trials.* [2] venenatis faucibus=*poisoned jaws.* [3] valetudo=*weakness.* [4] crediderit, 175. [5] mortalitas =*mortality*, i.e. *disease.* [6] Quoadusque=*so long as.* [7] separare=*to set apart.* [8] Et quando imbrem nubila serena=*and when fine weather keeps off the showers.* [9] siccitas=*drought.* [10] scopulosa=*precipitous.* [11] constringunt=*crush.* [12] naufragium=*shipwreck.* [13] habere, generasse, 117. [14] suboles subseciva=*surviving offspring.* [15] quis. Rare in Cl. except after 'si,' cf. Jas. v, 14, 69*a*. [16] dicat, 150 (1). [17] Collaudet, 101.

et invitet ad praemium dicens: "Venite, benedicti Patris mei, percipite regnum quod vobis paratum est ab origine mundi." His meditationibus corroborandus est animus, [1]ejusmodi exercitationibus contra omnia diaboli jacula firmandus. Sit in manibus divina lectio. Oratio [2]jugis [3]omnino non cesset. Spiritualibus semper actibus occupemur, ut quotiescunque inimicus [4]accesserit, et clausum adversum se pectus inveniat et armatum. [5]Non enim Christiani hominis corona est una, quae temporibus persecutionis accipitur. Habet et pax coronas suas, quibus [6]de variā et multiplici [7]congressione victores, prostrato et subacto adversario, coronantur. Libidinem subegisse continentiae corona est. Contra iram, contra injuriam repugnasse corona patientiae est. De avaritiā triumphus est pecuniam spernere. Laus est fidei fiduciā futurorum mundi adversa tolerare. Et qui superbus in prosperis non est, gloriam de humilitate consequitur. In hoc virtutum [8]stadio quotidie currimus, ad has justitiae palmas et coronas sine intermissione temporis pervenimus. Cogitemus ergo caeleste regnum. Cogitemus quod filii Dei hi soli possint vocari, qui nativitate caelesti et lege divinā ad similitudinem Dei Patris et Christi [9]respondeant adunati. Cogitemus sub oculis Dei nos stare, spectante et judicante ipso conversationis ac vitae nostrae curricula decurrere, pervenire nos tunc demum posse [10]ut eum videre contingat, si ipsum nunc videntem delectemus actibus nostris, si nos dignos gratiā ejus et indulgentiā praebeamus, si placituri semper in regno, in hoc mundo ante placeamus.

De zelo et livore (adapted).

Ambrose (died 397), the famous Bishop of Milan, was the son of the prefect of Gaul, and was educated with a view to his occupying a high administrative position in the state.

When still a young man he was made prefect of Liguria and Aemilia and, as such, was called upon to preside at the election of a bishop for Milan after the death of the Arian bishop Auxentius. His reputation among the people was such that, although he was a layman and unbaptized, he was himself elected bishop by popular acclamation much against his wish.

He disposed of his property and set himself to learn, in order

[1] ejusmodi = *such*, 71. [2] jugis = *continuous*. [3] omnino non cesset, 100. [4] accesserit, 88. [5] Non enim...accipitur = *For the crown which is received in time of persecution is not the only crown that a Christian man can win.* [6] de, 211. [7] congressione = *contest.* [8] stadio = *racecourse.* [9] respondeant, 150. [10] ut...contingat, a clause of consequence, 163.

that he might be able to teach the doctrines of Christianity. He became the most powerful champion of the Catholic party in the West against the Arians, and in the end secured the complete triumph of the Catholic doctrine in spite of much opposition and persecution. He also urged the Emperors Gratian, Valentinian and Theodosius to sweep away the last remains of paganism, to refuse the title of Pontifex Maximus, and to remove the altar of Victory from the Senate House. In the troubled times during which the young Emperors Gratian and Valentinian perished he was the most influential statesman in the West as well as the greatest bishop.

He is also famous as being the teacher who brought Augustine back to the Catholic faith, for his courage in making Theodosius do penance for the massacre of Thessalonica, and as being the founder of Latin Hymnology.

He has left many sermons and treatises written with a vigour and directness worthy of a Roman magistrate.

He was not an original thinker: his method of expounding Scripture was the allegorical method of Philo and Origen, and he copied Cicero in his ethical treatises.

He is nevertheless one of the greatest figures in the history of the Church, and in his capacity as a teacher and organiser sums up in himself the distinguishing characteristics of the Roman people.

Some of his works such as the De fide are published in Hurter's collection.

Ambrose in this piece imagines the pleas that the heretics will be constrained to make before the judgment seat of Christ. He is addressing the heretics throughout, and their appeals and the replies of Christ are in dialogue form. The heretics speak in the first person as well as Ambrose. Care must be taken to distinguish the speakers.

De judicio Domini in Arianos et alios haereticos.

Igitur [1]prosecutionem tuam videamus quemadmodum concilies tibi judicem. Dic, sane, dic, inquam: Ego te, Christe, puto esse dissimilem Patri. Respondebit et ille: Discerne, si potes: discerne, inquam, in quo putes me esse dissimilem.

Dic aliud: Creaturam, inquies, te arbitror. Respondebit et Christus: Si duorum hominum testimonium verum est, tu nec mihi nec Patri saltem credere debuisti, qui genitum nominavit?

Bonum, inquies, nego. Dicet et ille: Fiat tibi secundum fidem tuam, ut tibi bonus non sim.

[1] prosecutionem = *pleading.*

Omnipotentem non arbitror. Respondebit et ipse: Non possum ergo tibi tua peccata [1]donare.

[2]Subjectum dico. Referet ad hoc: Cur igitur libertatem ac veniam petis ab eo, quem putas pro servitio esse subjectum?

Video haerere prosecutionem tuam: non urgeo, quia peccatorum meorum ipse sum conscius. Non invideo veniam, quia ipse opto indulgentiam: votum tuum scire desidero. En allego apud judicem desideria tua; non prodo crimina, seriem tuorum expecto votorum.

Dic itaque ea [3]quae in communi voto sunt; dic, inquam: Domine, fac me ad imaginem Dei. Respondebit ille: Ad quem imaginem? Quam negasti? Dic: Fac me incorruptibilem. Referet utique: Quomodo te incorruptibilem facere possum, quem tu creaturam [4]dicendo, capacem corruptibilitatis esse voluisti? Mortui resurgent incorrupti, et tu corruptibilem dicis, quem Deum cernis?

Dic: Bonus esto mihi. Dicet tibi: Quid postulas quod negasti? Ego te bonum esse volui, ego dixi: Estote sancti, quoniam ipse sanctus sum; et tu mihi id negare contendis? Et tu expectas veniam peccatorum? Sed nemo potest donare peccata nisi solus Deus. Itaque cum verus et solus tibi Deus non sim, non possum utique tua peccata donare.

Haec Arianus dicat et Photinianus: Nego te, inquit, Deum.

Respondebit ei Dominus: Dixit insipiens in corde suo: Non est Deus. De quo dictum putas, de Judaeo, de Gentili, an de diabolo?

De quovis dictum sit, Photiniane, tolerabilior est ille, qui tacuit: tu vero et voce ausus es dicere, ut insipiente insipientior probareris.

Negas ergo, inquit, Deum, cum ego dixerim: [5]Dii estis, et filii Excelsi omnes. Et tu Deum negas, cujus opera divina circumspicis?

Dicat et Sabellianus: Ego te ipsum Patrem et Filium et Spiritum Sanctum arbitror. Respondebit et Dominus: Non audis Patrem, non audis Filium. Numquid hic ulla confusio est? Scriptura ipsa te docet Patrem esse, qui detulit judicium: Filium esse, qui judicat. Non audisti me [6]dicentem: Solus non sum; sed ego et qui misit me Pater?

Dicat et Manichaeus: Ego auctorem carnis nostrae diabolum credo. Respondebit ei: Ergo quid facies in caelestibus? Vade ad

[1] donare=*to forgive*, Eph. iv, 32. [2] Subjectum dico=*I say that thou art under authority.* [3] quae...sunt=*the things that men most commonly desire.* [4] dicendo 188. [5] In John x, 34; Ps. xxxii, 6. [6] dicentem 138.

auctorem tuum. Ego eos volo mecum esse, quos dedit mihi Pater. Tu te a diabolo creatum, Manichaee, arbitraris: ad illius ergo festina sedem, ubi ignis et sulphur, ubi non restinguitur ejus incendium, ne unquam poena moriatur.

[1]Mitto alia haereticorum portenta non nomina; quid eis erit judicii, quae erit forma sententiae? Respondebit his omnibus et ille moraliter: Populus meus, quid feci tibi, aut quid contristavi te? Nonne ex Aegypto eduxi te, et ex domo servitutis liberavi te?

Sed parum est ex Aegypto liberasse, et ex domo servitutis eripuisse: plus est te ipsum dedisse pro nobis. Dices ergo: Nonne vestras omnes suscepi injurias? Nonne corpus meum pro vobis obtuli? Nonne mortem appetivi, quod non erat [2]Divinitatis meae, sed vestrae redemptionis? Haeccine referuntur gratiae? Hoc profecit sanguis meus, sicut in propheta jam dixi: Quae utilitas in sanguine meo, quia descendi in corruptionem? Hoc ergo profecit, ut me impie negaretis, pro quibus ista sustinui.

Ego vero tunc, Domine Jesu, etsi gravium peccatorum mihi ipse sim conscius, dicam tamen: Non te negavi; habes quod [3]ignoscas fragilitati carnis. Delictum fateor, peccatum non abnuo: si vis, potes me mundare. Ne, quaeso, in judicium [4]intres cum servo tuo. Non quaero ut judices, sed ut ignoscas.

De fide, II, 13.

Jerome (died 420) was the greatest linguistic scholar among the Fathers. In early life he was educated in Rome by Donatus, and was well acquainted with Greek. He studied Hebrew with a Jew to enable him to make a new translation of the O.T. from the original.

In addition to his version of the Bible he wrote many commentaries and letters and made translations from the works of Origen. In his original writings his style is good and clear, but in his translation of the Bible he sacrificed the Latin language to his desire to make a literal version.

Even in his original writings he was no purist either in construction or vocabulary, and never shrunk from using many words, especially abstract nouns, compound nouns and diminutives,

Which would have made Quintilian stare and gasp.

He also frequently coined new words if the nature of the subject which he was treating demanded them.

[1] Mitto alia... = *I pass over the other nameless heretical monsters.* [2] Divinitatis, 27. [3] ignoscas... = *thou wilt have something to pardon*, 150 (1). [4] Ne intres, 99.

The influence of his writings on later Latin and the languages derived from it was very great.

In spite of the dream described in the next selection he never could get rid of his love for the Latin classics, for which he considered an elaborate apology necessary (see Ep. 70).

It should be remembered that he was of a vehement nature and that for the greater part of his life he lived as a hermit or a studious recluse in Syria or Palestine.

The best edition of his works is by Vallarsi, Verona 1734–42. It is carelessly reprinted in Migne, Pat. Lat.

There is a small selection of his letters in Hurter, and an edition of them has been published in the Vienna Corpus.

An elaborate account of his style, excluding the Vulgate, is given in Goelzer, La Latinité de St Jérôme. Hachette, Paris.

Somnium Hieronymi.

Cum ante annos plurimos domo, parentibus, sorore, cognatis, et quod his difficilius est, consuetudine [1]lautioris cibi propter caelorum me regna [2]castrassem: et Hierosolymam [3]militaturus pergerem, [4]bibliotheca, quam mihi Romae summo studio et labore confeceram, carere omnino non poteram: itaque miser ego, lecturus Tullium, jejunabam, post noctium crebras vigilias, post lacrymas, quas mihi praeteritorum recordatio peccatorum ex imis [5]visceribus eruebat, Plautus sumebatur in manus.

Si quando in memetipsum reversus, prophetas legere coepissem, [6]sermo horrebat incultus: et quia lumen caecis oculis non videbam, non oculorum putabam culpam esse, sed solis.

Dum ita me antiquus serpens illuderet, in mediā ferme quadragesimā medullis infusa febris corpus invasit exhaustum, et sine ullā requie, quod [7]dictu quoque incredibile est, sic infelicia membra [8]depasta est, ut ossibus vix haererem. Interim parantur exsequiae, et vitalis animae calor, toto frigescente jam corpore, in solo tantum tepente [9]pectusculo palpitabat; cum subito raptus in spiritu, ad

[1] lautioris cibi = *somewhat delicate food*, a Cl. use of the comparative. [2] castrassem = *I had deprived myself*. [3] militaturus = *to join the army of the Church*, i.e. *to become a monk*. Jerome often speaks of the monastic life in terms of military service. [4] bibliotheca = *library*, for the case see 57. [5] visceribus = *heart*. [6] sermo horrebat incultus = literally, *their uncultivated style bristled*, i.e. *repelled me*. [7] dictu, 193. [8] depasta *from* depascor. See Verg. Ec. i, 54, and Ps. ci, 5, and notice the mixture of literary reminiscences. [9] pectusculo, diminutive from pectus. The use of diminutives is characteristic of Late Latin.

tribunal judicis pertrahor; ubi tantum luminis, et tantum erat ex circumstantium claritate fulgoris, ut projectus in terram, sursum aspicere non auderem.

Interrogatus de conditione, Christianum me esse respondi. Et ille, qui praesidebat, Mentiris, ait; Ciceronianus es, non Christianus: ubi enim thesaurus tuus, ibi et cor tuum.

Illico obmutui, et inter verbera (nam caedi me jusserat) conscientiae magis igne torquebar illum mecum [1]versiculum reputans: In inferno autem quis confitebitur tibi? Clamare autem coepi et ejulans dicere: Miserere [2]mei, Domine, miserere mei. Haec vox inter flagella resonabat.

Tandem ad praesidentis genua [3]provoluti qui adstabant, precabantur ut veniam tribueret adulescentiae, et errori locum paenitentiae [4]commodaret, [5]exacturus deinde cruciatum, si gentilium literarum libros aliquando legissem. Ego qui in tanto constrictus [6]articulo, [7]vellem etiam majora promittere, [8]dejurare coepi, et nomen ejus obtestans dicere: Domine, si unquam habuero codices seculares, si legero, te negavi. In haec [9]sacramenti verba dimissus, revertor ad superos, et mirantibus cunctis oculos aperio, tanto lacrymarum imbre perfusos, ut etiam incredulis fidem facerem ex dolore. Nec vero sopor ille fuerat, aut vana somnia, quibus saepe deludimur; testis est tribunal illud, ante quod jacui: testis judicium triste, quod timui: ita mihi nunquam contingat in talem incidere quaestionem. [10]Liventes fateor habuisse me [11]scapulas, plagas sensisse post somnum, et tanto dehinc studio divina legisse, quanto non ante mortalia legeram. Ep. XXII, 30.

See the comment on this dream in Milton, Areopagitica, p. 18, in Temple Classics Edition.

De vita clericorum.

Igitur clericus, qui Christi servit ecclesiae interpretetur primum [12]vocabulum suum, et nominis definitione [13]prolatā, nitatur esse quod dicitur. Si enim κλῆρος Graece, "sors" Latine appellatur, propterea vocantur clerici, vel quia de sorte sunt Domini, vel quia

[1] See p. 126, n. 9. [2] mei, 29. [3] ad genua provoluti. A regular literary phrase, Livy, xxxiv, 11. [4] commodaret = *grant*. [5] exacturus = *and that he should exact*. [6] articulo = literally, *a joint*, hence *a point*, trans. *a critical condition*. [7] vellem, potential subj., 103. [8] dejurare = *to swear*. [9] sacramenti. Here in its Cl. sense of *an oath*. [10] Liventes = *black with blows*. [11] scapulas = *shoulders*. [12] vocabulum = *title*. [13] prolatā = *made known*.

ipse Dominus sors, id est, [1]pars clericorum est. Qui autem vel ipse pars Domini est, vel Dominum partem habet, talem se exhibere debet, ut et ipse possideat Dominum, et possideatur a Domino.

Qui Dominum possidet, et cum prophetā dicit: Pars mea Dominus, nihil extra Dominum habere potest: quod si quidpiam aliud habuerit praeter Dominum, pars ejus non erit Dominus. [2]Verbi gratiā: si aurum, si argentum, si possessiones, si variam [3]supellectilem, cum istis partibus Dominus pars ejus fieri non dignabitur. Si autem ego pars Domini sum, habens victum et vestitum, his contentus ero, et nudam crucem nudus sequar.

[4]Mensulam tuam pauperes et peregrini et cum illis Christus conviva [5]noverit. [6]Negotiatorem clericum, et ex inope divitem, ex ignobili gloriosum, quasi quandam pestem fuge. Corrumpunt mores bonos confabulationes pessimae.

* * * * * *

Divinas Scripturas saepius lege, imo nunquam de manibus tuis sacra lectio deponatur. [7]Disce quod doceas: obtine eum qui secundum doctrinam est fidelem sermonem, ut possis exhortari in doctrinā sanā, et contradicentes revincere. Non confundant opera tua sermonem tuum: ne, cum in ecclesiā loqueris, tacitus quilibet respondeat: Cur ergo haec, quae dicis, ipse non facis?

* * * * * *

[8]Hospitiolum tuum aut raro aut nunquam mulierum pedes terant. Omnes puellas et virgines Christi aut aequaliter ignora, aut aequaliter dilige. Si propter officium clericatūs aut vidua a te visitatur, aut virgo, nunquam domum solus [9]introeas. Solus cum solā, secreto et absque arbitro vel teste [9]non sedeas. Si familiarius est aliquid loquendum: habet nutricem majorem domus, virginem, viduam, vel maritam: non est tam [10]inhumana ut nullum praeter te habeat, cui se audeat credere. Caveto omnes suspiciones, et quidquid probabiliter fingi potest, ne fingatur ante devita. Crebra munuscula, et [11]sudariola, et [12]fasciolas, et vestes ori applicatas, et oblatos ac [13]degustatos cibos, blandas et dulces

[1] pars = *portion.* [2] Verbi gratiā = *for example.* [3] supellectilem = *furniture.* [4] Mensulam, diminutive of mensa. [5] noverit, 89. [6] Negotiatorem clericum = *a clergyman in business.* [7] Disce quod doceas = *learn that you may teach,* 159. [8] Hospitiolum = *home.* [9] nunquam introeas... non sedeas, 99. [10] inhumana = *cut off from human society.* [11] sudariola = *napkins.* [12] fasciolas = *garters.* [13] degustatos = *slightly tasted.*

litterulas sanctus amor non habet. "Mel meum, lumen meum, meum desiderium." Omnes delicias et [1]lepores et risu dignas [2]urbanitates et caeteras ineptias amatorum in comoediis erubescimus, in saeculi hominibus detestamur: quanto magis in monachis et clericis, quorum et sacerdotium [3]proposito, et propositum ornatur sacerdotio? Non hoc dico, quod aut in te, aut in sanctis viris ista [4]formidem: sed quod in omni proposito, in omni gradu et sexu et boni et mali reperiuntur, malorumque condemnatio laus bonorum [4]sit.

* * * * * *

Docente te in ecclesiā, non clamor populi, sed gemitus suscitetur: lacrymae auditorum laudes tuae sint: sermo presbyteri scripturarum lectione conditus sit. Nolo te declamatorem esse, et [5]rabulam garrulumque sine ratione, sed mysteriorum peritum, et sacramentorum Dei tui eruditissimum. Verba volvere, et celeritate dicendi apud imperitum vulgus admirationem sui facere, [6]indoctorum hominum est. Nihil tam facile, quam [7]vilem plebiculam et indoctam [8]concionem linguae volubilitate decipere, quae quidquid non intelligit, plus miratur.

* * * * * *

Vestes [9]pullas aeque devita, ut candidas. Ornatūs ut [10]sordes pari modo fugiendae sunt: quia alterum delicias, alterum [11]gloriam redolet. Non [12]absque amictu lineo incedere, sed pretium vestium linearum non habere laudabile est: alioquin ridiculum et plenum dedecoris est, referto [13]marsupio, quod sudarium [14]orariumque non habeas [15]gloriari. Sunt, qui pauperibus paulum tribuunt, ut amplius accipiant, et sub praetextu [16]eleemosynae quaerunt divitias, quae magis venatio appellanda est, quam eleemosynae genus. Sic bestiae, sic aves, sic capiuntur et pisces. Modica in hamo [17]esca ponitur, ut matronarum in eo [18]sacculi protrahantur.

* * * * * *

Cave ne hominum [19]rumusculos [20]aucuperis, ne in [21]offensum Dei populorum laudem commutes. Si adhuc, inquit Apostolus, homi-

[1] lepores=*facetiousness.* [2] urbanitates=*jokes.* [3] propositum=*profession.* [4] formidem, 156. [5] rabulam=*a bawler.* [6] indoctorum hominum est, 27. [7] vilem plebiculam=*the low common people.* [8] concionem=*audience.* [9] pullas=*dark.* [10] sordes=*untidiness.* [11] gloriam=*ostentation.* [12] absque=sine, 207. [13] marsupium=*a purse.* [14] orarium=*handkerchief.* [15] gloriari=*to boast.* [16] eleemosyna=*alms.* [17] esca=*a bait.* [18] sacculi=*money-bags.* [19] rumusculos=*applause.* [20] aucuperis=*fish for.* [21] offensum Dei. Objective Gen., 24.

nibus placerem, Christi servus non essem. Per bonam famam et malam, a dextris et a sinistris, Christi miles graditur, nec laude extollitur, nec vituperatione frangitur: non divitiis tumet, non [1]contrahitur paupertate, et [2]laeta contemnit et [2]tristia: per diem sol non urit eum, neque luna per noctem.

* * * * * *

Cave quoque, ne aut linguam, aut aures habeas [3]prurientes: id est, ne aut ipse aliis [4]detrahas, aut alios audias detrahentes. Parce a detractione linguae: custodi sermones tuos: et scito, quia per cuncta, quae de aliis loqueris, tuā sententiā judicaris, et in his ipse [5]deprehenderis, quae in aliis [6]arguebas. Neque vero illa justa est excusatio: [7]Referentibus aliis injuriam facere non possum. Nemo invito auditori libenter refert. Sagitta in lapidem nunquam figitur, interdum resiliens percutit dirigentem. Discat detractor, dum te videt non libenter audire, non facile detrahere. Cum detractoribus, ait Solomon, ne miscearis: quoniam repente veniet perditio eorum, et ruinam utriusque quis novit? tam videlicet ejus qui detrahit, quam illius qui accommodat aurem detrahenti.

Officii tui est visitare [8]languentes, nosse domos matronarum et liberos earum, et nobilium virorum custodire secreta. Officii tui sit, non solum oculos castos servare, sed et linguam. Nunquam de formis mulierum disputes, nec quid agatur in aliā, domus alia per te noverit. Hippocrates adjurat discipulos suos antequam [9]doceat, et in verba sua jurare compellit, [10]extorquet sacramento silentium, sermonem, incessum, habitum moresque praescribit. Quanto magis nos, quibus animarum medicina commissa est, omnium Christianorum domos debemus amare, quasi proprias? Consolatores potius nos in maeroribus suis, quam convivas in prosperis noverint. Facile contemnitur clericus, qui saepe vocatus ad prandium, ire non recusat.

Nunquam petentes, raro accipiamus rogati. Beatius enim est magis dare quam accipere. Nescio quo enim modo etiam ipse, qui deprecatur ut tribuat, cum acceperis, viliorem te judicat: et mirum in modum, si eum rogantem contempseris, plus te posterius veneratur.

Extracts from Ep. ad Nepotianum.

[1] contrahitur = *abased*. [2] laeta, tristia, 200. [3] prurientes = *itching*, II Tim. iv, 3. [4] detrahere = *slander*. [5] deprehenderis = *you are caught*. [6] arguebas = *you were reproving*. [7] Referentibus aliis = *when others tell stories*. [8] languentes = *the sick*. [9] doceat, 153. [10] extorquet = *exacts*.

Augustine (died 430), Bishop of Hippo, the most famous of the Latin Fathers, was born in Tagaste in Numidia. His father Patricius was a man of humble origin and indifferent character, his mother Monnica was a devout Christian woman who has been immortalised by her son in his Confessions. According to his own account he was not a diligent scholar, although his parents tried to give him the best education that was possible at the time. He never mastered Greek, much to his own disadvantage. After a dissolute youth he joined the sect of the Manichaeans, and, finally, after a long period of spiritual struggle, he was converted to Catholic Christianity by the influence of his mother and the teaching of Ambrose, Bishop of Milan. He was baptized in 387 in the 33rd year of his age, and gave up his profession as a teacher of rhetoric in order that he might retire from the world into a religious community. Shortly after this his mother died at Ostia and he returned to Africa where he was consecrated Bishop of Hippo in 395. His influence extended far beyond his unimportant see.

By his letters and his treatises he influenced the whole Christian world, and has influenced it ever since. Probably no Christian teacher after the time of the Apostles ever had such influence both for good and evil. Both the supporters of the ecclesiastical system of the middle ages and the German and French reformers claimed to found their teaching on the writings of Augustine.

Augustine's style is difficult and strikingly original. Only two passages from his voluminous writings are included here: both from the Confessions.

Of the two passages from the Confessions the first gives his account of his education, and is interesting because of his curiously modern views with regard to the "direct method" in language teaching, and for the preference which he shows for the Gradgrind type of education in "facts" in comparison with the training of the higher faculties of imagination and susceptibility through literature and humanism.

The general sentiment of the Church did not follow him in this: the common-sense of the Italian temperament prevailed over the rigor of the fiery African.

It would have been well for himself as well as for the Church at large if Augustine had not counted such natural feelings to be a sin, but had imbibed a little more of the humanity of Vergil,

> majestic in his sadness
> At the doubtful doom of human kind,

and of the spirit of the famous line

> Sunt lacrymae rerum, et mentem mortalia tangunt.

In the second extract we see Augustine at his best, not as the pitiless logician, or as the victorious controversialist, but as a man.

Augustine's works are accessible as a whole in Migne, Patrologia Latina, and portions of them are published in SS. Patrum Opuscula, by the Oxford and Cambridge Presses, and in the Loeb Library. An excellent translation of the Confessions by Dr Bigg is published by Methuen.

De miseriis Augustini in pueritia.

Deus, Deus meus, quas ibi miserias expertus sum et [1]ludificationes: [2]quandoquidem recte mihi vivere puero id proponebatur, [3]obtemperare monentibus, ut in hoc saeculo florerem, et excellerem [4]lignosis artibus, ad honorem hominum et falsas divitias [5]famulantibus. Inde in scholam datus sum ut discerem litteras, in quibus quid utilitatis esset ignorabam miser, et tamen si segnis in discendo [6]essem, [7]vapulabam. Laudabatur enim hoc a majoribus; et multi ante nos vitam istam agentes, praestruxerant [8]aerumnas vias, per quas transire cogebamur, multiplicato labore et dolore filiis Adam. [9]Invenimus autem, Domine, homines rogantes te, et didicimus ab eis, sentientes te, ut poteramus, esse magnum aliquem, qui posses, etiam non apparens sensibus nostris, exaudire nos, et subvenire nobis. Nam puer coepi rogare te, auxilium et refugium meum, et in [10]tuam invocationem rumpebam nodos linguae meae, et rogabam te parvus, non parvo affectu, ne in scholā vapularem. Et cum me non exaudiebas, [11]quod non erat ad insipientiam mihi, ridebantur a majoribus hominibus, usque ab ipsis parentibus, qui mihi accidere mali nihil volebant, [12]plagae meae, magnum tunc et grave malum meum.

* * * * * *

Quid autem [13]erat causae cur Graecas [14]litteras oderam, quibus puerulus imbuebar, ne nunc quidem mihi satis exploratum est.

[1] ludificationes = *delusions.* [2] quandoquidem... = *since this was set before me as the right way for a boy to live.* [3] obtemperare monentibus explains 'id,' 145. [4] lignosis artibus = *dry or tough studies.* [5] famulantibus agrees with artibus = *enslaved to.* [6] essem, 171. [7] vapulabam = *I was flogged.* [8] aerumnas, here used as an adjective = *grievous.* [9] Invenimus... = *Yet we found men, O Lord, who prayed to Thee, and we learnt from them, perceiving, as far as we were able, that Thou wert some great Being who couldst hear us.* [10] tuam invocationem. Possessive pronoun in sense of obj. gen., 25. [11] quod non erat ad insipientiam mihi. Cf. Ps. xxi, 3 Deus meus, clamabo per diem et non exaudies me: et nocte et non ad insipientiam mihi. Translate: *which Thou didst not reckon as folly to me.* [12] plagae meae. Subject of ridebantur. [13] erat. For the Ind. in indirect questions, see 143, 144. [14] litteras, trans. *studies.*

[1]Adamaveram enim Latinas, non quas primi magistri, sed quas docent qui [2]grammatici vocantur. Nam [3]illas primas ubi legere et scribere et numerare discitur, non minus onerosas poenalesque habebam, quam omnes Graecas. Unde tamen et hoc nisi de peccato et vanitate vitae, qua caro eram et spiritus ambulans et non revertens? Nam utique meliores, quia certiores erant primae illae litterae, quibus fiebat in me, et factum est, [4]et habeo illud ut et legam si quid scriptum invenio, et scribam ipse si quid volo, quam illae quibus [5]tenere cogebar [6]Aeneae nescio cujus errores, oblitus errorum meorum, et plorare Didonem mortuam, quia se occidit ob amorem, cum interea meipsum in his a te morientem, Deus vita mea, siccis oculis ferrem miserrimus.

* * * * * *

At enim [7]vela pendent liminibus grammaticarum scholarum: sed non illa magis honorem secreti, quam tegumentum erroris significant. Non clament adversum me venditores grammaticae vel emptores; quia, si proponam eis, interrogans utrum sit verum quod [8]Aeneam aliquando Carthaginem venisse poeta dicit; indoctiores se nescire respondebunt, doctiores autem etiam negabunt verum esse.

At si quaeram quibus litteris scribatur Aeneae nomen, omnes mihi, qui haec didicerunt, verum respondebunt, secundum id pactum et placitum, quo inter se homines ista signa [9]firmarunt.

[10]Item, si quaeram quid horum majore hujus vitae incommodo quisque obliviscatur, legere et scribere, an poetica illa figmenta, quis non videat quid responsurus sit, qui non est penitus oblitus sui? Peccabam ergo puer cum illa inania istis utilioribus amore praeponebam, vel potius ista oderam, illa amabam.

Jamvero unum et unum duo, duo et duo quatuor, odiosa cantio mihi erat, et dulcissimum spectaculum vanitatis equus ligneus plenus armatis et Trojae incendium, atque ipsius umbra Creusae.

Cur ergo Graecam etiam grammaticam oderam talia cantantem?

[1] Adamaveram=*I had taken a fancy to.* [2] grammatici=*teachers of literature.* [3] illas primas, understand litteras. [4] et habeo illud ut et legam, etc., 145. [5] tenere=*to remember.* [6] Aeneae nescio cujus=*of one Aeneas.* [7] vela=*curtains.* [8] Aeneam aliquando venisse, in apposition with 'quod.' [9] firmarunt =*have established.* [10] Item, si quaeram, etc. =*And if I ask which of these things, namely to read and to write, or these poetic fables, would cause the greatest inconvenience in this life to any one who should forget them.*

Nam et Homerus peritus texere tales fabulas, et dulcissime vanus est, et mihi tamen amarus erat puero.

[1]Credo etiam Graecis pueris Virgilius ita sit, cum eum sic discere coguntur, ut ego illum. Videlicet difficultas, difficultas omnino ediscendae peregrinae linguae, quasi [2]felle aspergebat omnes suavitates Graecas fabulosarum narrationum. Nulla enim verba illa noveram, et saevis terroribus ac poenis ut nossem [3]instabatur mihi vehementer. Nam et Latina aliquando infans nulla noveram; et tamen [4]advertendo didici sine ullo metu et cruciatu, inter etiam blandimenta nutricum et joca arridentium et laetitias alludentium. Didici vero illa sine poenali onere urgentium cum me urgeret cor meum ad parienda concepta sua, quae non possem, nisi aliqua verba didicissem, non a docentibus sed a loquentibus, [5]in quorum et ego auribus parturiebam quidquid sentiebam. Hinc satis elucet majorem habere vim ad discenda ista liberam curiositatem, quam [6]meticulosam necessitatem.

Confessions i, 14, 20, 22, 23 (selections).

AUGUSTINI ORATIO PRO MONNICA MATRE SUA.

Ego autem, jam sanato corde ab illo [7]vulnere in quo poterat [8]redargui carnalis affectus, fundo tibi, Deus noster, pro illā famulā tuā longe aliud lacrymarum genus, quod manat de concusso spiritu [9]consideratione periculorum omnis animae quae in Adam moritur. Quamquam illa in Christo vivificata, etiam nondum a carne resoluta, sic vixerit ut laudetur nomen tuum in fide moribusque ejus; non tamen audeo dicere, ex quo eam per Baptismum regenerasti, nullum verbum exisse ex ore ejus contra praeceptum tuum. Et dictum est a Veritate Filio tuo: Si quis dixerit fratri suo, Fatue, reus erit gehennae ignis.

Et vae etiam laudabili vitae hominum, [10]si, remotā misericordiā, discutias eam. Quia vero non exquiris delicta vehementer, [11]fiducialiter speramus aliquem apud te locum. Quisquis autem tibi

[1] Credo Graecis pueris... = *I believe that Vergil is as hateful to Greek boys when they are compelled to learn him in the same way, as I was compelled to learn Homer.* [2] felle = *with gall.* [3] instabatur = *pressure was brought to bear on me.* [4] advertendo = *by paying attention.* [5] in quorum auribus, etc. = *in whose ears I was travailing to express my thoughts.* [6] meticulosam necessitatem = *pedantic compulsion.* [7] vulnere, i.e. *the grief that he felt at the death of his mother.* [8] redargui = *be blamed.* [9] consideratione = *at the thought of.* [10] si, remotā misericordiā, discutias = *if thou shouldst sift it without pity.* [11] fiducialiter = *confidently.*

enumerat vera merita sua, quid tibi enumerat nisi munera tua? [1]O si cognoscant se homines homines; et qui gloriatur, in Domino glorietur.

Ego itaque, laus mea et vita mea, Deus cordis mei, sepositis paulisper bonis ejus actibus, pro quibus tibi gaudens gratias ago, nunc pro peccatis matris meae deprecor te: exaudi me per Medicinam vulnerum nostrorum, quae pependit in ligno, et sedens ad dexteram tuam interpellat te pro nobis. Scio misericorditer operatam, et ex corde dimisisse debita debitoribus suis: dimitte illi et tu debita sua, si quā etiam contraxit per tot annos post aquam salutis. Dimitte, Domine, dimitte obsecro, ne intres cum ea in judicium. [2]Superexaltet misericordia judicio, quoniam [3]eloquia tua vera sunt, et promisisti misericordiam misericordibus: quod ut essent, tu dedisti eis, qui misereberis cui misertus eris, et misericordiam praestabis cui misericors fueris.

Et credo [4]quod jam feceris quod te rogo, sed [5]voluntaria oris mei approba, Domine. Namque illā imminente die resolutionis suae non cogitavit suum corpus sumptuose contegi, aut condiri aromatibus, aut monumentum electum concupivit, aut curavit sepulcrum patrium; non ista mandavit nobis; sed tantummodo [6]memoriam sui ad altare tuum fieri desideravit, cui nullius diei praetermissione servierat, unde sciret dispensari victimam sanctam, quā deletum est [7]chirographum, quod erat contrarium nobis, quā triumphatus est hostis computans delicta nostra, et quaerens quid objiciat, et nihil inveniens in illo, in quo vincimus. Quis ei refundet innocentem sanguinem? Quis ei restituet pretium, quo nos emit, ut nos auferat [8]ei? Ad cujus pretii nostri sacramentum ligavit ancilla tua animam suam vinculo fidei. Nemo a protectione tuā disrumpat eam. Non se interponat nec vi nec insidiis leo et draco; neque enim respondebit illa nihil se debere, ne convincatur et obtineatur ab accusatore callido; sed respondebit dimissa debita sua ab eo, cui nemo reddet quod pro nobis, non debens, reddidit.

Sit ergo in pace cum viro, ante quem nulli, et post quem nulli, nupta est; cui servivit [9]fructum tibi afferens cum tolerantiā, ut eum quoque [10]lucraretur tibi.

[1] O si cognoscant, etc. = *O that men may know themselves to be but men.*
[2] Superexaltet misericordia judicio, Jas. ii, 13. [3] eloquia = *words.* [4] quod jam feceris, 112–115, 135. [5] voluntaria = *the free-will offerings of my mouth.*
[6] memoriam sui, objective gen., 24. [7] chirographum = *the handwriting,* Col. ii, 14. [8] ei: that is, *from the devil.* [9] fructum, i.e. *Augustine her son.*
[10] lucraretur = *that she might gain.*

Et inspira, Domine Deus meus, inspira servis tuis fratribus meis, filiis tuis, dominis meis, quibus et corde et voce et litteris servio, ut [1]quotquot haec legerint, meminerint ad altare tuum Monnicae famulae tuae, cum Patricio quondam ejus conjuge, per quorum carnem introduxisti me in hanc vitam, quemadmodum nescio.

Meminerint cum affectu pio parentum meorum in hāc luce transitoriā, et [2]fratrum meorum sub te Patre in matre Catholicā, et civium meorum in aeternā Jerusalem, cui suspirat [3]peregrinatio populi tui ab exitu usque ad reditum; ut, quod a me illa poposcit extremum, [4]uberius ei praestetur in multorum orationibus, per confessiones, quam per orationes meas.

Confessions ix, 34.

Bede (died 735), a monk of Jarrow, was among the greatest scholars of the early middle ages. He was acquainted with all the knowledge of his day although he never travelled out of England. He had read the Latin Classics as well as the Latin Fathers and had some knowledge of Greek and Hebrew. His most famous work is the History of the Saxon Church from which some extracts are here given.

His style shows considerable departure even from the Latin of the early Fathers, but this is only to be expected considering the barbarous times in which he lived and the distance that separated Jarrow from Italy. When he makes use of Classical expressions his correctness is rather that of a scholar who has learnt his style from books, than that of an original writer who is taking his part in the development of a language. The study of his works makes us marvel at the vigour of the Latin language which could extend its influence so far. The learning of Bede, handed on by Alcuin to the schools of Charlemagne, did much to help the first revival of letters in Europe.

De vita Beati Papae Gregorii.

Beatus papa Gregorius natione erat Romanus, a patre Gordiano, genus a [5]proavis non solum nobile sed [6]religiosum ducens. Felix denique ejusdem apostolicae sedis quondam episcopus, vir magnae gloriae in Christo et ecclesiā, ejus fuit [7]atavus. Nobilitatem vero

[1] quotquot = *as many as.* [2] fratrum. Augustine calls his parents his brethren because they had one Father in God and one Mother in the Church. [3] peregrinatio = *pilgrimage.* [4] uberius = *more abundantly.* [5] proavis = *ancestors.* [6] religiosum = *attached to the observances of religion.* [7] atavus = *the father of his great grandfather.*

illam quam ad [1]saeculum videbatur habere, totam [2]ad nanciscendam supernae gloriam dignitatis divinā gratiā [3]largiente convertit. Nam mutato repente habitu [4]saeculari, monasterium petiit, in quo tantā perfectionis gratiā coepit [5]conversari, ut, sicut ipse postea [6]flendo solebat adtestari, nulla nisi caelestia cogitare [7]soleret, ut etiam retentus corpore, ipsa jam carnis [8]claustra contemplatione transiret, ut mortem quoque, quae paene cunctis poena est, ut ingressum vitae, et laboris sui praemium amaret. Hoc autem ipse de se, non profecto [9]jactando virtutem, sed deflendo potius defectum, quem sibi per curam pastoralem incucurrisse videbatur, referre consueverat. Mox [10]pontificali functus officio domum suam monasterium facere curavit. Quin etiam dum alii pontifices construendis ornandisque ecclesiis auro vel argento operam dabant, hic autem quidquid pecuniae habuerat sedulus hoc dare pauperibus curabat, ut justitia ejus maneret [11]in saeculum saeculi, et cornu ejus exaltaretur in gloriā.

Ad cujus pietatis et justitiae opus pertinet etiam hoc, [12]quod nostram gentem per praedicatores quos huc direxit de dentibus antiqui hostis eripiens, aeternae libertatis fecit participem. Nec silentio praetereunda [13]opinio quae de beato Gregorio traditione majorum ad nos usque perlata est: quā videlicet ex causā admonitus, tam sedulam erga salutem nostrae gentis curam gesserit. [14]Dicunt quia die quādam cum, advenientibus nuper mercatoribus, multa [15]venalia in forum fuissent conlata, multique ad emendum confluxissent, et ipsum Gregorium inter alios advenisse, ac vidisse inter alia pueros venales positos, [16]candidi corporis et venusti

[1] saeculum=*an age*, hence *this life*. [2] ad nanciscendam supernae gloriam dignitatis=*to obtaining the glory of the heavenly crown*, 190. [3] largiente=*granting*. [4] saecularis=*worldly*. Compare the use of the expression *secular clergy* in opposition to *regular clergy*. [5] conversari=*to live, to behave one's self*. Compare the use of the word *conversation* in A.V. of Gal. i, 13, Jas. iii, 13. [6] flendo=*weeping*, 188. [7] soleret, transiret, amaret, consecutive, 163. [8] claustra=*bonds*. [9] jactando=*by way of boasting*, 191. [10] pontificali, i.e. *he was made Pope*. The Bishops of Rome took over this title from the ancient Romans. For the case see 57. [11] in saeculum saeculi=*for ever and ever*. [12] quod=*namely that*. It is easy to see from an example like this how clauses introduced by 'quod' came to be used as noun clauses. See 112–115. [13] opinio =*story*. [14] dicunt quia. Two const. are confused in this sentence. Bede began by writing a subordinate clause introduced by 'quia' after the verb 'dicunt' which should have contained verbs in the indicative or subj. mood: he however turned off into the ordinary Classical const. of the Acc. and Inf. and wrote the verbs in the Inf., leaving 'quia' in the air. See 112–115 and 130, 132. [15] venalia=*objects for sale*. [16] candidi corporis, 26.

vultūs, capillorum quoque [1]formā egregiā. Quos cum aspiceret, interrogavit, ut aiunt, de quā regione vel terrā [2]essent adlati. Dictumque est quod de Britanniā insulā, cujus incolae talis essent aspectūs. Rursus interrogavit utrum iidem insulani Christiani an paganis adhuc erroribus [2]essent implicati. Dictumque est quod essent pagani. At ille intimo ex corde longa trahens suspiria "Heu," inquit, "quod tam lucidi vultūs homines tenebrarum auctor possidet." Rursus ergo interrogavit, [2]quod esset vocabulum illius gentis. Responsum est quod Angli vocarentur. At ille "Bene," inquit, "nam et angelicam habent faciem, et tales angelorum in caelis decet esse coheredes. Quod habet nomen ipsa provincia de quā isti sunt adlati?" Responsum est quod Deiri vocarentur iidem provinciales. At ille: "Bene," inquit, "Deiri, de irā eruti, et ad misericordiam Christi vocati. Rex provinciae illius quomodo appellatur?" Responsum est quod Aella diceretur. At ille adludens ad nomen ait: "Alleluia: laudem Dei creatoris illis in partibus oportet cantari."

Accedensque ad pontificem Romanae et apostolicae sedis, nondum erat enim ipse pontifex factus, rogavit ut [3]genti Anglorum in Britanniam aliquos verbi ministros, per quos ad Christum converteretur, mitteret. Mox ipse, pontificatūs officio functus, perfecit opus diu desideratum, praedicatores ad Britanniam mittens, et ipse praedicationem, ut fructificaret, suis exhortationibus ac precibus adjuvans.

Rexit ecclesiam temporibus imperatorum Mauricii et Focatis. Secundo autem ejusdem Focatis anno transiens ex hāc vitā migravit ad veram quae in caelis est vitam. Sepultus vero est corpore in ecclesiā beati Petri apostoli; scriptum est in tumbā epitaphium hujusmodi:

Suscipe, terra, tuo corpus de corpore sumptum,
Reddere quod [4]valeas, vivificante Deo.
Spiritus astra petit, leti nil jura nocebunt
Cui vitae alterius mors magis ipsa via est.
Pontificis summi hoc clauduntur membra sepulcro,
Qui innumeris semper vivit ubique bonis.
[5]Esuriem [6]dapibus superavit, frigora veste,

[1] formā egregiā, 56. [2] essent adlati, essent implicati, quod esset vocabulum, 143. [3] genti, 39. [4] valeas... =*which thou mayest have power to give back when God quickeneth it*, 150 (2). [5] Esuriem =*hunger*. [6] dapibus =*by feasts*.

Atque animas monitis texit ab hoste sacris.
Implebat actu quidquid sermone docebat,
Esset ut exemplum, mystica verba loquens.
Ad Christum Anglos convertit pietate magistrā,
Adquirens fidei agmina gente novā.
Hic labor, hoc studium, haec tibi cura, hoc [1]pastor agebas,
Ut Domino offerres plurima lucra gregis.
Hisque, Dei consul, factus laetare triumphis:
Nam mercedem operum jam sine fine tenes.

Hist. Ecc., Book 2 (adapted).

De adventu Augustini ad praedicandum genti Anglorum.

Anno ab incarnatione Domini quingentesimo octogesimo secundo, regnante imperatore Mauricio, Gregorius, vir doctrinā et actione praecipuus, pontificatum Romanum et apostolicae sedis [2]sortitus, misit servum Dei Augustinum et alios plures cum eo monachos timentes Dominum [3]praedicare verbum Dei genti Anglorum.

[4]Qui cum jussis pontificalibus obtemperantes hoc opus adgredi coepissent, perculsi timore, redire domum potius, quam barbaram, feram, incredulamque gentem, cujus ne linguam quidem [5]nossent, adire cogitabant et hoc esse tutius communi consilio decernebant.

Nec mora, Augustinum, quem eis [6]episcopum ordinandum si ab Anglis susciperentur disposuerat, domum remittunt, qui a beato Gregorio humili supplicatu [7]obtineret ne tam periculosam, tam laboriosam, tam incertam peregrinationem adire deberent. [4]Quibus ille exhortatorias mittens litteras, in opus [8]eos verbi, divino confisos auxilio, proficisci suadet. Quarum videlicet litterarum ista est forma:

"Gregorius servus servorum Dei, servis Domini nostri. Quia melius fuerat bona non incipere, quam ab his quae coepta sunt, cogitatione retrorsum redire, summo studio, dilectissimi filii, oportet ut opus bonum, quod auxiliante Deo coepistis, impleatis.

[1] pastor=*as shepherd.* [2] sortitus=*having been allotted.* [3] praedicare, 157*a*, 162. [4] Qui=*but they*, 66. [5] nossent, the subj. is used because the words state their thought indirectly. Their actual thought was "Ne linguam quidem novimus." [6] episcopum ordinandum=*to be ordained bishop*, 188. [7] qui obtineret=*to obtain*, 150 (2). [8] eos, the acc. where the dat. would have been used in Cl. L., 37.

Nec labor ergo vos itineris, nec [1]maledicorum hominum linguae deterreant: sed omni instantiā, omnique fervore, quae inchoastis, Deo auctore, peragite: [2]scientes quod laborem magnum major aeternae retributionis gloria sequitur. [3]Remeanti autem Augustino, praeposito vestro, quem et abbatem vobis constituimus, in omnibus humiliter obedite. Omnipotens Deus suā vos gratiā [4]protegat, et vestri laboris fructum in aeternā me patriā videre concedat; quatenus etsi vobiscum laborare nequeo, simul in gaudio retributionis inveniar, quia laborare scilicet volo. Deus vos incolumes custodiat, dilectissimi filii."

Roboratus ergo confirmatione patris Gregorii, Augustinus cum famulis Christi, qui erant cum eo, rediit in opus verbi, pervenitque Britanniam. Erat eo tempore rex Aedilberctus in Cantiā potentissimus. Est autem ad orientalem Cantiae plagam Tanatos insula non modica. In hāc ergo [5]adplicuit Augustinus et socii ejus.

Acceperunt autem de gente Francorum interpretes, et mittens ad Aedilberctum, [6]mandavit se venisse [7]de Romā, ac nuntium ferre optimum, qui [8]sibi obtemperantibus aeterna in caelis gaudia, et regnum sine fine cum Deo vivo et vero futurum sine ullā dubietate [9]promitteret. [10]Qui haec audiens, manere illos in eā, quam aderant insulā, et eis necessaria ministrari, donec videret quid eis faceret jussit. Nam et antea fama ad eum Christianae religionis pervenerat, utpote qui uxorem habebat Christianam de gente Francorum regiā, [11]vocabulō Bercta; quam eā conditione a parentibus acceperat, ut ritum fidei ac religionis suae cum episcopo quem ei adjutorem fidei dederant, nomine Liudhardo, inviolatum servare licentiam haberet. Post dies ergo venit ad insulam rex, et residens [12]sub divo, jussit Augustinum cum sociis [13]ad suum ibidem advenire colloquium. Caverat enim ne in aliquam domum ad se introirent, vetere usus augurio, ne [14]superventu suo, si quid maleficae artis habuissent, eum superando deciperent. At illi non daemonicā sed divinā virtute praediti veniebant, crucem pro

[1] maledicorum=*men of strange speech.* [2] scientes=*because you know*, 183. [3] Remeanti. For the use of the present participle to denote action previous to the main verb see 177, 178. Trans. *When Augustine returns.* [4] protegat, 101. [5] adplicuit=*landed.* [6] mandavit=*he stated.* [7] de Roma, 45, 211. [8] sibi=*to those that obeyed it.* This is rather a loose use of 'sibi,' 61. [9] promitteret, 150 (1). [10] See p. 139, n. 4. [11] vocabulō Bercta=*Bertha by name.* [12] sub divo=*in the open air.* Cf. Vitamque sub divo et trepidis agat in rebus, Hor. 3. 2, 5. [13] ad suum colloquium=*to speak with him*, 25. [14] superventu suo=*by their craft.*

[1]vexillo ferentes argenteam, et imaginem Domini Salvatoris in tabulā depictam, [2]litaniasque canentes, pro suā simul et eorum ad quos venerant salute aeternā Domino supplicabant. Cumque ad jussionem regis residentes, verbum ei vitae praedicarent, respondet ille dicens: "Pulcra sunt quidem verba et promissa quae adfertis; sed quia nova sunt, et incerta, non his possum adsensum tribuere, relictis eis quae [3]tanto tempore cum omni Anglorum gente servavi. Verum quia de longe huc peregrini venistis, et ut ego mihi videor perspexisse, ea quae vos vera et optima credebatis, nobis quoque communicare desiderastis, nolumus molesti esse vobis: quin potius benigno vos hospitio recipere, et quae victui sunt vestro necessaria, ministrare curamus; nec prohibemus quin omnes quos potestis fidei vestrae religionis praedicando societis."

Dedit ergo eis mansionem in civitate Doruvernensi, quae imperii sui totius erat metropolis, eisque, ut promiserat, cum administratione victūs temporalis, licentiam quoque praedicandi non abstulit. Fertur autem quia adpropinquantes civitati, more suo cum cruce sanctā, et imagine magni regis Domini nostri Jesu Christi, hanc litaniam consonā voce modularentur: "Deprecamur te, Domine, in omni misericordiā tuā, ut auferatur furor tuus et ira a civitate istā, et de domo sanctā tuā, quoniam peccavimus. Alleluia."

At ubi datam sibi mansionem intraverant, coeperunt apostolicam primitivae ecclesiae vitam imitari; orationibus videlicet assiduis, vigiliis, et jejuniis [4]serviendo, verbum vitae quibus poterant praedicando, cuncta hujus mundi velut aliena spernendo, ea tantum quae victui necessaria videbantur, ab eis quos docebant, accipiendo, secundum ea quae docebant ipsi per omnia vivendo.

[5]Quid mora? Crediderunt nonnulli et baptizabantur, mirantes simplicitatem innocentis vitae, ac dulcedinem doctrinae eorum caelestis. Erat autem prope ipsam civitatem ad orientem ecclesia in honorem Sancti Martini [6]antiquitus facta dum adhuc Romani Britanniam incolerent, in quā regina, quam Christianam fuisse praediximus, orare consueverat. In hāc ergo et ipsi primo convenire, psallere, orare, missas facere, praedicare et baptizare coeperunt; donec, rege ad fidem converso, majorem praedicandi per omnia, et ecclesias fabricandi vel restaurandi licentiam acciperent.

[1] vexillum = *a banner.* [2] litaneas = *litanies.* [3] tanto tempore, 55. [4] serviendo, praedicando, spernendo, accipiendo, vivendo. For the use of the ablative of the Gerund in the sense of a present participle see 188. [5] Quid mora = *why say more?* [6] antiquitus, an adverb = *in ancient times.*

At ubi ipse etiam inter alios delectatus vitā mundissimā sanctorum, et promissis eorum suavissimis, quae vera esse miraculorum quoque multorum ostensione firmaverant, credens baptizatus est, coeperunt ad audiendum verbum confluere, ac, relicto gentilitatis ritu, unitati se sanctae Christi ecclesiae [1]credendo sociare.

Hist. Ecc. (adapted).

De colloquio Augustini cum Episcopis Brittonum.

Interea Augustinus [2]adjutorio usus Aedilbercti, convocavit [3]ad suum colloquium episcopos proximae Brittonum provinciae, coepitque eis fraternā admonitione suadere, ut pace catholicā secum habitā, communem evangelizandi gentibus pro Domino laborem susciperent. Non enim [4]Paschae Dominicum diem suo tempore, sed a quartā decimā usque ad vicesimam lunam observabant, et alia plurima unitati ecclesiasticae contraria faciebant. Qui cum longā disputatione habitā neque precibus, neque hortamentis, neque increpationibus Augustini ac sociorum ejus assensum praebere voluissent, sed suas potius traditiones universis, quae per orbem sibi in Christo concordant, ecclesiis praeferrent, sanctus pater Augustinus hunc laboriosi atque longi certaminis finem fecit [5]ut diceret: "Obsecremus Deum, qui habitare facit unanimes in domo Patris sui, ut nobis [6]insinuare caelestibus signis dignetur, quae sequenda traditio, quibus sit viis ad ingressum regni illius properandum. Adducatur aliquis aeger, et per cujus preces fuerit [7]curatus, hujus fides et [8]operatio Deo [9]devota atque omnibus sequenda credatur." Quod cum adversarii inviti licet concederent, allatus est quidam de genere Anglorum oculorum [10]luce privatus: qui cum oblatus Brittonum sacerdotibus, nil [11]curationis vel sanationis horum ministerio perciperet; tandem Augustinus justā necessitate compulsus, flectit genua sua ad Patrem Domini nostri Jesu Christi, deprecans ut visum caeco quem amiserat, restitueret, et per illuminationem unius hominis corporalem, in plurimorum corde fidelium spiritalis gratiam lucis accenderet. Nec mora, illuminatur caecus, ac verus summae lucis [12]praeco ab omnibus praedicatur Augustinus. Tum Brittones confitentur quidem in-

[1] See p. 141, n. 4. [2] adjutorio = *help*. [3] ad suum colloquium = *to converse with him*, 25. [4] Paschae Dominicum diem = *the feast of Easter*. [5] ut diceret = *by saying*; consecutive subj. [6] insinuare = *to explain*; Acts xvii, 3 Vg. [7] curare = *to cure*. [8] operatio = *practice*. [9] devota = *consecrated*. [10] luce privatus, 46. [11] curatio = *cure*. [12] praeco = *herald*.

tellexisse se veram esse viam justitiae, quam [1]praedicaret Augustinus: sed non se posse [2]absque suorum consensu ac licentiā priscis abdicare moribus. Unde postulabant ut secundus synodus pluribus advenientibus foret. Quod cum esset statutum, venerunt, ut perhibent, septem Brittonum episcopi et plures viri doctissimi, qui ad prefatum [3]ituri concilium, venerunt primo ad virum quendam sanctum et prudentem consulentes an ad praedicationem Augustini suas deserere traditiones deberent. Qui respondebat: "Si homo Dei est sequimini illum." Dixerunt: "Et unde hoc possumus probare?" At ille: "Dominus," inquit, "ait: 'Tollite jugum meum super vos, et discite a me quia mitis sum et humilis corde.' Si ergo Augustinus ille mitis est et humilis corde, credibile est [4]quia jugum Christi et ipse portet, et vobis [5]portandum offert: sin autem immitis ac superbus est, constat [6]quia non est de Deo, neque nobis ejus sermo [7]curandus." [8]Qui rursus aiebant, "Et unde vel hoc dinoscere valemus?" "Procurate," inquit, "ut ipse prior cum suis ad locum synodi adveniat, et si vobis adpropinquantibus adsurrexerit, scientes [4]quia famulus Christi est, obtemperanter illum audite: sin autem vos spreverit, nec coram vobis adsurgere voluerit, cum sitis numero plures, et ipse spernatur a vobis." Fecerunt ut dixerat. Factumque est, ut venientibus illis sederet Augustinus in sellā. Quod illi videntes mox in iram conversi sunt, [9]eumque notantes superbiae, cunctis quae dicebat contradicere laborabant. Dicebat autem eis, "In multis quidem nostrae consuetudini, immo [10]universalis ecclesiae contraria geritis: et tamen si in tribus his mihi obtemperare vultis; ut Pascha suo tempore celebretis, ut ministerium baptizandi, quo Deo renascimur, juxta morem sanctae Romanae et apostolicae ecclesiae compleatis, ut genti Anglorum unā nobiscum verbum Domini praedicetis, caetera quae agitis, quamvis moribus nostris contraria, aequanimiter cuncta tolerabimus."

At illi nil horum se facturos, neque illum pro archiepiscopo habituros esse respondebant: conferentes [11]ad invicem dicebant, "Si modo nobis adsurgere noluit, quanto magis si ei subditos esse coeperimus jam nos pro nihilo contemnet."

Hist. Ecc.

[1] praedicaret, 150 (3). [2] absque, 207. [3] ituri = *when they were about to go, or before they went*, 179, 183. [4] quia, 112–115. [5] portandum offert = *offers you to carry*, 192. [6] quia, 116. [7] curandus = *is any heed to be paid*, 192. [8] Qui, 66. [9] eumque notantes superbiae = *and censuring him for his pride.* [10] universalis ecclesiae, understand 'consuetudine.' [11] ad invicem, 70.

Adamnan (died 704), ninth abbot of Iona. Famous for his life of Columba the founder of that monastery. This work consists chiefly of a chronicle of the miracles of Columba; but the last chapters which tell the story of his death are so simple and beautiful as to warrant the inclusion of practically the whole of them in this book. The style is barbarous, so much so that a few alterations have been made to bring the more unusual expressions within the comprehension of the student.

De vita et de transitu ad Dominum Sancti Columbae.

Sanctus Columba, de stirpe nobile [1]Scoticae gentis ortus, anno aetatis suae quadringesimo secundo pro Christo [2]peregrinari volens, de [3]Scotiā in Britanniam demigravit. [4]Qui [5]et a puero Christiano deditus [6]tirocinio et sapientiae studiis, [7]integritatem corporis et animae puritatem, Deo donante, custodiens, quamvis in terrā positus, caelestibus se moribus aptum ostendebat. Nullum etiam [8]vel unius horae intervallum transiri poterat, quo non aut orationi aut lectioni aut scripturae aut alicui operi incumberet. [9]Jejunationum quoque et vigiliarum indefessis laboribus sine ullā intermissione die noctuque occupatus est. Et inter haec omnibus carus, [10]hilarem semper faciem ostendens, Spiritūs Sancti gaudio intimis laetificabatur [11]praecordiis. Diu insulam Ionam habitavit quae juxta oras terrae Pictorum in mare sita est, et ibi monasterium collocavit. Tum demum cum jam triginta annos in illā insulā complevisset, illo ipso die, sancta facies ejus mirificā hilaritate effloruit, oculisque ad caelum elevatis, incomparabili repletus gaudio, valde laetificabatur. Tum post modicum intervallum illa suavis laetitia in maestam convertitur tristitiam. At duo viri, qui eādem horā ejus [12]tugurii ad januam stabant, et ipsi cum eo valde tristificati, causam ipsius subitae laetitiae rogant et illius subsequentis tristitiae. Ad quos sanctus sic profatur "Ite in pace, nec illius laetitiae causam nec etiam tristitiae a me nunc rogate manifestari."

Quo audito, lacrimantes, prostratis in terrā vultibus humiliter rogant, scire volentes aliquid de illā re quae eādem horā sancto erat revelata. [4]Qui cum eos valde tristes esse vidisset, "Quia vos," ait, "amo, tristificare nolo. Promittere prius debetis ne ulli

[1] Scoticae. The Scotch race then inhabiting Ireland. [2] peregrinari = *to go abroad*. [3] Scotiā. Ireland was called 'Scotia' in the 6th cent. [4] Qui, 66. [5] et = *even*. [6] tirocinium = *service* (the state of being a recruit, 'tiro'). [7] integritas = *chastity*. [8] vel = *even*. [9] Jejunatio = *fasting*. [10] hilaris = *cheerful*. [11] praecordia = *heart*. [12] tugurium = *hut*.

hominum [1]sacramentum de quo rogatis in vitā meā prodatis" Qui cum secundum ejus mandatum prompte promisissent, vir venerandus sic ad eos proloquitur. "Usque in hunc, inquit, praesentem diem meae in Britanniā peregrinationis triginta completi sunt anni. [2]Interea multis ante diebus a Domino meo devote postulavi, ut in fine hujus praesentis anni me de meo absolveret incolatu, et ad caelestem patriam [3]illico advocaret. Et haec fuit causa meae laetitiae, de quā vos me maesti interrogatis. Angelos enim sanctos de ex els vidi missos throno ad meam de carne animam educendam. Sed ecce nunc subito retardati, ultra nostrae [4]fretum insulae stant in rupe, scilicet volentes, ut me de corpore advocent, adpropinquare. Sed propius accedere non permissi, mox ad caelum redituri sunt; quia Dominus quod mihi totis viribus roganti donavit, ut hāc in die ad ipsum de mundo transirem, multarum magis ecclesiarum pro me orationes audiens, [5]dicto citius immutavit. Quibus scilicet ecclesiis exorantibus sic a Domino donatum est ut quatuor ab hāc die mihi in carne manenti superaddantur anni. Haec mihi tam maesta retardatio hodiernae tristitiae [6]non immerito causa fuit. Quibus quatuor terminatis in hāc vitā annis, Deo propitio, nullā praecedente corporis molestiā, ad Dominum laetus emigrabo." Secundum igitur haec verba, vir venerabilis quatuor postea annos in carne mansit.

Annorum quatuor super memoratorum termino jam appropinquante, [7]die Sabbati vir sanctus et pius minister ejus Diormitius ad proximum pergunt benedicendum [8]horreum. Quod intrans Sanctus cum benedixisset, et videns in eo magnos [9]frugum acervos, "Valde congratulor meis familiaribus monachis, inquit, quia hoc etiam anno, si quidem a vobis emigrare me oportuerit, satis cibi habebitis." Quo audito verbo, Diormitius minister tristificari coepit, et sic locutus est, "Hujus anni tempore, pater, saepius nos contristas, quia de tuo transitu [10]crebro commemoras." Cui Sanctus hoc dedit responsum, "Aliquid [11]arcanum habeo, quod, si mihi firmiter promiseris, nemini ante meum revelare obitum, de meo tibi transitu aliquid manifestius [12]intimare potero. Haec in sacris voluminibus dies Sabbatum [13]nuncupatur, quod interpretatur 're-

[1] sacramentum = *sacred thing, mystery.* [2] Interea multis ante diebus = *For many days past.* [3] illico = *straightway.* [4] fretum = *strait.* [5] dicto citius = *more quickly than a word can be uttered.* [6] non immerito = *not without good cause.* [7] die Sabbati = *Saturday.* [8] horreum = *barn.* [9] frugum acervos = *heaps of corn.* [10] crebro = *frequently.* [11] arcanum = *secret.* [12] intimare = *to make known.* [13] nuncupare = *to call.*

quies.' Et mihi vere est Sabbatum haec hodierna dies, quia hujus praesentis laboriosae vitae mihi ultima est, in quo post meos labores [1]sabbatizo, et hāc mediā nocte, [2]secundum eloquia Scripturarum, patrum gradiar viam. Jam enim Dominus meus Jesus Christus me invitare dignatur; ad quem, inquam, hāc ipsā nocte, ipso me invitante, emigrabo." Haec maesta minister audiens verba, coepit [3]amare flere. Quem Sanctus [4]in quantum potuit consolari conabatur.

Post haec Sanctus horreum egreditur, et ad monasterium revertens, mediā residet viā, in quo loco postea crux, [5]molari infixa lapide, hodieque stans, in margine cernitur viae. Dumque ibidem Sanctus, ut praefatus sum, senio fessus, paululum sedens, requiesceret, ecce albus occurrit [6]caballus, obediens servitor, qui scilicet [7]lactaria vascula ad monasterium gestare consueverat. Hic ad Sanctum accidens, [8]mirum dictu, caput in sinum ejus ponens, dominum a se mox emigraturum, et ipsum ultra non visurum sciens, coepit plangere, [9]ubertimque, quasi homo, lacrimas in gremium Sancti fundere. Quod videns minister coepit illum lamentatorem repellere. Sed Sanctus prohibuit eum dicens, "Sine hunc, sine nostri amatorem, ut in hunc meum sinum fletūs effundat amarissimi [10]plangoris. Ecce tu, homo cum sis, et rationalem animam habeas, nullo modo scire de meo exitu potuisti, nisi quod tibi ego ipse nuper manifestavi: huic vero bruto et irrationali [11]animanti, quoque modo ipse Conditor voluit, egressurum a se dominum manifeste revelavit." Et haec dicens maestum a se revertentem equum benedixit.

Et inde egrediens, et [12]monticellum monasterio supereminentem ascendens, in vertice ejus paululum stetit, et stans, ambas elevans palmas, suum benedixit [13]coenobium his verbis, "Huic loco, quamquam angusto et vili, non tantum Scotorum reges, cum populis, sed etiam barbararum et exterarum gentium regnatores cum plebibus sibi subjectis, grandem et non mediocrem conferent honorem: a sanctis quoque etiam aliarum ecclesiarum non mediocris veneratio conferetur."

[1] sabbatizare=*to rest.* [2] secundum eloquia Scripturae=*in the words of Scripture.* [3] amare=*bitterly.* [4] in quantum potuit=*as well as he could.* [5] molari lapide=*in a mill-stone.* [6] caballus=*horse.* The vernacular word; Fr. *cheval.* [7] lactaria vascula=*milk-pails.* [8] mirum dictu=*wonderful to say*, 193. [9] ubertim=*copiously.* [10] plangor=*lamentation.* [11] animans=*animal.* [12] monticellum=*a little hill.* [13] coenobium=*community.*

Post haec verba, de illo descendens monticellulo, et ad monasterium revertens, sedebat in tugurio Psalterium scribens; et ad illum tricesimi tertii psalmi versiculum perveniens ubi scribitur, "Inquirentes autem Dominum non deficient [1]omni bono," "Hic," ait, "in fine cessandum est paginae: quae vero sequitur Baithereus scribat." Sancto convenienter congruit [2]decessori novissimus versus quem scripserit, cui nunquam bona deficient aeterna: successori vero sequens aeque versus congruit, spiritualium doctori filiorum, "Venite, filii, audite me, timorem Domini docebo vos."

Post haec Sanctus ad vespertinalem [3]Dominicae noctis [4]missam ingreditur ecclesiam, quā consummatā, ad tugurium revertens in lectulo residet, ubi pro [5]stramine nudam habebat petram, et pro [6]pulvillo lapidem, qui hodie juxta sepulcrum ejus stat.

Ibique residens ultima ad fratres mandata, solo audiente ministro, commendat ita loquens, "Haec vobis, O filioli, novissima commendo verba, ut inter vos mutuam et non fictam habeatis caritatem cum pace: et si ita, juxta sanctorum exempla patrum, observaveritis, Deus, confortator bonorum, vobis auxiliabitur, et ego, cum ipso manens, pro vobis interpellabo; et non solum praesentis vitae necessaria ab eo sufficienter administrabuntur, sed etiam aeternalium bonorum praemia, divinorum observatoribus praeparata, tribuentur."

Post quae, felici appropinquante novissimā paulisper horā, Sanctus conticuit. Tum mediā nocte [7]festinus surgens ad ecclesiam pergit, citiorque ceteris currens, solus ingressus juxta altare flexis in oratione genibus recumbit; Diormitius minister, tardius prosecutus, eodem momento totam ecclesiam angelicā luce repleri videt. Diormitius ergo, ecclesiam ingrediens, flebili ingeminat voce, "Ubi es, pater?" Et, necdum allatis fratrum lucernis, per tenebras [8]palpans, Sanctum ante altarium recumbantem invenit: quem paululum erigens, et juxta sedens, sanctum in suo gremio posuit caput. Et inter haec [9]coetus monachorum cum luminaribus accurrens, patre viso moriente, coepit plangere. At Sanctus, necdum egrediente animā, apertis sursum oculis, ad utrumque latus cum mirā vultūs hilaritate et laetitiā circumspiciebat; sanctos scilicet obvios intuens angelos. Diormitius tum sanctam dexteram manum Sancti

[1] omni bono, 46, 202. [2] decessori = *the departing saint.* [3] Dominicae noctis = *Saturday night* (the eve of the Lord's day). [4] missa = *mass.* [5] stramen = *bed.* [6] pulvillum = *pillow.* [7] festinus = *suddenly.* [8] palpans = *feeling.* [9] coetus = *crowd.*

ad benedicendum monachorum chorum sublevat. Sed et ipse venerabilis pater in quantum poterat, simul suam movebat manum ut videlicet quod voce in egressu non valebat animae etiam motu manūs fratres videretur benedicere.

Et post sanctam benedictionem ita significatam, continuo spiritum exhalavit. Quo tabernaculo corporis egresso, facies rubens, et mirum in modum angelicā visione [1]exhilarata remansit, ut non quasi mortui sed dormientis videretur viventis. Tota interea personabat maestis plangoribus ecclesia.

Itaque hymnis matutinalibus terminatis, sacrum corpus de ecclesiā ad tugurium unde paulo ante vivens venerat, cum [2]canorā fratrum reportatum psalmodiā, et post tres dies sancti et beati patroni venerabile corpus mundis [3]involutum sindonibus, debitā humatur cum veneratione, in luminosā et aeternali resurrecturum claritudine.

Vita S. Columbae (adapted).

Thomas Aquinas (died 1274), the Angelic Doctor, was the most influential Church writer of the middle ages. He was born of a noble family at Aquino near Naples, joined the Dominican order and was a pupil of Albertus Magnus at Cologne. He taught at Paris, Bologna and Rome and finally settled at Naples. Like the other Schoolmen he devoted his life and writings to the defence of the doctrines of the Church as then understood, following the methods of Aristotle in argument and using the Sentences of Peter the Lombard as the groundwork of his teaching.

He was made a Doctor of the Church by Pius V and his works have been specially commended by Leo XIII to the Catholic seminaries and theological faculties throughout the world.

He is still studied even by theologians who do not belong to the Roman obedience, while the writings of the other Schoolmen are for the most part neglected and forgotten.

His great work was the Summa Theologiae and he also compiled a commentary on the Gospels from the writings of the Fathers which goes by the name of the Catena Aurea.

Editions of these works may easily be had. It has been doubted if the pieces that follow were written by him, or not. They are ascribed to him by Hurter in the SS. Patrum Opuscula, and in any case they are interesting examples of mediaeval Latin and of the discussion of subjects that still excite interest.

[1] exhilaratus = *brightened.* [2] canorus = *tuneful.* [3] involutum sindonibus = *wrapped in linen.*

De bono fidei.

Primum quod est necessarium Christiano est fides, sine quā nullus dicitur fidelis Christianus. Fides autem facit quatuor bona. Primum est [1]quod per fidem anima conjungitur Deo: nam per fidem anima Christiana facit quasi quoddam matrimonium cum Deo: "Sponsabo te mihi in fide." Et inde est quod quando homo baptizatur, primo confitetur fidem, cum dicitur ei: "Credis in Deum?" quia baptismus est primum sacramentum fidei. Et ideo dicit Dominus: "Qui [2]crediderit et baptizatus fuerit salvus erit." Baptismus enim sine fide non prodest. Et ideo sciendum est quod nullus est acceptus a Deo sine fide. "Sine fide impossibile est placere Deo." Et ideo dicit Augustinus [3]super illud, "Omne quod non est ex fide, peccatum est": "Ubi non est aeternae et incommutabilis veritatis [4]agnitio, falsa est virtus etiam in optimis moribus."

Secundo quia per fidem inchoatur in nobis vita aeterna: nam vita aeterna nihil aliud est quam cognoscere Deum: unde dicit Dominus: "Haec est vita aeterna, ut cognoscant te solum verum Deum." Haec autem cognitio Dei incipit [5]hic per fidem, sed perficitur in vitā futurā, in quā cognoscimus eum sicuti est: et ideo dicitur, "Fides est substantia sperandarum rerum." Nullus ergo potest pervenire ad beatitudinem, quae est vera cognitio Dei, nisi primo cognoscat per fidem. "Beati qui non viderunt, et crediderunt."

Tertio quod fides dirigit vitam praesentem: nam [6]ad hoc quod homo bene vivat, [7]oportet quod sciat necessaria ad bene vivendum: et si deberet omnia necessaria ad bene vivendum per studium addiscere, vel non potest pervenire, vel post longum tempus. Fides autem docet omnia necessaria ad bene vivendum. Ipsa enim docet quod est unus Deus, qui est remunerator bonorum et punitor malorum, et quod est alia vita, et [8]hujusmodi; quibus satis [9]allicimur ad bonum et vitamus malum. "Justus meus ex fide vivit."

Notice the very frequent use of 'quod' in these selections where 'ut' or an Inf. would be used in Cl. L.

[1] quod=*namely that*. The clause 'quod...Deo' is the complement of the predicate, 116. [2] crediderit, 88. [3] super=*with reference to the passage*, 236. [4] agnitio=*recognition*. [5] hic=*here*, in this world. [6] ad hoc quod homo bene vivat. The clause introd. by 'quod' is in apposition to 'hoc,' 145. [7] oportet quod sciat, 118. [8] hujusmodi=*of such a kind*. [9] allicimur=*we are enticed*.

Et hoc etiam patet [1]quia nullus philosophorum ante adventum Christi cum toto conatu suo potuit tantum scire de Deo, et de necessariis ad vitam aeternam, quantum post adventum Christi scit una [2]vetula per fidem: et ideo dicitur: "repleta est terra scientiā Domini."

Quarto quia fides est quā vincimus tentationes. "Sancti per fidem vincerunt regna." Et hoc patet, [1]quia omnis tentatio vel est a diabolo, vel a mundo, vel a carne. Diabolus tentat ut non obedias Deo, nec subjiciaris ei. Et hoc per fidem removetur: nam per fidem cognoscimus quod ipse est Dominus omnium, et ideo [3]sibi est obediendum. "Adversarius vester diabolus circuit quaerens quem devoret: cui resistite fortes in fide." Mundus autem tentat vel alliciendo prosperis, vel terrendo adversis. Sed haec vitamus per fidem, quae facit nos credere aliam vitam meliorem istā: et ideo prospera mundi hujus despicimus, et non formidamus adversa. "Haec est victoria quae vicit mundum, fides nostra": et etiam quia docet nos credere alia majora mala, scilicet inferni. Caro vero tentat inducendo nos ad delectationes vitae praesentis momentaneas. Sed fides ostendit nobis quod per has, si eis [4]indebite adhaeremus aeternas delectationes amittimus. "In omnibus sumentes scutum fidei." Sic ergo patet quod multum est utile habere fidem. Sed si dicit aliquis: "Stultum est credere quod non videtur, et non sunt credenda quae non videntur," respondeo dicendum quod hoc dubium primo tollit imperfectio intellectūs nostri: nam si homo posset perfecte per se cognoscere omnia visibilia et invisibilia, stultum esset credere quod non videmus; sed cognitio nostra est adeo debilis, [5]quod unus philosophus fuit triginta annis in solitudine, ut cognosceret naturam apis. Si ergo intellectus noster est ita debilis, nonne stultum est nolle credere de Deo nisi illa tantum quae homo potest cognoscere per se? Et ideo contra hoc dicitur: "Ecce Deus magnus, vincens scientiam nostram."

Secundo potest responderi, [6]quia, [7]dato quod aliquis magister aliquid diceret in suā scientiā, et aliquis rusticus diceret non esse ita sicut magister doceret, eo quod ipse non intelligeret, multum reputaretur stultus ille rusticus.

[1] quia = *because*. [2] vetula = *old woman*. [3] sibi, 61. [4] indebite = *excessively*. [5] quod unus philosophus, a curious use of 'quod' in the sense of 'ut' consecutive. [6] quia, here used to introduce an object clause, 112. [7] dato quod aliquis magister aliquid diceret in suā scientiā = *let it be granted that any master makes a statement in his own subject*, 51.

Constat autem quod intellectus angeli excedit magis intellectum optimi philosophi, quam intellectus optimi philosophi intellectum rustici. Et ideo stultus est philosophus, si nolit credere ea quae angeli dicunt, et multo magis si nolit credere ea, quae Deus dicit.

Et contra hoc dicitur, "Plurima supra sensum hominum ostensa sunt tibi."

Tertio responderi potest, quia, si homo nollet credere nisi ea, quae cognosceret, certe non posset vivere in hoc mundo. Quomodo etiam aliquis vivere posset nisi crederet alicui? Quomodo etiam crederet quod talis est pater suus?

Et ideo est necesse quod homo credat alicui de iis, quae perfecte non potest scire per se: sed nulli est credendum sicut Deo; et ideo illi qui non credunt dictis fidei, non sunt sapientes, sed stulti et superbi, sicut dicit Apostolus, "Superbus est, nihil sciens." Propterea dicebat: "Scio cui credidi, et certus sum."

Quarto potest etiam responderi, quia Deus probat quod ea, quae docet fides, sunt vera.

Si enim rex mitteret litteras cum sigillo suo sigillatas, nullus auderet dicere, quod illae litterae non processissent de regis voluntate. Constat autem quod omnia quae sancti crediderunt, et tradiderunt nobis de fide Christi, signata sunt sigillo Dei: quod sigillum ostenderunt illa opera, quae nulla [1]pura creatura facere potest: et haec sunt miracula, quibus Christus confirmavit dicta apostolorum et sanctorum. Si dicas quod miraculum nullus vidit fieri, respondeo ad hoc: "Constat quod totus mundus colebat idola, et fidem Christi persequebatur, sicut paganorum etiam historiae tradunt. Sed modo omnes conversi sunt ad Christum, et sapientes, et nobiles, et divites, et potentes, et magni ad praedicationem simplicium, et pauperum, et paucorum praedicantium Christum. Aut ergo hoc est miraculose factum, aut non."

Si miraculose, habes propositum. Si non, dico quod non potuit esse majus miraculum quam quod mundus totus sine miraculis converteretur. Non ergo quaerimus aliud. Sic ergo nullus debet dubitare de fide, sed credere ea quae fidei sunt magis quam ea quae videt: quia visus hominis potest decipi, sed Dei scientia nunquam fallitur.

[1] pura = *mere*.

De fructibus Incarnationis.

Possumus autem sumere ex his aliqua ad eruditionem. Primo enim confirmatur fides nostra. Si enim aliquis diceret aliqua de aliquā terrā remotā, et ipse non fuisset ibi, non crederetur ei sicut si ibi fuisset. Antequam ergo veniret Christus in mundum, patriarchae et prophetae et Johannes Baptista dixerunt aliqua de Deo; sed tamen non ita crediderunt eis homines, sicut Christo, qui fuit cum Deo, imo unum cum ipso: unde multum firma est fides nostra ab ipso Christo nobis tradita. "Deum nemo vidit unquam: unigenitus Filius, qui est in sinu Patris, ipse enarravit." Et inde est quod multa fidei secreta sunt manifesta nobis post adventum Christi, quae ante occulta erant.

Secundo ex iis elevatur spes nostra. Constat enim [1]quod Dei Filius non pro parvo ad nos venit, sumens carnem nostram, sed [2]pro magnā utilitate nostrā: unde fecit quoddam [3]commercium scilicet quod assumpsit corpus animatum, et de virgine nasci dignatus est, ut nobis largiretur suam deitatem: et sic factus est homo, ut hominem faceret Deum. "Per quem habemus accessum per fidem in gratiam istam in quā stamus, et gloriamur in spe gloriae filiorum Dei."

Tertio ex hoc accenditur caritas. Nullum est tam evidens caritatis indicium, quam quod Deus creator omnium factus est creatura, Dominus noster factus est frater noster, Filius Dei factus est filius hominis. "Sic Deus dilexit mundum, ut Filium suum unigenitum daret." Et ideo ex hujus consideratione amor noster [4]reaccendi debet, et inflammari ad Deum.

Quarto inducimur ad servandam puram animam nostram. In tantum enim natura nostra fuit nobilitata et exaltata ex conjunctione ad Deum, quod fuit ad consortium divinae personae suscepta: unde angelus post incarnationem noluit sustinere quod beatus Johannes adoraret eum, quod ante sustinuerat etiam a maximis patriarchis. Ideo homo hujus exaltationem recolens et attendens, debet [5]dedignari vilificare se et naturam suam per peccatum: ideo dicit beatus Petrus: "Per quem maxima et pretiosa promissa nobis donavit, ut per haec efficiamur divinae consortes naturae, fugientes ejus quae in mundo est concupiscentiae corruptionem."

[1] See paragraph 127. [2] pro magnā utilitate nostrā = *to our great benefit.* [3] commercium = *union.* [4] reaccendi = *to be kindled afresh.* [5] dedignari = *to disdain.*

Quinto ex his inflammatur desiderium nostrum ad perveniendum ad Christum. Si enim aliquis rex esset frater alicujus et esset remotus ab eo, desideraret ille, cujus frater esset rex, ad eum venire, et apud eum esse et manere. Unde cum Christus sit frater noster, debemus desiderare esse cum eo et conjugi ei. "Ubicunque fuerit corpus, illuc congregabuntur et aquilae," et Apostolus desiderium habebat dissolvi, et esse cum Christo: quod quidem desiderium crescit in nobis considerando incarnationem ejus.

De Symb. Apost.

Quare orare debemus ut fiat voluntas Dei.

Sed quid est quod dicitur "Fiat voluntas tua"? Nonne dicitur "Omnia quaecumque voluit fecit"? Si omnia facit quae vult in caelo et in terrā, quid est hoc quod dicit "Fiat voluntas tua sicut in caelo et in terrā"? Ad hoc sciendum est quod Deus tria vult de nobis, et nos petimus [1]quod haec impleantur.

Primum quidem quod Deus vult de nobis est [2]quod nos habeamus vitam aeternam. Cum ergo consequimur vitam aeternam, salvamur, et hoc vult Dominus. "Haec est voluntas Patris mei qui misit me, ut omnis qui videt Filium, et credit in eum, habeat vitam aeternam." Haec autem voluntas jam completa est in angelis et in sanctis qui sunt in patriā, quia vident Deum, et cognoscunt et fruuntur eo. Sed nos desideramus quod sicut voluntas Dei completa est in beatis, ita compleatur in nobis.

Alia voluntas Dei de nobis est, ut servemus mandata ejus. Sic ergo cum dicimus "Fiat voluntas tua," oramus ut impleamus mandata Dei. Haec autem voluntas Dei fit in justis, sed in peccatoribus nondum fit. Notandum est quod ex modo loquendi datur nobis [3]doctrina. Non enim dicit fac, nec etiam faciamus: sed dicit "Fiat voluntas tua," quia ad vitam aeternam duo sunt necessaria, scilicet gratia Dei et voluntas hominis; et licet Deus fecerit hominem sine homine, non tamen justificat eum sine eo. Sic enim dicit Augustinus "Qui creavit te sine te non justificabit te sine te," quia vult quod homo coöperetur. "Convertimini ad me, et ego convertar ad vos."

[1] quod haec impleantur: 'quod' is here used as a substitute for 'ut' after a verb of requesting, 142. [2] quod nos habeamus vitam aeternam, 145.
[3] doctrina = *teaching*.

"Gratiā Dei sum id quod sum, et gratia ejus in me vacua non fuit." [1]Non ergo presumas de te, sed confidas de gratiā Dei; nec negligas, sed adhibeas studium tuum. Et ideo non dicit "faciamus," ne videretur quod nihil faceret gratia Dei; nec dicit "fac," ne videretur quod nihil faceret voluntas et conatus noster: sic dicit "fiat," per gratiam Dei, adhibito studio et conatu nostro.

De Oratione Dominica (adapted).

Thomas a Kempis, who is generally supposed to be the author of the "Imitation of Christ," was a monk in the Augustine convent of Zwolle in the Netherlands in the first half of the 15th century. His book is perhaps the most popular devotional treatise in existence. Notice the number of abstract nouns used and their approximation in sense to the words in English derived from them.

Qualiter homo desolatus se debet in manus Dei offerre.

Domine Deus, sancte Pater, sis nunc et in aeternum benedictus, quia sicut vis, sic factum est, et quod facis bonum est. Laetetur in te servus tuus, non in se, nec in aliquo alio, quia tu solus laetitia vera. Quid habet servus tuus, nisi quod a te accepit, etiam sine merito suo? Tua sunt omnia, quae dedisti et quae fecisti. Pauper sum et in laboribus a juventute meā, et contristatur anima mea nonnunquam usque ad lacrimas, quandoque etiam conturbatur spiritus meus a se propter imminentes passiones. Pater juste, sancte et semper laudande, venit hora [2]ut probetur servus tuus. Pater amande, dignum est ut hāc horā patiatur pro te aliquid servus tuus. Pater perpetuo venerande, venit hora, quam ab aeterno praesciebas affuturum, [2]ut ad modicum tempus succumbat foris servus tuus, vivat vero semper apud te intus; paululum [3]vilipendatur, humiliatur et deficiat coram hominibus, passionibus conteratur et languoribus, ut iterum tecum in aurorā novae lucis resurgat et in caelestibus clarificetur. Pater sancte, tu sic ordinasti et sic voluisti; et hoc factum est quod ipse praecepisti.

Haec est enim gratia ad amicum tuum pati et tribulari in mundo pro amore tuo, quotiescumque et a quocumque et quomodocumque id permiseris fieri. Sine consilio et providentiā tuā et sine causā

[1] Non presumas, 44. [2] ut probetur, 147. [3] vilipendatur = *that he should be despised.*

nihil fit in terrā. Bonum mihi, Domine, quod humiliasti me, ut discam [1]justificationes tuas, et omnes elationes cordis atque praesumptiones abjiciam.

Utile mihi quod confusio cooperuit faciem meam, ut te potius quam homines ad consolandum requiram. Didici etiam ex hoc inscrutabile judicium tuum expavescere, qui affligis justum cum impio, sed non sine aequitate et justitiā.

Gratias tibi ago, quia non pepercisti malis meis, sed attrivisti me verberibus amaris, infligens dolores et immittens angustias foris et intus. Non est qui me consoletur ex omnibus, quae sub caelo sunt, nisi tu, Domine Deus meus, caelestis medicus animarum, qui percutis et sanas, deducis ad inferos et reducis. Disciplina tua super me, et virga tua me docebit.

Ecce, Pater dilecte, in manibus tuis sum ego, sub virgā correctionis tuae me inclino. Percute dorsum meum et collum meum, ut incurvem ad voluntatem tuam [2]tortuositatem meam. Fac me pium et humilem discipulum, sicut bene facere consuevisti, ut ambulem ad omnem [3]nutum tuum. Tibi me et omnia mea ad corrigendum commendo; melius est hic corripi quam in futuro. Tu scis omnia et singula, et nil te latet in humanā conscientiā. Antequam fiant nosti ventura, et non opus est tibi ut quis te doceat aut admoneat de his, quae geruntur in terrā.

Tu scis quid expedit ad profectum meum, et quantum deservit tribulatio ad [4]rubiginem vitiorum purgandam. Fac meum desiderium beneplacitum tuum, et ne despicias peccaminosam vitam meam, nulli melius nec clarius quam tibi notam.

Da mihi, Domine, hoc scire quod sciendum est, hoc amare, quod amandum est, hoc laudare, quod tibi summe placet. Falluntur saepe hominum sensus in judicando; falluntur amatores saeculi visibilia sola amando. Quid est homo inde melior quia reputatur ab homine major?

Fallax fallacem, vanus vanum, caecus caecum, infirmus infirmum decipit, dum exaltat: nam quantum unusquisque est in oculis tuis, tantum est et non amplius, ut ait humilis Sanctus Franciscus.

[5]Fili, non vales semper in ferventiori desiderio virtutum stare, nec in altiori gradu contemplationis consistere; sed necesse habes

[1] justificationes = *righteousness.* [2] tortuositatem = *my crooked ways.* [3] nutum = *nod, i.e. will.* [4] rubiginem = *rust* or *stain.* [5] Fili, here Christ speaks.

interdum ob originalem corruptelam ad inferiora descendere, et onus corruptibilis vitae etiam invite et cum taedio portare.

Tunc expedit tibi ad humilia et exteriora opera confugere, et in bonis actibus te recreare, adventum meum et supernam visitationem firmā confidentiā expectare, exilium tuum et ariditatem mentis patienter sufferre, donec a me iterum visiteris et ab omnibus anxietatibus libereris. Nam faciam te laborum oblivisci et internā quiete perfrui. Expandam coram te prata scripturarum, ut dilato corde currere incipies viam mandatorum meorum. Et dices: Non sunt condignae passiones hujus praesentis temporis ad futuram gloriam, quae revelabitur nobis.

De Imitatione Christi III, 50, 51 (abridged).

APPENDIX OF LATIN HYMNS

THE object of this Appendix is to make available to students of Ecclesiastical Latin a few of its treasures which are now, with a few exceptions, only to be found in books which are out of print and, in some cases, rare.

No attempt has been made to provide a critical text or to write elaborate notes. Those who desire a scholarly edition of the earlier hymns will find it in *Early Latin Hymns* by A. S. Walpole published by the Cambridge University Press. The author is indebted to this book for a few statements in his notes. An attempt has been made to give at least one example from the best known Christian Latin poets from the time of St. Ambrose to the era of the Schoolmen.

SCHOOL OF ST. AMBROSE

St. Ambrose (born 340, died 397), is the first great writer of Latin hymns. Many of the hymns attributed to him were probably written in imitation of his austere and objective style. He was the principal champion of the Catholic Faith in the West against the Arian heresy, and introduced the Eastern custom of antiphonal singing into his diocese of Milan to encourage his flock under persecution by the Arians.

Hymnus ad Galli Cantum

Aeterne rerum Conditor,
noctem diemque qui regis,
et temporum das tempora,
ut alleves fastidium.

Praeco diei jam sonat,
noctis profundae pervigil,
nocturna lux viantibus,
a nocte noctem segregans.

Hoc excitatus Lucifer
solvit polum caligine,
hoc omnis errorum chorus
viam nocendi deserit.

Hoc nauta vires colligit,
pontique mitescuntque freta,
hoc, ipse petra Ecclesiae
canente, culpam diluit.

Surgamus ergo strenue;
gallus jacentes excitat,
et somnolentos increpat,
gallus negantes arguit.

Gallo canente, spes redit,
aegris salus refunditur,
mucro latronis conditur,
lapsis fides revertitur.

Jesu, labentes respice,
et nos videndo corrige.
Si respicis, lapsūs cadunt,
fletuque culpa solvitur.

Tu, Lux, refulge sensibus,
mentisque somnum discute;
te nostra vox primum sonet,
et vota solvamus tbi.

3 *Et temporum das tempora* and givest the fixed times of the seasons. 4 *Fastidium* weariness. See Vergil, Eclogue IV, 61 5 *Praeco* herald. 6 *Noctis profundae pervigil* watchful throughout the depth of night. 8 *A nocte noctem segregans* dividing one part of the night from another. 9 *Hoc* with this word when used in this line and when used in lines 11, 13 and 15 it is possible to understand *canente* in line 16. It may also be understood as an Ablative of the Agent, a construction not uncommon in late Latin. Compare: *Et laureatus Spiritu scriptis coronatus suis* in another of the Ambrosian hymns. *Lucifer*. See note on line 5 of *Lucis Largitor splendide*. 11 *Errorum chorus*. This is said by Walpole to be the correct reading. He interprets *errorum* as the abstract for the concrete, and gives it the sense of 'roving demons'. Compare 1 Pet. v, 8 and *Hamlet*, Act I, Scene I, 147 sqq. In the Roman Breviary these words are corrected into *erronum cohors* which is said to mean 'a band of vagabonds, or evil men'. 15 *Ipse petra Ecclesiae*, i.e. St. Peter. The masculine pronoun is *a constructio ad sensum*. 16 *Diluit* washes away.

20 *Arguit* convicts. Compare Jn. xvi, 8. 25 *Respice* Compare Lk. xxii, 60 and Prudentius, *Cathermerinon*, I, 49 sqq. 27 *Lapsus cadunt* our failings fall from us. The cock is prominent in early Christian art in representations of the denial of St. Peter. It was regarded in the Middle Ages as the type of the Christian preacher. The ancients believed that a lion could not bear the sight of a cock (Lucretius, IV, 710) and this idea was readily applied to the flight of Satan (the roaring lion of 1 Pet. v, 8) from the faithful preaching of the Gospel. See St. Gregory, *Regula Pastoralis*, III, 40.

Hymnus Matutinus

Lucis largitor splendide,
cuius sereno lumine
post lapsa noctis tempora
dies refulsus panditur.

Tu verus mundi Lucifer
non is qui parvi sideris
venturi lucis nuntius
angusto fulget lumine.

Sed toto sole clarior
Lux ipse totus et dies
interna nostri pectoris
illuminans praecordia.

Adesto rerum conditor,
paternae lucis gloria,
cuius remota gratia
patescunt nostra corpora.

Tuoque plena Spiritu
secum Deum gestantia,
ne rapientis perfidi
diris pateant fraudibus.

Ut inter actūs saeculi
vitae quos usus exegit
omni carente crimine
tuis vivamus legibus.

Probrosas mentis castitas
carnis vincat libidines,
sanctumque puri corporis
delubrum servet Spiritūs.

Haec spes precantis animae,
haec sunt votiva munera,
ut matutina nobis sit
lux in noctis custodiam.

1 *Largitor splendide* glorious bestower. 2 *Sereno* bright. 3 *Post lapsa noctis tempora* after the night-time has passed. 5 Understand *es*. Notice the play on the word Lucifer. This word means literally 'the light-bearer' or 'the morning star'. See Vergil Eclogue, VIII, 17. The use of Lucifer in English as a name for the devil arose from a misunderstanding of Isaiah xiv, 17, which was supposed in the Middle Ages to refer to the fall of Satan. The word *lucifer* is used in its proper sense in 2 Pet. i, 19. 6 *Parvi sideris*. These words qualify *lumine*. 8 *Angusto* meagre. 12 *Praecordia* the inmost depths. Strictly speaking it means the midriff or diaphragm. 16 *Patescunt* lie open to. Another reading is *pavescunt*.

19 *Perfidi* the deceiver, i.e. the devil. 21 *Actus saeculi* the business of the world. 23 *Crimine.* In Classical Latin this word means 'accusation', but in late and especially Church Latin it commonly means 'sin' or 'crime'. 27 *Sanctum* is the completion of the predicate and not the attribute of *delubrum.* 32 *In noctis custodiam* until the night-watch.

PRUDENTIUS

Prudentius is generally believed to have been born in Spain about 348. He was educated as a lawyer and filled important civil and military positions. In his fifty-seventh year he determined to devote his literary talents to the service of Christ.

He did much to give the Latin of his time a form suitable for sacred poetry. Selected verses from some of his long lyric poems have been used in the services of the Church in their original form and are also found translated in Hymns Ancient and Modern and other English collections.

Hymnus Omni Hora

Corde natus ex Parentis
ante mundi exordium,
A et O cognominatus,
ipse fons et clausula
omnium quae sunt, fuerunt
quaeque post futura sunt.

Ipse jussit, et creata,
dixit ipse, et facta sunt
terra, coelum, fossa ponti
trina rerum machina
quaeque in his vigent sub alto
solis et lunae globo.

Corporis formam caduci,
membra morti obnoxia
induit, ne gens periret
primoplasti a germine,
merserat quam lex profundo
noxialis Tartaro.

Psallat altitudo coeli,
psallant omnes angeli,
quidquid est virtutis usquam
psallat in laudem Dei:
nulla linguarum silescat,
vox et omnis consonet.

Ecce quem vates vetustis
concinebat saeculis,
quem prophetarum fideles
paginae spoponderant
emicat, promissus olim,
cuncta collaudent eum.

Tu cibus, panisque noster,
tu perennis suavitas,
nescit esurire per aevum
qui tuam sumit dapem
nec lacunam ventris implet,
sed fovet vitalia.

Clausus aurium meatus
et sonorum nescius
purgat ad praecepta Christi
crassa quaeque obstacula,
vocibus capax fruendis,
ac susurris pervius.

Omnis aegritudo cedit,
languor omnis pellitur,
lingua fatur, quam veterna
vinxerant silentia:
gestat et suum per urbem
laetus aeger lectulum.

Quin et ipsum, ne salutis
inferni expertes forent,
Tartarum benignus intrat,
fracta cedit janua,
vectibus cadit revulsis
cardo dissolubilis.

Illa prompta ad irruentes,
ad revertentes tenax,
obice retrorsum pulso,
porta reddit mortuos,
lege versa, et limen atrum
jam recalcandum patet.

Sed Deus dum luce fulva
mortis antra illuminat,
dum, stupentibus tenebris,
candidum praestat diem,
tristia squalentis aethrae
palluerunt sidera.

Sol refugit, et lugubri
sordidus ferrugine
igneum relinquit axem
seque moerens abdidit.
Fertur horruisse mundus
noctis aeternae chaos.

Solve vocem, mens, sonoram
solve linguam nobilem:
dic tropeum passionis,
dic triumphalem crucem
pange vexillum, notatis
quod refulget frontibus.

Macte, judex mortuorum,
macte, rex viventium:
dexter in Parentis arce
qui cluis virtutibus
omnium venturus inde
justus ultor criminum.

Te senes, et te juventus,
parvulorum te chorus
turba matrum virginumque
simplices puellulae
voce concordes pudicis
perstrepant concentibus

Fluminum lapsūs et undae,
litorum crepidines,
imber, aestus, nix, pruina,
silva et aura, nox dies
omnibus te concelebrent
saeculorum saeculis.

Notes on Hymnus Omni Hora

3 A et O, cf. Rev. I, 8. 4 *Clausula* 'ending'. 10 *Trina rerum machina,* 'the triple fabric of the universe'. Cf. *Quod superest, ne te promissis plura moremur, Principio maria ac terras coelumque tuere: Horum naturam triplicem tria corpora, Memmi, Tres species tam dissimiles, tria talia texta Una dies dabit exitio: multosque per annos Sustentata ruet moles et machina mundi.* Lucretius, V, 91-97. 13 *Caduci* 'frail'. 14 *Obnoxia* 'liable to'. 16 *Primoplasti* 'first formed'. A word half Latin and half Greek, formed for Christian use. 18 *Noxialis* 'baleful'. 21 *Virtutis* 'power'. 23 *Nulla linguarum* 'no tongue', an extension of the use of the partitive genitive. 33 *Nescit esurire* 'He cannot hunger'. The subject of this verb is the antecendent of *qui.* 37 *Meatus* 'opening, or passage'. 41 *Vocibus capax fruendis* 'Capable of hearing voices'. 45 *Veterna* 'Long standing'. 50 *Expertes* 'Without a share in'. 54 *Cardo* properly 'a hinge'. May be translated 'door' here. *Dissolubilis,* properly 'that which may be dissolved', perhaps may be translated 'broken open' here. 55 *Prompta* 'Readily opened'. Cf. Vergil, Aen. VI, 126. 60 *Recalcandum*

'To be trodden again'. 65 *Squalentis aethrae* 'Of the mourning sky'. The Romans, when in mourning, went about with unkempt hair and torn garments. 66 *Sidera* i.e. the sun and moon. 67 *Sol refugit*—'The sun fled away, and in trappings of woe left his fiery course.' Cf.

Ille etiam extincto miseratus Caesare Roman
Cum caput obscura nitidus ferrugine texit,
Impiaque aeternum timuerunt saecula noctem.

Vergil, Georgics I, 466.

77 *Pange* celebrate. 79 *Macte* 'Hail' (Virgil, Aen. IX, 641). 82 *Cluis* 'Excellest'. An old word used by Plautus and Lucretius and revived in later Latin. *Virtutibus,* 'Works of power'. Cf. Mt. vii, 22. 92 *Crepidines* 'Margins, banks'. The above verses are selected from the ninth poem in the Cathemerinon. See Hymns Ancient and Modern for a translation of part of it.

Hymnus in exequiis Defuncti

Deus ignee fons animarum,
duo qui socians elementa
vivum simul et moribundum
hominem, Pater, effigiasti,

Tua sunt, tua, rector, utraque;
tibi copula jungitur horum;
tibi, dum vegitata cohaerent,
et spiritus et caro servit.

Rescissa sed illa seorsum
solvunt hominem perimuntque,
humus suscipit arida corpus
animae capit aura liquorem.

Quia cuncta creata necesse est
labefacta senescere tandem,
compactque dissociari
et dissona texta retexi.

Hanc tu, Deus optime, mortem
famulis abolire paratus,
iter inviolabile monstras
quo perdita membra resurgant

Ut, dum generosa caducis
ceu carcere clausa ligantur,
pars illa potentior extet,
quae germen ab aethere traxit.

Si terrea forte voluntas
luteum sapit et grave captat,
animus quoque pondere victus
sequitur sua membra deorsum.

At si generis memor ignis
contagia pigra recuset,
vehit hospita viscera secum,
pariterque reportat ad astra.

Nam quod requiscere corpus
vacuum sine mente videmus,
spatium breve restat, ut alti
repetat collegia sensūs.

Hinc maxima cura sepulcris
impenditur: hinc resolutos
honor ultimus accipit artūs
et funeris ambitus ornat.

Quidnam sibi saxa cavata,
quid pulchra volunt monumenta
nisi quod res credita illis
non mortua, sed data somno?

Jam maesta compesce, querella,
lacrimas suspendite, matres,
nullus sua pignora plangat,
mors haec reparatio vitae est.

Sic semina sicca virescunt,
jam mortua, jamque sepulta,
quae redita caespite ab imo
veteres meditantur aristas.

Nunc suscipe, terra, fovendum,
gremioque hunc concipe molli:
hominis tibi membra sequestro
generosa et fragmina credo.

Animæ fuit haec domus olim
factoris ab ore creatae,
fervens habitavit in istis
sapientia, principe Christo.

Tu depositum tege corpus,
non immemor illa requiret
sua munera fictor et auctor
propriique aenigmata vultūs.

Veniant modo tempora justa,
cum spem Deus impleat omnem,
reddas patefacta necesse est
qualem tibi trado figuram.

Non si cariosa vetustas
dissolverit ossa favillis,
fueritque ciniscculus arens
minimi mensura pugilli.

Nec, si vaga flamma et aurae,
vacuum per inane volantes,
tulerint cum pulvere nervos,
hominem periisse licebit.

Sed dum ressolubile corpus
revocas, Deus, atque reformas,
quanam regione jubebis
animam requiescere puram?

Gremio senis addita sancti
recubabit, ut est Eleazar,
quem floribus undique septum
dives procul aspicit ardens.

Sequimur tue dicta Redemptor,
quibus atra morte triumphans
tua per vestigia mandas
socium crucis ire latronem.

Patet ecce fidelibux ampli
via lucida jam Paradisi
licet et nemus illud adire
homini quod ademerat anguis.

Nos tecta fovebimus ossa
violis et fronde frequente
titulum et frigida saxa
liquido spargemus odore.

NOTES ON HYMNUS IN EXEQUIIS DEFUNCTI

6 *Tibi* may be a dative of the agent which is a rare use, or it may be a dative of advantage. 7 *Vegitata* 'quickened', or 'in life'. Augustine, Confessions, x, 10. 11 The earth is spoken of as 'dry' when compared with the 'fluid' nature of the soul. It was a commonplace of ancient thought that the body returned to the earth and the soul to the sky. Ecclesiastes xii, 7. 1 Cor. xv, 47. Euripides, Supplices 531, Lucretius, II, 999. 16 *Et dissona texta retexi.* 'and that the discordant strands which are woven together should be rewoven.' 21 *Generosa* 'the noble elements'. *Caducis* 'the part destined to decay'. 23 'that part may show itself more powerful'. The next stanzas show that the poet taught that this should be done while the union of soul and body existed. 26 'tastes of the clay and desires what is base'. 29 'But if the fire, mindful of its nature.' The soul is regarded as part of the eternal fire. Cf. line 1. 31 *Viscera* flesh. 36 *Collegia* Neut. Pl. 'union, partnership'. 40 *Funeris ambitus* 'a stately funeral'. 41 *Quidnam sibi volunt* 'What is the meaning of?' 45 *Compesce* is used

intransitively here and *querella* is in the Vocative case. 47 *Pignora* 'dear ones'. *Nunc tibi commendo communia pignora natos.* Propertius IV, 11, 73. 49 *Semina* Cf. 1 Cor. xv, 36 sqq. 51 *Caespite* 'sod'. 52 *Meditantur* 'prepares', cf. Horace, Odes III, 6, 23. The sense is that the buried grain is preparing again to be the full ear of corn that it once was. 55 *Sequestro* 'deposit'. 56 *Generosa et fragmina credo* 'Noble are the remains that I entrust to thee'. 58 *Ab ore* Cf. Genesis ii, 7. 59 *Istis* in later Latin *iste* lost its proper sense and could be used as if equivalent to *hic*, or *ille.* 64 *Propriique aenigmata vultus* 'The dim outline of his own face.' Genesis i, 27. Cf. *Videmus nunc per speculum in aenigmate,* 1 Cor. xiii, 12. 65 *Veniant mods tempora justa* 'Only let the appointed time arrive . . . then laid open thou must restore the form which I now entrust to thee just as it once was.' 69 *Cariosa* 'withered'. 71 *Cinisculus* a diminutive from *cinis.* 72 *Pugilli* 'a handful'. 74 *Inane* 'the void', as often in Lucretius. 81 *Senis* Abraham, Lk. xvi, 22. 82 *Eleazar* i.e. Lazarus. 86 *Quibus atra morte triumphans* this seems to mean 'to triumph over' on the analogy of *triumphare de.* 92 *Homini* 'from man' the usual construction with *adimo. Anguis,* Genesis iii. 95 *Titulum* 'the tomb stone'. Cf. *Surgens ergo Jacob mane, tulit lapidem quem supposuerat capitti suo, et erexit in titulum.* Genesis xxviii, 18. The above verses are selected from the tenth poem in the Cathemerinon.

SEDULIUS

Selected Passages from the Carmen Paschale

Little is known about Sedulius. He lived in the middle of the fifth century and was a Presbyter.

The long poem from which these extracts are made is an excellent example of the way in which Christian poets who were steeped in Vergil in their school days tried to make the Scriptures attractive to their contemporaries by re-writing them in verse. This poem was popular in the Middle Ages, but is little known now.

Voce coelesti testimonium Christo perhibetur.

Has inter virtutis opes, jam proxima Paschae
coeperat esse dies, Domini cum gloria vellet
ponere mortalem, vivamque resumere carnem,
non aliam sed rursus eam, quam munere plenam
lucis ab infernis relevans ad sidera vexit.
Exclamans palam: 'Pater, ista memet ab hora
salvifica, sed in hanc ideo veni tamen horam.
Clarifica,' dixit, 'nomen tuum': Magnaque coelo
vox resonans venit per nubila: 'Clarificavi,
clarificabo iterum.' Quid apertius est, Patre teste
coelo assertore? At nec sic cognoscere Christum

gens voluit Judea Deum. Pars esse ferebat
hoc tonitrum, pars angelicam crepuisse loquellam.
O gens caeca oculis, O gens durissima corde
Non tonitrus potuit Christum sive angelus ullus
auctorem generasse suum, qui, nomine Patris
audito, responsa daret, sed ab ore Tonantis
Natum agnoscentis, populus quo crederet adstans,
vox emissa suo respondit consona Verbo.

Christus pedes descipulorum lavat.

Annua tunc sacrae celebrans per munera caenae
Paschales ex more dapes, humilemque ministrum
se faciens, et grata suis exempla relinquens
assurgit, famulisque libens famulatur, et omnem
linteolo accinctus tantum inclinavit honorem,
discipulis ut sponte lavans vestigia cunctis,
nec Judam exciperet, quem proditionis iniquae
noverat auctorem. Sed nil tibi gloria, saeve
traditor, illa dabit pedibus consistere mundis
qui sensu pollutus eras, velut omne sepulchrum
exteriora gerens albae velamina formae,
sordibus interius foedoque cadavere plenum.

Christus traditus inimicis, servi summi sacerdotis auriculam curat.

Traditus ergo viris Operator sanctus iniquis
consuetam non liquit opem, pueroque revulsam
ense Petri, ne qua pius a pietate vaceret,
reddidit auriculam: nec enim vindicta Tonanti
conveniens humana fuit, qui milia Patrem
angelicas sibimet legiones poscere posset
plus duodena dari, si mallet sumere poenas
de meritis quam sponte suis ignoscere plagis.
Tunc parci mucroni jubet, quia venerat ipse
ponere pro cunctis animam, non tollere cuiquam.

Christus ad aedes Caiphae ducitur.

Continuo ad tristes Caiphae deducitur aedes.
Ille sacerdotum fuerat tunc denique princeps,
et princeps scelerum, namque hoc residente cathedra
pestifera, falsis agitatum testibus ardet
concilium, jamjamque volant mendacia mille
in Dominum, vanis hominum conflata cavillis,
quae periunt levitate sua, velut ignis oberrans
ardentes stipulas, vires cui summa cremandi
materies infirma rapit, victoque furore
labitur invalidae deformis gloria flammae.

Christus a Judeis illuditur.

Postquam nulla dolis patuit via, brachia tolli
armat in insontem saevus furor: heu mihi quantis
impedior lacrimis rabidum memorare tumultum.
Sacrilegas movisse manūs non denique passim
vel colphis pulsare caput, vel caedere palmis,
aut spuere in faciem plebs execranda quievit.
Ille tamen patiens subjecto corpore totum
sustinuit, nostraeque dedit sua membra saluti.
Namque per hos colophos caput sanabile nostrum,
sputa haec per Dominum nostram lavere figuram,
his alapis nobis libertas maxima plausit.

Christus ante tribunal praesidis.

At Dominus patiens, cum praesidis ante tribunal
staret, ut ad jugulum ductus mitissimus agnus,
nil inimica cohors insontis sanguine dignum
comperiens, regem quod se rex diceret esse,
objicit, et verum mendax pro crimine ducit.
Heu falx torva patrum, segitem caesura nepotum.
Heu facinus, Pilate, tuum, quot gesseris uno
crimina judicio; vigili si mente notares,
non solas lavasse manūs, sed corpore toto
debueras sacrum veniae sperare lavacrum.

Christus suspenditur in cruce.

Protinus in patuli suspensus culmine ligni
hujus in exuviis sors mittitur, ut sacra vestis
intemerata manens a Christo schisma vetaret.
Quin etiam insontis latere ex utroque cruentos
constituere viros, sed dispar causa duorum.
Suppliciis tamen rerum Dominator in ipsis
jura potestatis non perdidit: aequus utrumque
judex namque tuens, hunc eligit, hunc reprobavit.
Unus enim quem vita ferox nec morte relinquit,
in Dominum sceleratis movens convicia dictis
mordebat propriis, et tantum setiger hircus
ore veneneso vitem lacerabat amoenam.
Alter, adorato per verba precantia Christo,
saucia dejectus flectabat lumina, tantum
lumina, nam geminas arcebant vincula palmas.
Quem Dominus, ceu pastor ovem deserta per arva
colligit errantem, secumque adducere gaudet
in campos, Paradise, tuos ubi flore perenni
gramineus blanditur ager, nemorumque voluptas
irriguis nutritur aquis, interque benigne
conspicuos pomis non deficientibus hortos
ingemit antiquum serpens habitare colonum.

Mors Christi.

Ergo, ubi cuncta boni completa est passio Christi,
ipse animam proprio dimisit corpore sanctam.
Dic ubi nunc tristis victoria, dic ubi nunc sit
mors, stimulus, horrenda, tuus, quae semper opimis
instaurata malis cunctas invadere gentes
poenali ditione soles. En, pessima, non tu
pervenis ad Christum, sed Christus pervenit ad te,
cui licuit sine morte mori, quique omnia gignens
omnia constituens, te non formavit ut esses
semine viperio. Culpa genitrice crearis,
et venia regnante peris. Jam spiritus artūs
liquerat ad tempus, patulo jam frigida ligno
viscera pendebat, et adhuc arma furor ministrans
cuspide perfossum violat latus: ecce patente
vulnere purpureus cruor et simul unda cucurrit.
Haee sunt quippe sacrae pro religionis honore,
corpus, sanguis, aqua, tria vitae munera nostrae.
Fonte renascentes, membris et sanguine Christi
vescimur, atque ideo templum Deitatis habemur.
Quod servare Deus nos annuat immaculatum,
et faciat tenues tanto Mansore capaces.

Resurrectio Christi.

Coeperat interea post tristis Sabbata felix
irradiare dies, culmen qui nominis alti
a Domino domiante trahit, primusque videre
promeruit nasci mundum, atque resurgere Christum.
. . . Hoc luminis ortu
virgo parens aliaeque simul cum munere matres
messis aromaticae notum venere gemantes
ad tumulum, vacuumque vident sine corpore factum,
sed plenum virtute locum, nam missus ab astris
angelus amoti residebat vertice saxi,
flammeus aspectu, niveo praeclarus amictu,
qui gemina specie terrorem et gaudia portans,
cunctaque dispensans custodibus igne minaci
venerat in forma Christi quaerentibus alba.
Illae igitur Dominum calcata vivere morte
angelica didicere fide: perterritus autem
miles in ancipiti retinet discrimine vitam,
deserta statione fugax, testisque timoris
vera refert gratis, sed post data munera fallit.
Discipulum globum placidi sub tempore somni
clam se nocturna Christum rapuisse rapina
compositus simulator ait. Fare, improbe custos,
responde, scelerata cohors, si Christus, ut audes

dicere, concluso furtim productus ab antro
sopitos latuit, cujus jacet intus amictus,
cujus ad exuvias sedet angelus? Anne beati
corporis ablator velocius esse putavit
solvere contectum quam devectare ligatum
cum mora sit furtis contraria? Cautius ergo
cum Domino potuere magis sua lintea tolli.
Mentita est vox vana sibi: tamen ista figuram
res habet egregam; Judeis constat ademptum
quem nos devoto portamus pectore Christum.

Christus ascendit ad Patrem.

Haec ubi dicta pio Dominus sermone peregit,
Bathaniae mox arva petit: coramque beatis
qui tantum meruere viris spectare triumphum
aetherias subvectus abit sublimis in auras.
Ad dextram sedet ipse Patris, mundumque gubernat
jure suo, qui cuncta tenens excelsa et ima
Tartara post coelum penetrat, post Tartara coelum.
Illi autem laetis cernentes vultibus altas
ire super nubes Dominum tractūsque coruscos
vestigiis calcare suis, venerantur, adorant,
sidereasque vias alacri sub corde reportant,
quas cunctis doceant. Testes nam jure fideles
divinae virtutis erunt, qui plura videntes
innumerabilum scripserunt pauca bonorum.
Nam si cuncta sacris voluissent tradere chartis
facta Redemptoris, nec totus cingere mundus
sufficeret densos per tanta volumina libros.

Notes on the Carmen Paschale

1 *Virtutis opes* 'Mighty deeds of power.' 3 *Vivam* as this is opposed to *mortalem*, it may perhaps be translated, 'Ever living'. 7 The words *salvifica* and *clarifica* are taken from the Vulgate of Jn. xii. 10 *Quid apertius* etc. 'What could be more plain, when the Father gave his witness from heaven?' 12 *Ferebat* 'Was saying', as often in Vergil. 13 *Crepuisse loquellam* 'That some angelic voice had sounded forth.' A characteristic use of two unusual words, one of which is an unnecessary diminutive. 16 *Qui . . . daret* 'To give a reply when the name "Father" was heard.' 17 *Tonantis* Here we see the beginning of the application of the names and attributes of pagan gods to God and Christ which is so marked a feature of Renaissance Latin. Even Dante speaks of Christ as *Il sommo Giove per noi crocifisso.* 18 *Populus quo crederet adstans* 'That the people standing by might believe.' Jn. xii, 30. 19 *Verbo* Cf. Jn. i sqq. *Tantum inclinavit honorem* This seems to

mean, 'He brought the honour that he showed them to such a point that washing of his own accord the feet of all his disciples, he did not even leave Judas out.' Note how often *vestigium* is used in the sense of 'foot' in this poem. 33 The word *pius* is just as difficult to translate here as it is in Vergil. Perhaps it might be translated 'kind'. *Vacaret,* 'Cease'. 34 *Vindicta* 'Vengeance'. *Tonanti* seems to refer to Christ in this passage. It is even more out of place than it was in line 17. 39 *Parci mucroni jubet* 'He commands him to put up his sword.' The Infinitive *parci* is an impersonal passive, such as is found in verbs governing a Dative case. See note on line 9 of *Aterne rerum Conditor.* 46 *Vanis hominum conflata cavillis* 'Fanned to a flame by the vain scoffing of men. 47 *Velut ignis ...* 'Like a fire twisting among the blazing stubble from which the feeble ends of the burning straw snatch away the power of burning and the smothered glory of the weakened flame slips away and its fury is overcome.' 51 *Tolli* This Infinitive may be used to express Result in imitation of the Greek construction. Cf. the Vulgate of Acts v, 3. 1 Thess. i, 9. Translate: 'So that arms were raised.' 54-56 The main verb in this sentence is *non quievit* which may be translated 'did not cease'. *Passim* means 'here and there'. *Colaphis* means 'blows'. 59 *Sanabile* 'Healed' cf. Wisdom I, 14 (Vulgate). 61 *His alapis* etc. Translated literally this means, 'The greatest liberty applauded for us with these slaps.' An excellent example of a false straining after effect in later Latin poetry. 63 *Jugulum* properly means 'throat'. Translate 'to the slaughter'. 67 *Falx torva* 'the ill-omened sickle'. 71 The Indicative is used because the verb is a modal verb. Compare: *Nisi his esset a Deo, onn poterat facere quicquam.* Jn. ix, 33. *Lavacrum,* compare Titus III, 5. 73 *Sors mittitur* the 'lot is cast'. 74 This is a common mystical interpretation of the seamless garment of Christ. 75 *Cruentos* 'blood-guilty'. 76 *Causa* 'condition or state'. 82 *Setiger* 'hairy'. 85 *Lumina* 'eyes'. 86 Compare Vergil, Aeneid II, 406. 90 *Blanditur* 'invites'. 97 *Quae semper opimis instaurata malis* 'who ever renewed with the extreme of evil'. 99 *Ditione* 'sway'. 106 *Viscera* 'body'. 107 *Cuspide* 'lance'. 111 *Fonte renascentes* etc. 'being born in the fountain, we feed on the body and blood of Christ, and, on this account, are considered to be the temple of the Divinity. May God be pleased to enable us to keep that temple undefiled, and make us able, unworthy though we be, to receive so great a guest.' 116 *Culmen qui nominis alti* 'who draws the crowning glory of an exalted name from the Lord's triumph.' 130 *In ancipiti discrimine* 'in the doubtful crisis'. 132 *Gratis* 'without a reward being given them.' 134 *Clam se* 'without their knowledge' or 'while they slept'. 135 *Compositus* 'agreed'. *Fare* Imperative from *for fare fatus.* 138 *Sospitos latuit* 'was stolen while you slept'. 144 *Tamen ista figuram* etc. 'Yet this event has a notable signification.' *Figura* properly means the outward aspect of a thing. It is used in a number of different senses in the Vulgate to translate several Greek words which have no exact equivalent in Latin. Compare 1 Cor. vii, 31, *Praeterit enim figura hujus mundi,* where it is used in its proper sense. In 1 Cor. x, 6 and 11 it is used in the sense of type or symbol. *Haec autem in figura facta sunt.* The meaning of the word in these passages approximates to its meaning in this passage in Sedulius. In Acts vii, 43 it is used in the sense of an image. This well illustrates the difficulty which the translators of the Latin New Testament found in dealing with even a simple form of Greek.

VENANTIUS FORTUNATUS

Venantius Fortunatus was born in 530 in Italy. He spent most of his life in Gaul and died in 609 as Bishop of Poitiers.

He was one of the last writers who retained some traces of Classical culture and marks a turning point between a feeble and barbarous imitation of the Classics and the freedom which the Latin of the Middle Ages was shaping for itself.

These hymns are given here rather because of their celebrity than because of their excellence. They are translated in Hymns A. and M., Nos. 96 and 97.

De Cruce

Pange, lingua, gloriosi proelium certaminis,
et super crucis tropaeo dic triumphum nobilem,
qualiter Redemptor orbis immolatus vicerit.

De parentis protoplasti fraude Factor condolens,
quando poma noxialis morsu in mortem corruit,
ipse lignum tunc notavit damna ligni ut solveret.

Hoc opus nostrae salutis ordo depoposcerat,
multiformis proditoris ars ut artem falleret,
et medellam ferret inde hostis unde laeserat.

Quando venit ergo sacri plenitudo temporis,
missus est ab arce Patris Natus orbis conditor,
atque ventre virginali caro factus prodiit.

Vagit infans inter arcta conditus praesepia,
membra pannis involuta virgo mater alligat,
et pedes manūsque crura stricta cingit fascia.

Lustra sex qui jam peracta tempus implens corporis,
se volente, natus ad hoc, passioni deditus
agnus in cruce levatur, immolatus stipite.

Hic acetum, fel, arundo, sputa, clavi, lancea,
mite corpus perforatur, sanguis unda profluit,
terra, pontus, astra, mundus quo lavantur flumine.

Crux fidelis inter omnes, arbor una nobilis
nulla talem silva profert fronde, flore, germine:
dulce lignum, dulci clavo dulce pondus sustinens.

Flecte ramos, arbor alta, tensa laxa viscera,
et rigor lentiscat ille quem dedit nativitas,
ut superni membra Regis miti tendas stipite

Sola digna tu fuisti ferre pretium saeculi,
atque portum praeparare nauta mundo naufrago
quem sacer cruor perunxit fusus agni corpore.

Notes on De Cruce

1 *Pange* sing or celebrate. 2 *Super* about. 3 *Qualiter* how. 4 *Fraude* sin: *protoplasti* first formed. 7 *Nostri salutis ordo* the plan of our salvation. 9 *Medella* remedy. 13 *Arcta* narrow. 14 *Pannis* rags. 15 *Fascia* bandage, the swaddling clothes. 16 *Lustra sex* six times five years. These words are probably in apposition with *tempus*. *Qui* refers to *agnus* in line 18. *Tempus corporis* the time of His life in the body. 18 *Stipite* on the tree. 19 Understand *sunt*. 25 *Viscera* fibres. 28 *Pretium* ransom. 29 *Nauta* is said by Walpole to refer to the cross: 'And swimming on the waves to prepare a harbour for the wrecked world.' Neale translates *nauta* by the word 'Ark' which also gives good sense and is quite in keeping with the symbolic language common in Fortunatus' hymns.

De Cruce II

Vexilla Regis prodeunt,
fulget crucis mysterium,
quo carne carnis conditor
suspensus est patibulo.

Quo vulneratus insuper
mucrone diro lanceae,
ut nos lavaret crimine
manavit unda et sanguine.

Impleta sunt quae cecinit
David fideli carmine,
dicens, 'In nationibus
regnavit a ligno Deus.'

Arbor decora et fulgida,
ornata Regis purpura,
electa digno stipite
tam sancta membra tangere

Beata cuius brachiis
pretium pependit saeculi,
statera facta corporis
tulitque praedam Tartaris

Notes on De Cruce II

1 *Vexilla* banners. This line is parodied in Dante's Inferno, XXXIV, 1. 4 *Patibulum* gallows. 10 In the Italic version of Ps. xcvi, 10 the reading is: 'Tell it out among the heathen that the Lord reigneth from the tree.' This reading is also found in some MSS. of the LXX. Justin Martyr accused the Jews of corrupting the text. Dialogue 73. 19 *Statera* the arm of a balance. Some of the Fathers regarded the death of Christ as a price paid to the devil that he might free men from bondage. The cross is here spoken of as the balance on which the price was weighed. 20 *Tulit* took away.

INCERTI AUCTORIS

Hymnus quando communicant sacerdotes

A hymn by an unknown author found in the Bangor Antiphonary. An Irish legend says that it was sung by the angels to celebrate the cessation of a quarrel between St. Sechnall and St. Patrick.

Sancti venite,
Christi corpus sumite,
sanctum bibentes
quo redempti sanguinem.

Salvati Christi
corpore et sanguine,
a quo refecti
laudes dicamus Deo.

Dator salutis
Christus Filius Dei
mundum servavit
per crucem at sanguinem.

Pro universis
immolatus Dominus
ipse sacerdos
extitit et hostia.

Lege praeceptum
immolari hostias
qua adumbrantur
divina mysteria.

Lucis indultor
et salvator omnium
praeclaram sanctis
largitus est gratiam.

Accedant omnes
pura mente creduli
sumant aeternam
salutis custodiam.

Sanctorum custos
rector quoque Dominus
vitam perennem
largitur credentibus

Coelestem panem
dat esurientibus
de fonte vivo
praebet sitientibus.

Alpha et Omega
ipse Christus Dominus
venit venturus
judicare homines.

Notes on Hymnus quando communicant sacerdotes

See the translation of this hymn A.M., 313. 21 *Indultor* giver. 26 *Creduli* believers. 39 *Venturus* he that shall come, see Lk. vii, 19.

De Die Judicii

This poem is by an unknown author, probably of the seventh century. It is mentioned by Bede. The poem is acrostic, and the necessity ot finding words beginning with all the letters of the alphabet which already corresponded with the alphabet now in use made the poet spell *caritate* with a K, use *Xristum* for *Christum* and use the Greek word Ydri in line 43.

Apparebit repentina dies magna Domini,
  fur obscura velut nocte improvisos occupans.
Brevis totus tunc parebit prisci luxus saeculi,
  totum simul cum clarebit praeterisse saeculum.
Clangor tubae per quaternas terrae plagas concinens
  vivos una mortuosque Christo ciet obviam.
De caelesti Judex arce majestate fulgidus
  claris angelorum choris comitatus aderit.
Erubescet orbis lunae, sol et obscurabitur,
  stellae cadent pallescentes, mundi tremet ambitus,
Flamma ignis anteibit justi vultum Judicis
  caelum, terras et profundi fluctūs ponti devorans.
Gloriosus in sublimi Rex sedebit solio,
  angelorum tremebunda circumstabunt agmina.
Hujus omnes ad electi colligentur dexteram,
  pravi pavent a sinistris, haedi velut foetidi.
Ite, dicet Rex, a dextris, regnum coeli sumite,
  Pater vobis quod paravit ante omne saeculum.
Karitate qui fraterna me juvistis pauperem
  caritatis nunc mercedem reportate divites.
Laeti dicent: Quando, Christe, pauperem te vidimus,
  te, Rex magne, vel egentem miserati juvimus?
Magnus illis dicet Judex: Cum juvistis pauperem,
  panem, domum, vestem dantes, me juvistis humiles.
Nec tardebit a sinistris loqui justus Arbiter:
  in Genennae, maledicti, flammas huc discedite.
Obsecrantem me audire despexistis mendicum,
  nudo vestem non dedistis, neglexistis languidum.
Peccatores dicent: Christe, quando te vel pauperem,
  te, Rex magne, vel infirmum contemplantes sprevimus?
Quibus contra Judex altus: Mendicanti quamdiu
    opem ferre despexistis, me sprevistis, improbi.
Retro ruent tum injusti ignes in perpetuos,
  vermis quorum non morietur, flamma nec restinguitur.
Satan atro cum ministris quo tenetur carcere,
  fletus ubi mugitusque, strident omnes dentibus.
Tunc fideles ad coelestem sustollentur patriam,
  choros inter angelorum regni patent gaudia.

Urbis summae Hierusalem introibunt gloriam,
vera lucis atque pacis in qua fulget visio.
Xristum regem jam paterna claritate splendidum,
ubi celsa beatorum contemplantur agmina.
Ydri fraudes ergo cave, infirmantes subleva,
aurum temne, fuga luxūs, si vis astra petere.
Zona clara castitatis lumbos nunc praecingere
in occursum magni Regis fer ardentes lampadas.

Notes on De Die Judicii

2 *Occupans* coming upon. 4 *Clarebit* it shall be made manifest. See Lucretius, VI, 937. 5 *Quaternas plagas* the four quarters. 6 *Ciet* will summon. 9 *Et* even. 10 *Ambitus* the circuit. 15 *Ad* to be taken with *dexteram*. 16 *Foetidus* foul. 17 *Dicet Rex a dextris* for *Dicet Rex his qui a dextris erunt*. See the Vulgate of Mt. xxv, 34. 20 *Divites* proleptic—so that you become rich. 28 *Languidus* sick. See Juvenal I, 122. 29 *Hierusalem* this is one of many Hebrew names which are not declined in Latin. 43 *Ydri* the Hydra, the old serpent, that is the devil. 46 *In occursum* in order to meet.

De Spiritu Sancto

It is not known by whom this celebrated hymn was written. It was probably composed in the ninth century.

It is the only ancient Latin hymn which has been retained in the Prayer Book of the Church of England where it was used in the ordination services. The longer version in the Prayer Book first appeared in the second Prayer Book of Edward VI. The shorter version was inserted in 1662 and is by Bishop Cousin. Dryden's hymn "Creator Spirit, by whose aid" was founded on it.

Veni, Creator Spiritus,
mentes tuorum visita,
imple superna gratia
quae tu creasti pectora.

Qui Paracletus diceris,
altissimi donum Dei,
fons vivus, ignis, caritas,
et spiritalis unctio.

Tu septiformis munere,
dextrae Dei tu digitus,
tu rite promissum Patris
sermone ditans guttera.

Accende lumen sensibus,
infunde amorem cordibus,
infirma nostri corporis
virtute firmans perpeti.

Hostem repellas longius,
pacemque dones protinus,
ductore te sic praevio
vitemus omne noxium.

Per te sciamus da Patrem
noscamus atque Filium
te utriusque Spiritum
credamus omni tempore

Notes on Creator Spiritus

9 *Septiformis munere* seven-formed in thy gifts. Isaiah xi, 2. 10 *Dextra Dei tu digitus* Compare Matt. xii, 28 with Lk. xi, 20. 12 *Ditans* endowing. *Guttera* properly throats: here trans. tongues. Mk. xiii, 11. 17 *Repellas, dones* present Subjunctive in sense of Imperative, as is usual in late Latin. 19 *Ductore sic te previo* with such a leader as thee going before. 21 *Sciamus da* grant us to know. 24 Understand *esse.*

PETRUS DAMIANI

Peter Damiani, the author of this hymn, was born at Ravenna in 988. He was noted for his extreme asceticism, for his devotion to the Papacy and his opposition to the marriage of the clergy. He was the friend and helper of Hildebrand (Gregory VII) and was made Cardinal Bishop of Ostia. He resigned this position in 1062 and died in 1072 as Abbot of Sta. Croce d'Avellano.

De Gloria Paradisi

Ad perennis vitae fontem mens sitivit arida,
claustra carnis praesto frangi clausa quaerit anima:
gliscit, ambit, eluctatur exul frui patria.

Dum pressuris ac aerumnis se gemit obnoxiam,
quam amisit, dum deliquit, contemplatur gloriam
praesens malum auget boni perditi memoriam.

Nam quis promat summae pacis quanta sit laetitia,
ubi vivis margaritis surgunt aedificia,
auro celsa micant tecta, radiant triclinia:

Solis gemmis pretiosis haec structura nectitur,
auro mundo tanquam vitro urbis via sternitur;
abest limus, deest fimus, lues nulla cernitur.

Hiems horrens, aestas torrens illic nunquam saeviunt;
flos perpetuus rosarum, ver agit perpetuum,
candent lilia, rubescit crocus, sudat balsamum.

Virent prata, vernant sata, rivi mellis influunt;
pigmentorum spirat odor, liquor et aromatum;
pendent poma floridorum non lapsura nemorum.

Non alternat luna vices sol vel cursus siderum;
agnus est felicis urbis lumen inocciduum,
nox et tempus desunt ei, diem fert continuum.

Nam et sancti quique velut sol praeclarus rutilant,
post triumphum coronati mutue coniubilant
et prostrati pugnas hostis iam securi numerant.

Omni labe defaecati carnis bella nesciunt,
caro facta spiritalis et mens unum sentiunt,
pace multa perfruentes scandalum non perferunt.

Mutabilibus exuti repetunt originem,
et praesentem veritatis contemplantur speciem,
hinc vitalem vivi fontis hauriunt dulcedinem.

Inde statum semper idem existendi capiunt,
clari, vividi, iucundi nullis patent casibus:
absunt morbi semper sanis, senectus iuvenibus.

Hinc perenne tenent esse, nam transire transiit;
inde virent, vigent, florent: corruptela corruit,
immortalitatis vigor mortis ius absorbuit.

Qui scientem cuncta sciunt, quid nescire nequeunt;
nam et pectoris arcana penetrant alterutrum?
unum volunt, unum nolunt, unitas est mentium.

Licet cuiquam sit diversum pro labore meritum,
caritas hoc facit suum quod amat in altero:
proprium sic singulorum fit commune omnium.

Ubi corpus, illic iure congregantur aquilae,
quo cum angelis et sanctae recreantur animae,
uno pane vivunt cives utriusque patriae.

Avidi et semper pleni quod habent desiderant,
non satietas fastidit, neque fames cruciat:
inhiantes semper edunt et edentes inhiant.

Novas semper melodias vox meloda concrepat,
et in iubilum prolata mulcent aures organa,
digna per quem sunt victores regi dant praeconia.

Felix coeli quae praesentem regem cernit anima
et sub sede spectat alta orbis volvi machinam,
solem, lunam et globosa cum planetis sidera

Christe, palma bellatorum, hoc in municipium
introduc me post solutum militare cingulum,
fac consortem donativi beatorum civium.

Probes vires inexhausto laboranti proelio
nec quietem post procinctum denegas emerito
teque merear potiri sine fine praemio.

Notes on De Gloria Paradisi

1 *Ad* with a view to, for. Compare Col. II, 25. *Sitivit* this use of the past tense is an imitation of the timeless Greek Aorist. See Ps. xli, 3 and Jas. i, 11. 2 *Praesto* straightway. 3 *Gliscit* burns with desire. *Ambit* literally goes round, hence canvass for votes or desire which is the meaning here. 4 *Obnoxium* exposed to. 5 *Dum* used in the sense of *cum*. 6 *Micant* shine. *Tricliniis* banqueting hall. 11 *Mundo* fine or pure, Rev. xxi, 21. 12 *Limus* mud. *Fimus* filth. *Lues* disease. 16 *Vernant sata* the crops flourish. 17 *Pigmentorum* this properly means colours, it may mean unguents here. *Aromatum* spices. 19 *Non alternat luna vices* the mood does not change her phases. 20 *Inocciduum* that sets not. 24 *Hostis jam securi* now without fear of the enemy. 25 *Omni labe defaecati* cleansed from all stain. 27 *Scandalum* cause of stumbling. Compare Matt. xvi, 23, xviii, 7. 28 *Mutabilibus exuti* having put off the things that change. 32 *Nullis patent casibus* they are exposed to no accidents. 34 *Esse* and *transire* are Infinitives used in the sense of abstract nouns. *Esse* means being and *transire* transience or succession. 37 *Qui scientem cuncta*, etc. What can those who know Him who knoweth all things fail to know, for they penetrate the secrets of each other's hearts? 40 *Licet cuiquam*, etc. Even though it be that the merit of each is diverse in proportion to his labour, love makes that which he loves in another to be his own, so that that which is peculiar to each becomes the common property of all. Dante, Paradiso III, 70, expresses the same thought. 43 One of the mediaeval interpretations of the difficult saying in Matt. xxiv, 28 was that where Christ is His saints will be gathered by a similar instinct to that which gathers together eagles to their prey. 45 *Pane* see Jn. vi, 31, 33 sqq. 48 *Inhiantes* desiring. 49 *Concrepat* resounds. 52 *Praeconia* proclamation, may perhaps be translated celebration. 53 *Machinam* fabric. 55 The metaphors of the last two verses are taken from the discharge of a soldier. Christ is the palm and reward of his service. He is to be made a citizen of the *municipium* of Heaven after he has loosed and laid aside his belt, the emblem of military service. The *donativum* was the money given to discharged soldiers who have served their time (*emeritare*). *Quies* means rest. Christ is the eternal reward of faithful service. 59 *Procinctum* readiness for battle.

PETER ABELARD

De Sabbatis Patriae Caelestis

Peter Abelard (1079-1142), the author of this hymn, was a celebrated teacher in the University of Paris and one of the founders of the scholastic theology. On account of his rationalizing tendencies he was condemned as a heretic at the instance of St. Bernard, but was protected by Peter the Venerable in the famous monastery of Cluny. The story of his stormy and unhappy life may be read in Milman's History of Western Christianity, vol. IV.

O quanta qualia
sunt illa Sabbata,
quae semper celebrat
superna curia;
quae fessis requies,
quae merces fortibus,
cum erit omnia
Deus in omnibus.

Quis rex, quis curia,
quale palatium
quae pax, quae requies,
quod illud gaudium?
Hujus participes
exponant gloriae,
si quantum sentiunt
possint exprimere.

Vere Hierusalem
est illa civitas,
cujus pax jugis est,
summa jucunditas,
ubi non praevenit
rem desiderium
nec desiderio
minus est praemium.

Ibi molestiis
finitis omnibus,
securi cantica
Sion cantabimus,
et juges gratias
de donis gratiae
beata referet
plebs tibi, Domine.

Illic nec Sabbato
succedit Sabbatum
perpes laetitia
sabbatizantium,
nec ineffabiles
cessabunt jubili
quos decantabimus
et nos et angeli.

Nostrum est interim
mentes erigere,
et totis patriam
votis appetere,
et ad Hierusalem
a Babylonia
post longa regredi
tanquam exilia

Perenni Domino
perpes sit gloria
ex quo, per quem sunt,
in quo sunt omnia;
ex quo sunt, Pater est,
per quem sunt, Filius,
in quo sunt, Patris
et Filii Spiritus.

There is an admirable translation of this hymn in A.M. 235 by Dr. Neale.

Notes on O quanta qualia

This hymn is one of the best examples of mediaeval hymnology with occasional rhymes and written in a style which is at once compressed and yet quite intelligible.

The use of terms peculiar to the city of Rome such as *curia*, properly the Senate house, *palatium*, properly the residence of the Emperors on the Palatine hill, and *plebs* is remarkable.

19 *Jugis* everlasting. 21 *Ubi non praevenit rem desiderium* where the thing desired does not surpass the reality. Cf. Lucretius III, 58. *Eripitur persona, manet res.* 28 *Sion* is an indeclinable noun and is here in the Genitive case. 41 *Nostrum est* our part in the meantime is to lift up our minds. 50 *Perpes* everlasting. 55 *Omnia* is to be understood as the subject of *sunt* in this and the following lines.

De Spiritu Sancto

This hymn has been attributed to King Robert of France and to Pope Innocent III. It is not known who wrote it.

Veni, Sancte Spiritus,
et emitte caelitus
lucis tuae radium;
veni, pater pauperum;
veni, dator munerum;
veni, lumen cordium.

Consolator optime,
dulcis hospes animae,
dulce refrigerium;
in labore requies,
in aestu temperies,
in fletu solacium

O lux beatissima,
reple cordis intima
tuorum fidelium.
Sine tuo numine
nihil est in homine
nihil est innoxium.

Lava quod est sordidum,
riga quod est aridum,
rege quod est devium,
fove quod est languidum,
flecte quod est rigidum,
sana quod est saucium.

Da tuis fidelibus
in te confidentibus
sacrum septenarium.
Da virtutis meritum,
da salutis exitum,
da perenne gaudium.

Notes on De Spiritu Sancto

2 *Caelitus* an adverb, translated from heaven. 9 *Refrigerium* refreshment. A word often used in the inscriptions in the Catacombs. 17 *Nihil est in homine* Archbishop Trench suspects that the text is corrupt in this line and the next. 18 *Innoxium* etc. This line appears to mean that without the Spirit the nature of man is full of sin. 21 *Devium* amiss, out of the true way. 27 *Sacrum septenarium* the sacred seven-fold gifts. 29 *Salutis exitum* the way of escape to salvation. See for a translation A. and M., 156.

De Domino Jesu

This and the following hymn were long ascribed to St. Bernard, but now it is stated in Raby's Christian Latin Poetry that the real author of *Salve caput cruentatum* is the Cistertian Arnulf of Louvain.

Jesu dulcis memoria is said to be inspired by Bernard's prose writings, but not to be by him in the form in which we have it.

Both hymns are, however, a reflection of his mysticism and austerity. The first is taken from a long poem on the Name of Jesus, and the verses have been chosen because they are translated in Hymns A. and M., 178 and 190. This accounts for the repetition of a stanza which is found in both translations.

Jesu, dulcis memoria,
dans vera cordi gloria;
sed super mel et omnia
ejus dulcis praesentia.

Nil canitur suavius,
nec auditur jucundius,
nec cogitatur dulcius,
quam Jesus Dei filius.

Jesu, spes poenitentibus,
quam pius es petentibus,
quam bonus te quaerentibus,
sed quid invenientibus?

Nec lingua valet dicere,
nec littera exprimere;
expertus potest credere
quid sit Jesum deligere.

Sis, Jesu, nostrum gaudium,
qui es futurum praemium;
sit nostra in te gloria
per cuncta semper saecula.

Jesu, dulcedo cordium,
fons vivus, lumen mentium,
excedens omne gaudium
et omne desiderium.

Jesu, spes pœnitentibus,
quam pius es petentibus,
quam bonus te quaerentibus,
sed quid invenientibus?

Qui te gustant, esuriunt,
qui bibunt, adhuc sitiunt,
desiderare nesciunt
nisi Jesum quem diligunt.

Quoqcenque loco fuero
mecum Jesum desidero,
quam laetus cum invenero,
quam felix cum tenuero.

Mane nobiscum, Domine,
et nos illustra lumine,
pulsa noctis caliginem
mundum replens dulcidine.

Ad faciem Christi in cruce pendentis

Salve, caput cruentatum,
totum spinis coronatum,
conquassatum, vulneratum,
arundine vulneratum,
facie sputis illita.
Salve, cujus dulcis vultus,
immutatus et incultus,
immutavit suum florem,
totus versus in pallorem,
quem coeli tremit curia.

Omnis vigor atque viror
hinc recessit, non admiror,
mors apparet in aspectu,
totus pendens in defectu,
attritus aegra macie.
Sic affectus, sic despectus,
propter me sic interfectus,
peccatori tam indigno
cum amoris in Te signo
appare clara facie.

In hac tua passione
me agnosce, Pastor bone,
cujus sumpsi mel ex ore,
haustum lactis cum dulcore,
prae omnibus deliciis.
Non me reum asperneris,
nec indignum dedigneris;
morte tibi jam vicina
tuum caput hic inclina,
in meis pausa brachiis.

Tuae sanctae passioni
me gauderem interponi,
in hac cruce tecum mori
praesta crucis amatori,
sub cruce tua moriar.
Morti tuae tam amarae
grates ago, Jesu care,
qui es clemens, pie Deus,
fac quod petit tuus reus,
ut absque te non finiar.

Dum me mori est necesse,
noli mihi tunc deesse;
in tremenda mortis hora
veni, Jesu, absque mora,
tuere me et libera
Cum me jubes emigrare,
Jesu care, tum appare;
O amator amplectande,
temetipsum tunc ostende
in cruce salutifera.

Notes on Salve, caput cruentatum

This hymn is part of a long poem in seven sections each of which is addressed to some part of the body of Christ.

It finds its expression in art in the frescoes of Fra Angelico in the convent of S. Marco in Florence.

The hymn O sacred head, surrounded by crown of piercing thorn (A. and M., 111), is translated from it through the German.

3 *Conquassatum* bruised. 5 *Illita* defiled. 7 *Immutatus et incultus* changed and uncared for. 10 *Curia* properly the senate house at Rome used here as in the hymn of Abelard *O quanta qualia* either in the sense of the Court of Heaven or of the Heavenly Host. 11 *Viror* manly strength. 14 *Defectu*

weakness. 15 *Macie* leanness. 30 *Pausare* to rest. A colloquial word used in this sense in late Latin. 26 and 27 Note the use of *non* where *ne* would be used in Cl. Latin. 32 *Interponi* to take my share. 34 and 35 *Praesta . . . moriar* Grant to the lover of the cross that I may die under the cross. 40 and 44 *Absque=sine* as often in the Vulgate.

De contemptu mundi

Cum sit omnis homo foenum,
et post foenum fiat coenum,
ut quid, homo, extolleris?
cerne quid es, et quid eris;
modo flos es, et verteris
in favillam cineris.

Per aetatum incrementa,
immo magis detrimenta,
ad non-esse traheris.
velut umbra, cum declinat,
vita surgit et festinat
claudit meta funeris.

Homo dictus es ab humo;
cito transis, quia fumo
similis effeceris.
nunquam in eodem statu
permanes, dum sub rotatu
hujus vitae volveris.

O sors gravis, O sors dura,
O lex dira, quam natura
promulgavit miseris.
homo nascens cum moerore,
vitam ducis cum labore,
et cum metu morieris.

Ergo si scis qualitatem
tuae sortis, voluptatem
carnis quare sequeris?
memento te moriturum
et post mortem id messurum
quod hic seminaveris.

Terram teris, terram geris,
et in terram reverteris
qui de terra sumeris.
cerne quid es et quid eris,
modo flos es, et verteris
in favillam cineris.

Notes on De contemptu mundi

1 *Foenum* see Jas. i, 10. 2 *Coenum* filth. 3 *Ut quid* wherefore? 4 *Quid es* etc. The Indicative mood in an Indirect question is quite common in late Latin. 7 *Incrementa* growth. 8 *Detrimenta* decline. 9 *Non-esse* an interesting example of the use of the Infinitive as an abstract noun. Trans. annihilation. 13 An example of mediaeval etymology. 25 *Qualitatem* nature.

PETRUS VENERABILIS

De Resurrectione

Peter the Venerable, the author of this hymn, was Abbot of Cluny in the first half of the twelfth century.

Mortis portis fractis, fortis
Fortior vim sustulit;
et per crucem regem trucem
infernorum perculit.
Lumen clarum tenebrarum
sedibus resplenduit;
dum salvare, recreare
quod creavit voluit.
Hinc Creator, ne peccator
moreretur moritur;
cujus morte nova sorte
vita nobis oritur.

Inde Sathan victus gemit
unde Victor nos redemit;
illud illi fit letale
quod est homini vitale,
qui cum captat, capitur,
et dum mactat, moritur.
Sic decenter, sic potertcr
Rex devincens inferos,
linquens ima, die prima
rediit ad superos.
Resurexit et revexit
secum Deus hominem
Reparando quam creando
dederat originem.
Per Auctoris passionem
ad amissam regionem
primus redit nunc colonus,
unde laetus fit hic sonus.

Notes on De Resurrectione

1 *Mortis portis fractis, fortis Fortior vim sustulit* This is the kind of play on words which delighted some mediaeval writers. Compare: Mors mortis mortem norti nisi morte dedisset, aeternae vitae janua clausa foret. See Lk. xi, 21 sqq. 17 *Qui* refers to Satan. 25 *Reparando, creando* these ablatives of the Gerund are equivalent to a Present Participle, as often in late Latin. 29 *Colonus* i.e. Adam.

ADAM OF ST. VICTOR

De SS. Evangelistis

It is perhaps advisable to include a poem by Adam of St. Victor, whom Archbishop Trench regarded as the greatest of mediaeval poets. Certainly no other poet has preserved more of the allegorical interpretation of scripture in a terser form than he has.

He lived in the twelfth century and was a member of the Abbey of St. Victor in Paris.

Jucundare, plebs fidelis,
cujus Pater est in coelis,
recolens Ezechielis
Prophetae praeconia:
est Johannes testis ipse,
dicens in Apocalypsi,
Vere vidi, vere scripsi
vera testimonia.

Circa thronum majestatis,
cum spiritibus beatis
quatuor diversitatis
adstant animalia.
Formam primum aquilinam,
et secundum leoninam,
sed humanam et bovinam
duo gerunt alia.

Formae formant figurarum
formas Evangelistarum,
quorum imber doctrinarum
stillat in Ecclesia:
hi sunt Marcus et Matthaeus,
Lucas et quem Zebedaeus
pater misit tibi, Deus,
dum laxaret retia.

Formam viri dat Mattheo,
quia scripsit sic de Deo
sicut descendit ab eo,
quem plasmavit homine.
Lucas bos est in figura,
ut praemonstrat in Scriptura
hostiarum tangens jura
legis sub velamine.

Marcus leo per desertum
clamans, rugit in apertum
iter fiet Deo certum,
mundum cor a crimine.
Sed Johannes ala bina
caritatis aquilina
forma fertur in divina
puriore lumine.

Quatuor describunt isti
quadriformes actus Christi,
et figurant, ut audisti,
quisque sua formula.
Natus homo declaratur,
vitulus sacrificatur,
leo mortem depraedatur,
et ascendit aquila.

Ecce forma bestialis,
quam Scriptura prophetalis
notat: sed materialis
haec est impositio.
Currunt rotis, volant alis,
inest sensus spiritalis,
rota gressus est aequalis
ala contemplatio.

Paradisus his rigatur,
viret, floret, foecundatur,
his abundat, his laetatur
quatuor fluminibus.
Fons est Christus, hi sunt rivi
fons est altus, hi proclivi,
ut saporem fontis vivi
ministrent fidelibus.

Horum rivo debriatis
sitis crescat caritatis,
ut de fonte pietatis
satiemur plenius.
Horum trahat nos doctrina
vitiorum de sentina,
sicque ducat ad divina
ab imo superius.

Notes on De SS. Evangelistis

3 See Ezechiel xi, 14. 17 *Figurarum* see note on line 144 of the Carmen Paschale. 25 Jerome, Ambrose and Gregory assigned the symbolic animals to the Evangelists as they are assigned in this hymn and as we now assign them. Irenaeus who first made the application assigned them differently. (Adv. Haer. III, 2, 8). 28 *Plasmavit* formed. 35 See Matt. iii, 3. 44 Trench marks suâ formulâ as an ablative. Figurant must then be used intransitively. 47 *Depraedatur* preys on. 52 *Impositio* interpretation. 55 *Rota gressus est aequalis* Trench says that this means that all four Evangelists agree in their account of the earthly life of Christ. 60 *Fluminibus* Genesis ii, 10. In early Christian art either a symbol or a figure of Christ was often represented standing on a hill from which the four rivers of Paradise are flowing. 65 *Debriatis* is a late Latin word meaning intoxicated. 70 *Sentina* cesspool.

THOMAS OF CELANO

Dies Irae

It seems impossible to exclude from any anthology of Latin hymns the greatest and best known of all merely because its text is easily accessible. It is generally attributed to Thomas of Celano, the friend and biographer of St. Francis of Assisi. It is more remarkable for its intense earnestness and forcible, yet compressed expression than for any elegance of language. It is, however, one of those poems which is so great as to defy translation, though many attempts have been made to translate it into both German and English.

Dies irae, dies illa,
solvet saeclum in favilla
teste David cum Sibylla.

Quantus tremor est futurus,
quando judex est venturus
cuncta stricte discussurus.

Tuba mirum spargens sonum
per sepulcra regionum
coget omnes ante thronum.

Mors stupebit et natura,
cum resurget creatura
judicanti responsura.

Liber scriptus proferetur,
in quo totum continetur
unde mundus judicetur.

Judex ergo cum sedebit,
quidquid latet apparebit;
nil inultum remanebit.

Quid sum miser tunc dicturus,
quem patronum rogaturus,
cum vix justus sit securus?

Rex tremende majestatis,
qui salvandos salvas gratis,
salva me, fons pietatis.

Recordare, Jesu pie,
quod sum causa tuae viae;
ne me perdas illa die.

Quaerens me sedisti lassus,
redemisti crucem passus;
tantus labor non sit cassus.

Juste judex ultionis,
donum fac remissionis
ante diem rationis.

Ingemisco tamquam reus,
culpa rubet vultus meus
supplicanti parce, Deus.

Qui Mariam absolvisti
et latronem exaudisti,
mihi quoque spem dedisti.

Oro supplex et acclinis,
cor contritum quasi cinis;
gere curam mei finis.

Lacrimosa dies illa,
qua resurget ex favilla
judicandus homo reus.
huic ergo parce, Deus.

Notes on the Dies Irae

1 *Dies irae, dies illa* see Zephanaiah I, 15 sqq. 2 *David* Like most Hebrew names this name is treated as indeclinable in Latin. *Sibylla.* The so called Sibylline Oracles were treated in the early Church and in the Middle Ages as prophecies of Christ. The Sibyls take their place with the Prophets even in the ceiling of the Sistine Chapel painted by Michael Angelo and they appeared as prophetesses in many miracle plays. 8 *Per sepulchra regionum* through the sepulchres of all lands. 10 *Mors stupebit* see 1 Cor. xv, 26. 13 Notice that, although the endings of the three verbs on this stanza are the same, the first is Future Indicative, the second is Present Indicative and the third is Present Subjunctive and denotes purpose. 21 See 1 Pet., iv, 18. 20 *Patronum* a protector, a reference to the Roman custom that every alien must have a Roman citizen as his *patronus.* 23 *Salvandos* a paraphrase of the Vulgate version of Acts ii, 47 *qui salvi firent,* which is a mistranslation of the Greek. *Gratis* freely. 24 *quod* see note on line 32 of next hymn. 30 *Cassus* vain, or in vain. 31 *Ultionis* a descriptive Genitive. 33 *Rationis* reckoning. 34 *Ingemisco tanquam reus* I groan as being one who is guilty. 37 *Qui Mariam absolvisti* see Lk. vii, 37. It was generally taken for granted in the Middle Ages that 'the woman who was a sinner' was Mary Magdalene. 40 *Acclinis* prostrate. 42 *Gere curam* have a care for.

Thomas Aquinas who lived during the middle of the thirteenth century was the greatest of the Schoolmen and is still regarded even outside the Roman Church as one of the greatest of mediaeval philosophers and theologians. In the two hymns printed below he sets forth the doctrine of Transubstantiation with remarkable terseness.

De Eucharistia

Lauda, Sion, Salvatorem,
lauda Ducem et Pastorem
in hymnis et canticis;
quantum potes, tantum aude,
quia major omni laude,
non laudare sufficis.

Laudis thema specialis
Panis vivus, et vitalis
hodie proponitur,
quem in sacrae mensa caenae
turbae fratrum duodenae
datum non ambigitur.

Sit laus plena, sit sonora,
sit jocunda, sit decora
mentis jubilatio!
dies enim solemnis agitur,
in qua mensae prima recolitur
hujus institutio.

In hac mensa novi Regis
novum pascha novae legis,
phase vetus terminat.
vetustatem novitas,
umbram fugat veritas,
noctem lux eliminat.

Quod in caena Christus gessit,
faciendum hoc expressit
in sui memoriam:
docti sacris institutis,
panem vinum in salutis
consecramus hostiam.

Dogma datur Christianis,
quod in carnem transit panis
et vinum in sanguinem:
quod non sapis, quod non vides,
animosa firmat fides
praeter rerum ordinem.

Sub diversis speciebus,
signis tamen et non rebus,
latent res eximiae:
caro cibus, sanguis potus,
manet tamen Christus totus
sub utraque specie.

A sumente non concisus,
non confractus, non divisus,
integer accipitur:
sumit unus, sumunt mille,
quantum isti, tantum ille,
nec sumptus consumitur.

Sumunt boni, sumunt mali,
sorte tamen inaequali
vitae vel interitūs:
mors est malis, vita bonis;
vide, paris sumptionis
quam sit dispars excitus.

Fracto demum sacramento
ne vacilles, sed memento,
tantum esse sub fragmento
quantum toto tegitur:
nulla rei fit scissura,
signi tantum fit fractura,
qua nec status nec statura
signanti minuitur.

Ecce, panis angelorum
factus cibus viatorum,
vere panis filiorum
non mittendus canibus:
in figuris praesignatur,
cum Isaac immolatur,
agnus paschae deputatur,
datur manna patribus.

Bone Pastor, Panis vere,
Jesu, nostri miserere,
tu nos pasce, nos tuere,
tu nos bona fac videre
in terra viventium.

tu qui cuncta scis et vales,
qui nos pascis hic mortales,
tu nos ibi commensales,
coheredes et sodales
fac sanctorum civium.

Notes on Lauda, Sion, Salvatorem

7 *Thema* notice this Greek word and also the word *phase* in line 21. They may be translated by their English transliterations. 8 *Vitalis* lifegiving. 12 *Ambigitur* understand *esse*: trans. it is not doubted. 32 *Quod* this is the late Latin way of introducing a noun clause which is here in apposition to *dogma*. Trans. namely that. It is curious that this construction which is so common in prose so rarely occurs in these hymns. In line 34 *quod* has its usual sense as a relative pronoun. 35 *Animosa* courageous. 38 *Rebus* realities. 42 *Specie* like *speciebus* above is here obviously used in its theological sense. 47 *Isti* and *ille* these are used as personal pronouns with exactly the same meaning in different numbers. The distinction in meaning found in Cl. Latin has disappeared. 56 *Vacilles* do not be doubtful. 69 *Deputatur* is slain.

De Eucharistia II

Adoro te devote, latens Deitas,
quae sub figuris vere latitas,
tibi se cor meum totum subjicit,
quia te contemplans totum deficit.

Visus, gestus, tactus in te fallitur,
sed solo auditu in te creditur;
credo quidquid dixit Dei Filius,
nihil veritatis verbo verius.

In cruce latebat sola Deitas,
sed hic latet simul et Humanitas,
ambo tamen credens atque confidens
peto quod petivit latro poenitens.

Plagas sicut Thomas non intueor,
Deum tamen meum te confiteor,
fac me in te semper pie credere,
in te spem habere, te deligere.

Pie Pellicane, Jesu Domine,
me immudum munda tuo sanguine,
cuius una gutta salvum facere
totum mundum posset omni scelere.

Jesu, quem velatum nunc aspicio,
quando fiet illud quod jam sitio,
ut te revelata cernens facie
visu sim beatus tuae gloriae?

Notes on De Eucharistia II

17 *Pellicane* It was believed in the Middle Ages that the pelican fed her young with her own blood taken from her breast. She is consequently often represented in mediaeval art as a type of Christ. 24 *Revelata* unveiled, 11 Cor. iii, 18.

Bernard of Morlaix

De Contemptu Mundi

We conclude with a few well-known verses selected from the long poem generally attributed to Bernard of Morlaix who was monk at Cluny.

They are familiar to many in the translation by Dr. Neale, A. and M., 225, 226, 227, 228. The verses here given set forth the joys of heaven which Bernard contrasts with the evils of the world in his day.

Hic breve vivitur, hic breve plangitur, hic breve fletur;
non breve vivere, non breve plangere retribuetur.

O retributio, stat brevis actio, vita perennis;
O retributio, coelica mansio stat lue plenis.

Sunt modo praelia, postmodo praemia. Qualia? Plena:
plena refectio, nullaque passio, nullaque poena.

Spe modo vivitur, et Sion angitur a Babylone;
nunc tribulatio, tunc recreatio, sceptra coronae.

Qui modo creditur, Ipse videbitur, atque scietur,
Ipse videntibus atque scientibus attribuetur.

Hora novissima, tempora pessima sunt, vigilemus.
ecce minaciter imminent Arbiter ille supremus.

Imminet, imminet, ut mala terminet, aequa coronet,
recta remuneret, anxia liberet, aethera donet.

O bona patria, lumina sobria te speculantur,
ad tua nomina sobria lumina collacrymantur.

Est tua mentio pectoris unctio, cura doloris,
concipientibus aethera mentibus ignis amoris.

Urbs Sion aurea, patria lactea, cive decora,
omne cor obruis, omnibus obstruis et cor et ora.

Nescio, nescio quae jubilatio, lux tibi qualis,
quam socialia gaudia, gloria quam specialis.

Stant Sion aurea conjubilantia, martyre plena,
cive micantia, Principe stantia, luce serena.

O bona patria, num tua gaudia teque videbo?
O bona patria, num tua praemia plena tenebo?

Dic mihi, flagito, verbaque redito, dicque, Videbis;
spem solidam gero, remne tenens ero? dic, Retinebis.

O sacer, O pius O ter et amplius ille beatus,
cui sua pars Deus; O miser, O reus, hac viduatus.

NOTES ON DE CONTEMPTU MUNDI

3 *Stat* equivalent to *est.* 4 *Lue* defilement. 14 *Aethera* Heaven. 15 *Sobria* sad.

INDEX OF TEXTS QUOTED

The numbers on the right of each column refer to paragraphs

[1] The Psalms are quoted according to the numbering in the Vulgate.